BTS

Blood, Sweat & Tears

BTS

Blood, Sweat & Tears

Tamar Herman

VIZ MEDIA

CONTENTS

at No. 8, while "ON" would become their first Top 5 hit, debuting at No. 4 on the Hot 100 following its release in February 2020.

Each turn of their career has moved the act along a historic path. This book explores BTS and their impact on the world, with a particular focus on their rise in the U.S. through the *Love Yourself* and *Map of the Soul* eras. Part music bio, part analysis, *BTS: Blood, Sweat & Tears* aims to be a thorough introduction to the South Korean septet and their discography for new audiences and long-time fans who are curious about their rise to unprecedented fame, and how they have, with diligence, dedication, and talent, created a new music world order.

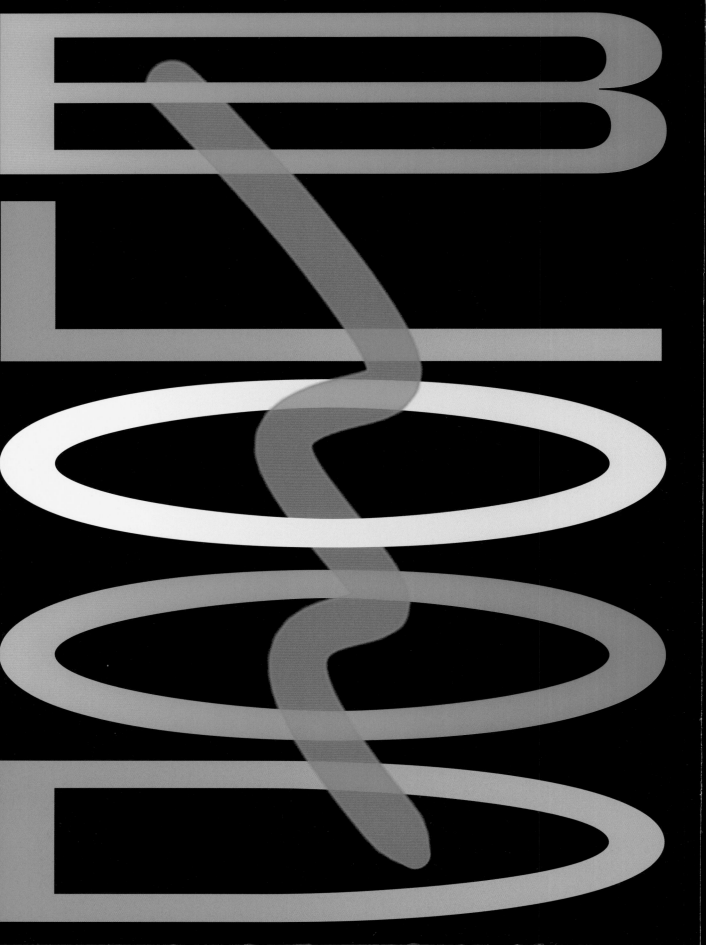

THE ORIGINS AND HISTORY OF BTS

1

BTS MEETS THE WORLD

Chapter One

At the time BTS debuted in 2013 under Big Hit Entertainment, their name evoked confusion, especially among English-language media covering the phenomenon we know generally as "K-pop." Their Korean name, *Bangtan Sonyeondan*, doesn't roll off the tongue in English, and its most commonly used translation, "Bulletproof Boy Scouts," seemed almost comical at the time. "Bangtan Boys" was thrown around for a moment, and often makes reappearances, but in the end, the three-letter acronym "BTS" reigned supreme. Over the years, the men of BTS have come to embody the meaning of every variation on their name, and—in addition to their international names, like *Bodan Shonendan* in Japan—have even expanded on it. For example, "Beyond the Scene" nods to their unique place as a vastly popular South Korean act, operating in the international music scene unhindered by previous geographic and sociological barriers.

While the band is best known globally as "BTS," each name has come to represent different elements of BTS and remains integral to their identity. As "Bulletproof Boy Scouts," BTS convey a sense of protection, reliability, resilience, and independence. During their early days, the group described their music as offering "protection against the bias and negative criticisms of teenagers," while the official English tagline, as translated in the release of the *BTS World* game in 2019, was "A bulletproof shield against the prejudice and oppression being thrown at the younger generation, standing strong against the world armed with your own music, knowing your own value." As "BTS," the act has lived up to the acronym's traditional meaning with a behind-the-scenes bond that's helped them stick to their career path for years, surpassing all limitations K-pop artists previously experienced to achieve global success.

BTS debuted in 2013, just as the music industry in South Korea was undergoing significant change. K-pop had already found its way around the globe in the late '00s and early '10s, largely thanks to the advent of YouTube, which spurred numerous viral hits and widening interest in what was taking place in the bottom half of the Korean Peninsula. But though K-pop gained popularity in many markets across the globe, it didn't achieve long-lived traction in English-speaking countries. As BTS arrived on the scene, there was a generational shift in the South Korean music world. The K-pop acts that had dominated over the past few years were beginning to lose their edge even as the industry continued to do well and see financial gains, expanding its reach further than ever before. The viral success of Psy's "Gangnam Style" in 2012 drew even greater international attention to South Korea's music industry.

It was into this burgeoning scene that BTS arrived, the first boy band formed wholly by Big Hit Entertainment. Featuring members from the underground hip-hop scene as well as some with backgrounds in more typical K-pop fare, like dancing and acting, BTS was a brand-new venture for Big Hit.

The company had been founded in 2005 by long-term K-pop hitmaker Bang Si-hyuk and up until that point had a roster primarily filled with ballad singers, like co-ed trio 8Eight and popular vocal pop quartet 2AM, the latter of which was co-managed by JYP Entertainment. There was a single girl group, GLAM, which began their career in 2012 and was, along with 8Eight, jointly managed by Big Hit and Source Entertainment. But BTS was set to be something new: the company's first solo-managed act, and a hip-hop-oriented boy band. The idea for the group originated a few years before 2013, with early iterations of the band's name, which was created in 2010,[3] appearing on albums in 2010–11 from the likes of Lim Jeong-hee, Kan Mi-youn, Lee Hyun, 2AM, and Lee Seung-gi when potential members of the act appeared as featured artists. But between 2010, when the act's first member RM (known as Rap Monster in the early days of BTS's career) joined the label, and BTS's debut in 2013, there were several changes to the lineup as the act became more pop-oriented.

Intended to be a hip-hop group rather than a more typical idol boy band, the original BTS lineup emphasized rap over singing. RM was the first to join the company and, over the years, Suga and J-Hope joined the initial group along with the likes of Supreme Boi, who would later go on to produce for BTS. Several other rappers such as Iron, i11evn, and Kidoh, the latter of whom debuted in Topp Dogg, were also apparently involved with the BTS project at some point. Over the years, the identity of the group shifted and the final lineup featured both hip-hop artists and more traditional pop singers, with three members focusing on the former and four on the latter (though several of the vocalists—or vocal line—also rapped in the group's early days, and the rappers—rap line—all sing). Accordingly, at the start of their career the emphasis was on hip-hop: "BTS is a hip-hop group," said Suga during an interview with LOEN TV (later 1theK) backstage at their MelOn debut showcase on June 12, 2013. "There are many idols doing hip-hop music nowadays, but we will do the most authentic hip-hop music."

Though Big Hit had prominent names both behind the scenes and on its roster, it was still a small label compared to much of its competition at the time, and putting out a new boy band that looked a lot like other recently arrived hip-hop-leaning groups, like Block B (2011), B.A.P (2012), and Topp Dogg, was perhaps a sign of the times. Ever since K-pop had found its feet in the '90s, elements of hip-hop had been incorporated into acts and most teams, especially boy bands, featured designated rappers. In the previous K-pop generation, BIGBANG was recognized for featuring talented hip-hop artists in its lineup, while even earlier K-pop groups like H.O.T (1996–2001, 2018—), Sechs Kies (1997–2000, 2016—), and g.o.d (1999—2005, 2014—) set the industry standard for most K-pop groups featuring designated rappers. Some early acts, such as 1TYM (1998–2005) were entirely hip-hop-based, though that was increasingly rare in the late '00s and early '10s, when idol groups shifted more predominantly towards pop and dance music. But by the time of BTS's debut, hip-hop had begun to rise in popularity, meaning that multiple acts weren't just drawing inspiration from the genre but were leaning into it as the very essence of their brand identity, drawing on it both musically and for its forthright approach to lyrics, meshing these elements with those more typical of K-pop. When BTS arrived it was one of many rookie boy bands drawing on hip-hop, but the group quickly separated itself from the crowd.

Fresh out of the gate, BTS laid the groundwork for the messaging they would include in many of their releases as their career progressed.

BTS drew on talent with backgrounds typical of potential K-pop stars, like Jimin and Jin, who had studied dancing and acting respectively, but also featured members who had participated in underground hip-hop scenes throughout Korea: rapper-songwriters RM and Suga had performed with crews and produced for others, while J-Hope had been a breakdancer. But this underground Korean hip-hop street cred didn't particularly help the new group BTS stand out at a time when every male K-pop team was embracing hip-hop and the genre was on the rise in the country, largely thanks to the popularity of the Mnet competition series, *Show Me the Money.*

The popular hip-hop series blew up shortly after it began airing in 2012. While hip-hop had been popular in South Korea in the '90s and early '00s, with several hip-hop artists, like Drunken Tiger, Verbal Jint, Tasha (aka Yoon Mi-rae), Epik High, and others rising to prominence, by the mid to late '00s the Korean music scene had shifted to pop and some R&B, with only a handful of hip-hop artists remaining popular. Following the rise of *Show Me the Money*, hip-hop saw a revival in South Korea, creating an environment where K-pop could delve freely into the genre.

BTS's debut with "No More Dream" and *2 Cool 4 Skool* on June 12, 2013 might not have been enough to set them apart from the crowd of boy bands leaning into hip-hop, decked out in black athleisure outfits, gold chains, and fierce accessories. However, the septet distinguished themselves with the message of the song and the album, which relayed a realistic commentary on students not being given freedom to dream and pursue their own desires. Fresh out of the gate, BTS laid the groundwork for the messaging they would include in many of their releases as their career progressed. Though it didn't bring the act to the top charts straightaway, *2 Cool 4 Skool* was still the 65th best-selling album of 2013 on South Korea's end-of-year Gaon albums chart, the first sign of BTS's burgeoning popularity. Its successor, September's *O!RUL8,2?*, would land at No. 55, showing that the band had a dedicated, growing fanbase from the onset of their career.

But not only did BTS face the challenges that are innately part of the competitive K-pop world, they also had to contend with hostility from South Korea's increasingly mainstream hip-hop scene. The first few years of their career were filled with tension as the act figured out how to navigate this space. They were K-pop idols, but not idol enough. They were leaning heavily into hip-hop, but hip-hop's foundation as a genuine form of musical expression seemed to contradict the corporate approach of entertainment companies forming idol groups and pop music in general. This dichotomy

18

Blood

has carried on throughout BTS's career, with the group exploring the issue in their music and eventually releasing the single "IDOL" in 2018. In the single, the band declared that they didn't care what others called them, because they're proud of what they've achieved regardless. Their music speaks for itself.

In November 2013, a notable challenge to BTS's identity came up. During an event for the first anniversary of hip-hop journalist Kim Bong-hyeon's podcast *Hip-Hop Invitational*, which RM and Suga attended, the conversation shifted to the question of whether "idols" in Korea were industrial products rather than musical talent. Rapper B-Free questioned whether the pair could legitimately call themselves hip-hop artists, essentially calling them sell-outs and questioning why they would want to pursue a career in the idol industry where they would have to wear makeup. In response, RM and Suga explained how they went from being underground artists to pursuing their careers in a more straightforward, lucrative way. RM shared how he had unsuccessfully auditioned to join several hip-hop crews before one rapper, The Untouchable's Sleepy, introduced him to Bang Si-hyuk; Suga revealed that he used to write music but could not make a living from it. Rather than sell out, they had chosen a path that, yes, included makeup and synchronized dancing as K-pop idols, but still kept the pair in charge of their own artistic expression while straddling the two different worlds. It was a relatively short conversation, but the hip-hop artist was clearly hostile about BTS's direction, and the incident became a notable example of BTS staying true to themselves while challenging music world norms.

(In January 2016, B-Free apologized on Twitter and in 2018, he addressed the situation in an interview with *W Magazine*, where he described his questioning of their hip-hop idoldom as a "harsh joke" and recanted his previous stance towards men wearing makeup.[4] He apologized again on Twitter in 2019.)

K-pop groups often encounter this reductive perception of their artistry, and many factors affect it, ranging from modern-day sensibilities about artistic integrity to racism, to the commonly held view that the entire industry is taking advantage of young talent and building entertainment empires on their backs. Whether or not this is true (and it is to some degree, just as most industries take advantage of their workers), it necessitates a conversation about what K-pop is and what it is not.

20

WHAT IS
K-POP?

K-pop is not a single genre of music, but rather a collection of associated elements that encapsulate a brand of music coming out of South Korea. At its most basic, the term "K-pop" is a catchall phrase used in English to refer to artists, music, music videos, performances, and other multimedia content featuring young stars, typically known as "idols," who are managed by entertainment companies in South Korea; it is often also more generally used to refer to popular music from South Korea. During a 2018 talk BTS held at the Grammy Museum in Los Angeles, Suga put it more concisely and said K-pop is a form of "integrated content" born out of the South Korean mainstream music industry. This multi-pronged approach to content creation is where BTS have excelled, particularly since the creation of the "BU," or the creative narrative of the "BTS Universe" that's featured throughout BTS's discography and videography.

Though it has a sizable, incredibly diverse following around the world, the K-pop idol industry is built on young stars shaped and managed by entertainment companies, where the stars are typically seen as performers rather than artists. The industry primarily revolves around boy bands and girl groups. Though many groups, including BTS, participate in songwriting, there is a distinct difference, both in South Korea and beyond, between a Korean pop musician and a K-pop idol, though in English the term "K-pop" is typically applied to everything coming out of the Korean mainstream pop music industry, while in Korea "K-pop idol" is a distinct entity from a typical pop performer. A stigma applies to the term, just as it does to the terms "boy band" and "girl group." This is, at least in part, due to the perceived lack of authenticity inherent in corporately sponsored and created acts, as all but a few K-pop idols are handpicked, trained, and invested in by entertainment companies as a cultural product rather than a wholly artistic production. It is additionally stigmatized because stars are frequently mistreated in the K-pop industry, which has a historic legacy of overworking talent and underpaying them, though in recent years the larger entertainment companies' contracts have become more legally regulated. However, abuse, overwork, and irregular working conditions are still widespread.

In general, "idol" music in South Korea is considered a subgenre of pop music, and singles are typically electropop dance tracks infused with hip-hop, R&B, EDM, or alternatively poignant ballads. Catchy hooks are integral for dance tracks, and many singles are crafted to be performed with intricate accompanying choreography. BTS's music is not technically very different from most other pop music, but the members, particularly RM and Suga, have been strongly involved in writing their music since the band's earliest days, and over the years have helped craft and refine the group's musical identity. That, as well as working with a dedicated team of songwriters since the start, has helped the group develop their authentic brand of artistry in a way that few K-pop groups can, particularly because most K-pop groups base new releases on one-off concepts rather than growing their artistic identity in a linear fashion. That's not true for everyone—many acts like BIGBANG, Highlight, B1A4, Seventeen, and even newer groups like Stray Kids, ATEEZ, and (G)I-DLE have carved out a distinct sound for themselves thanks to members who write songs—but BTS's roots, with two members who were already writing songs before the group formed, and the participation of other members in songwriting over the years, have played a key role in making the group shine especially brightly in a crowded global music industry.

Many of BTS's early days were spent attempting to carve out a place for themselves in a highly competitive field, where young pop idols are rarely just singers but also dancers, models, actors, and television personalities. K-pop is the epitome of cross-platform marketing in the era of globalization, and even before the arrival of their debut release (known as their "debut" in the K-pop world) BTS had begun to develop their social media footprint, which would eventually grow to include not only one of the most impactful Twitter accounts of the late 2010s but also hundreds of videos on YouTube that shared moments of their careers and lives with audiences across the world. This early adoption of social media as a way of sharing snapshots of the group's daily life rapidly began to gain BTS a small, dedicated following for their relatable, authentic content and early performance videos, including numerous covers.

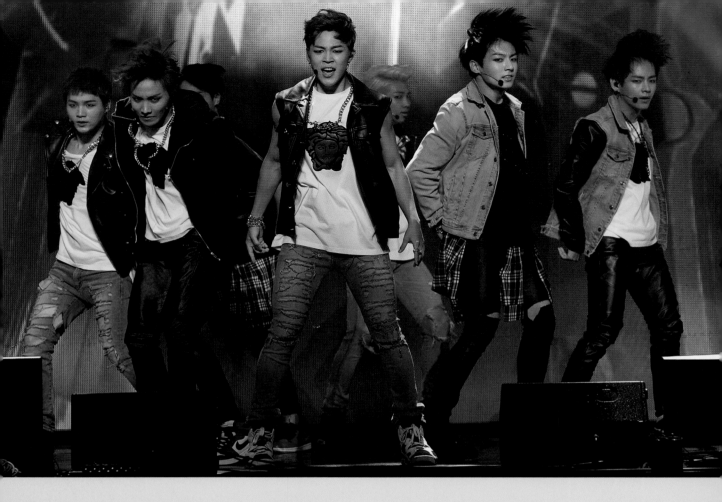

BTS at their *Dark & Wild* album showcase in August 2014.

Blood

THE EARLY SKOOL & WILD DAYS

Between 2010 and June 2013, Big Hit Entertainment put together the group that would go on to become BTS. Through auditions, recommendations, and street casting, members of the team were discovered and introduced to the company, after which they went through rigorous training. Over the years, members were occasionally seen serving as backup dancers or featured artists in content put out by other artists. The release of BTS's first music video was preceded by a variety of content shared on BTS's social media, SoundCloud, and YouTube channels, wherein all the members but the "hidden card" V, who was kept out of the spotlight until just before their debut, introduced themselves to the world through a wide array of content, including covers of many iconic hip-hop songs, such as "Graduation Song," a song by Jimin, Jungkook, and J-Hope about the feelings of being free from school after graduating based on Snoop Dogg & Wiz Khalifa's "Young, Wild & Free" with Bruno Mars, and "A Typical Trainee's Christmas," which was a blend of Kanye West's "Christmas in Harlem" and "Last Christmas" by Wham!

For their official debut on June 13, BTS appeared on a K-pop music broadcast show, Mnet's *M Countdown*, after premiering "No More Dream," and the album's other tracks at their first showcase event the day before. (Because of this, they commemorate June 13 as their debut rather than the album release date.) Due to the competitive state of the Korean music world, BTS flew relatively under the radar in their early days, to the degree that their song "Sea," released as a hidden track on the physical version of 2017's *Love Yourself 承 Her*, referred to how the septet eagerly anticipated other acts pulling out of televised appearances so that they could fill their place.

Through their *Skool* album trilogy releases in 2013 and 2014, BTS actively addressed questions of their identity and worldview, putting forth a concept that balanced impish rebellion and sentimental schoolboy charm. *2 Cool for Skool*, the start of this trio, saw them acknowledged at Gaon Chart's year-end awards as the top new boy band of 2013, and its lead single "No More Dream" showed the group had generated sizable interest in the U.S. when it landed on *Billboard*'s World Digital Song Sales chart shortly after its release, peaking at No. 14.

About a month into BTS's formal career, the group announced the name of their fandom ARMY (formally stylized as A.R.M.Y) or Adorable Representative MC of Youth. Introduced on July 9, just a few days before the group released a music video for their second single "We Are Bulletproof Pt. 2" on July 16, the fandom name would prove prophetic as a term used to represent the massive, dedicated, protective following that BTS would accrue in the coming years.

Barely a month after the release of the music video for "We Are Bulletproof Pt. 2," BTS began teasing their first comeback. While in the Western world a "comeback" typically means a long-awaited return to the spotlight, in the K-pop world it refers to the next release from an act. On August 27, BTS released their first conceptual "comeback trailer" for what they'd later announce as their *O!RUL8,2?* album. The idea of a comeback trailer, which hinted at the thematic identity of the upcoming release, would go on to become a mainstay of BTS's promotions ahead of many of their releases over the years. The initial animated trailer was followed on September 4 by the album's "concept trailer" that featured a cover of Kanye West's 2013 song "BLKKK SKKKN Head," and showed the group performing theatrical choreography, including them facing down the police and being shot, then band member RM reviving them. Though it was one of many covers of iconic hip-hop songs that BTS put out over the years, the trailer didn't explicitly credit West when they released it, a point of contention during that pivotal conversation with B-Free a few weeks later, as he had previously tweeted out that he felt it bordered on plagiarism. But, rather than copying, BTS were paying homage to the legacy of hip-hop, and the trailer video was a dynamic display of the group's sharp, theatrical choreography and emphasized their anti-establishment messaging.

BTS's second album dropped on September 11 of that year with similar themes to their first one, cementing the group's position as a hip-hop-oriented boy band railing against society, particularly the struggles of students in academically aggressive South Korea. Lead single "N.O" was released on September 10 through a music video that showed the members in a futuristic, authoritarian state being educated in a classroom filled with armed guards in riot gear. Rebelling against the guards and their instructor, the song again addressed a social issue as "No More Dream" did, leaning in to

BTS's desire to become a voice for their generation. The album debuted at No. 4 on the Gaon Chart the week of its release, and ended up at No. 55 on Gaon's album chart for the entirety of 2013, ten places ahead of *2 Cool 4 Skool*, which ranked at No. 65.

Along with *O!RUL8,2?*, September marked a new beginning for BTS with the launch of their first reality show (often called a variety show in the Korean entertainment world). *Rookie King: Channel Bangtan* aired on September 3 on Korean cable broadcaster SBS MTV. Over the next few months, the group would appear on a variety of programs and release several covers, as well as receive their first year-end award at the 2013 Melon Music Awards (MMAs) on November 14, when they took home the best new artist of the year award for a group (Lim Kim was chosen as the top new soloist). While this was a major win and one to be applauded, a frank conversation was recorded between V and another off-screen member and featured during a *Bangtan Bomb* (a series of videos shared on YouTube) where they acknowledged that the awards system seemed to be based upon playing by the industry's rules, such as participating in events that are broadcast to help TV channels bring in viewers, rather than solely rewarding talent and musical accolades. This conversation showed from the very early days of BTS's career that both the band and Big Hit, which uploaded the content, would have to fight even harder to be recognized for their worth beyond the traditional wheeling and dealing of the K-pop world. The award became the first of many and will always be important for the group and their history. BTS went on to win several rookie awards throughout that season in South Korea, each a nod of industry recognition to BTS's potential, and an acknowledgment that their brand of hip-hop idoldom was gaining attention and traction.

They began to tease the third and final part of their *Skool* trilogy on February 4 of 2014, when the *Skool Luv Affair* comeback trailer dropped, a colorful animated clip that featured the final part of "Intro: Skool Luv Affair," revealing an upbeat rap track that relayed what it means to be "Bangtan Style." But despite the introductory film's heavy hip-hop leanings, it was with this album that BTS began to step away from their more swaggering, gangster rap-inspired styling and sonic inspiration. Instead, they followed up with the music video for "Boy In Luv" (also known as "Real Man" in Korean ["상남자"]) on February 11 and the album on February 12, this time blending vibrant rock with their hip-hop and pop influences, and putting forth romantic, rather than sociological, lyricism.

BTS Meets The World

27

Shortly after the release of "Boy In Luv," BTS announced what would go on to become their annual fanmeeting event: BTS Global Official Fanclub A.R.M.Y 1st Muster, with the name referring to a military term for troops assembling. It took place on March 29 in Seoul's Olympic Hall, and would become the first of many such events.

Following their first Muster, BTS dropped the "Just One Day" music video on April 6, making the R&B-infused track the second single from *Skool Luv Affair*. Both it and "Boy In Luv" ended up on Billboard's World Digital Song Sales chart, with the second single charting at No. 25 and the first one landing at No. 5 upon its release. The album ended up rising to No. 1 on Gaon's weekly music chart following the release of "Just One Day," after originally debuting at No. 3. *Skool Luv Affair* also became BTS's first album to place on international charts, appearing on both Billboard's World Albums chart in the U.S. and Japan's Oricon Chart. And there was more to come: the group released a repackage, or reissue, of *Skool Luv Affair* on May 14 featuring two new songs, "Miss Right" and "Like (Slow Jam Remix)." The album ended 2014 as the 20th best-selling album of the year in South Korea, as tracked by the Gaon Chart. Around this time, the group began pursuing overseas markets, with a Japanese version of "No More Dream" released through a music video on May 25, and on June 2 they announced what would go on to become their annual two-week-long Festa event series, leading up to their anniversary on June 13. They released their first Japanese single album *No More Dream*, featuring Japanese versions of three previously released songs including the title track, on June 4, and then the Japanese music video for "Boy In Luv" a month later on July 4.

One of BTS's biggest early career moments was when the group went to study hip-hop in the U.S. through the television program *American Hustle Life*, which aired on Korean cable channel Mnet. Filmed in the summer of 2014, it began airing on July 24, and took BTS to Los Angeles, where they studied hip-hop from the likes of Coolio, Warren G, and a variety of other artists, learning about the history of the genre and its relationship with Black American culture and history, breakdancing, beatboxing, R&B and soul music, and more. While it had its moments of uncomfortable culture clash and over-dramatization, the eight-episode reality show presented the group's dedication to learning about hip-hop's roots in a respectful manner. The series ended with the group's first-ever show in the U.S.—their Show & Prove showcase held at Los Angeles' Troubadour nightclub on July 14. With only two days' notice and BTS taking to the streets of L.A. to advertise, local ARMY came out in droves, with far more than the expected 200 attendees arriving. The venue, which holds 500, eventually permitted the extra fans into the hall after they had waited eagerly to see if they too would be lucky enough to be allowed in.

Dark & Wild

During their time in Los Angeles, BTS worked on their fourth Korean album, which would end up becoming *Dark & Wild*, their first LP (full-length album), released on August 19. The album continued to explore BTS's diversifying sound, incorporating rock elements into the singles "Danger" and "War of Hormone," while still featuring their hip-hop roots, such as on the aptly named "Hip-Hop Phile," during which BTS's rappers name-dropped the hip-hop icons who had inspired them. The album ended up peaking at No. 2 on Gaon's weekly album chart and at No. 3 on Billboard's World Albums Chart, and at No. 27 on Billboard's Heatseekers chart, showing the increasing U.S. interest in the group—no surprise considering how popular the group had proved during their first KCON (a popular Korean music festival) appearance immediately preceding its release. The septet performed at the Korean pop culture music convention and music festival's headlining concert at the Los Angeles Memorial Sports Arena on August 10, 2014, a date that many see as the moment it became apparent that BTS and their music had a sizable following in the U.S., based on the passionate response to their performance. The group's first LP would go on to be the 14th best-selling album of 2014 in South Korea, according to Gaon.

Following the release of *Dark & Wild*, which, with its hip-hop vibes and youth-oriented depictions of romance, could be seen as the extension of or sequel to the *Skool* album trio, BTS launched their first concert tour on October 17. Titled the 2014 Live Trilogy Episode II: The Red Bullet Tour—a bit of a misnomer since an Episode I would take place in Seoul the following March, in the middle of the larger tour—it would continue throughout 2014 and 2015, as BTS held 22 shows across 13 countries, including four shows in the U.S., through the following August. Throughout it all, BTS would be kept busy, and the end of 2014 was especially full of new content from the group: along with the "War of Hormone" music video, the septet dropped the Japanese version of "Danger" on November 9, and the corresponding single album on November 19, before releasing a remix of "Danger," known as the "Mo-Blue-Mix," featuring songwriter Thanh Bùi on November 20. It was followed by the release of their Japanese single album *Danger* the next day. The end of the year would bring their first full Japanese album in the form of *Wake Up* on December 24. Throughout 2014, the septet had released a large amount of new music and focused heavily on touring, and their stalwart fanbase grew with each release, bolstered by the act's presence on social media and through several TV series revolving around the septet.

Changes at Big Hit

As much as it was a period of post-debut development and growth, this period wasn't easy for BTS for a variety of reasons. As the new group tried to find its footing and make its way in the world, major changes took place at Big Hit, and the company's artist roster began to crumble, putting an emphasis, and what must have been immense pressure, on BTS. First, April of that year saw three 2AM members leave Big Hit and return to JYP, leading to a perpetual hiatus and essentially marking the end of the quartet's career together; only Lee Chang-min, who worked with 8Eight's Lee Hyun under the duo name Homme, remained, until he started his own one-man agency at the start of 2018. Then, in September, an industry-shaking news story unfolded: GLAM's Dahee, later known as Kim Si-won, was accused of attempted blackmail along with model Lee Ji-yeon.

According to media reports, the pair had threatened to release a compromising video of *G.I. Joe* star, actor Lee Byung-hun, discussing sexual content with them, while married to actress Lee Min-jung. In court, it was revealed that Dahee and Lee Ji-yeon had deliberately arranged the situation to try to get money out of Lee Byung-hun. According to reports based on court papers, Dahee owed Big Hit Entertainment over 300 million won (around 300,000 USD). On January 15, 2015, Dahee was sentenced to one year and Lee Ji-yeon a year and two months in prison—though both served reduced sentences. The same day, Big Hit announced that GLAM was disbanding.

A shocking affair, it meant that the start of 2015 began with a major blow to Big Hit, which lost most of its roster: BTS and Homme's Lee Chang-min and Lee Hyun were all that remained, and agency focus shifted almost entirely to the group.

With the release of *The Most Beautiful Moment in Life, Pt. 1* in April 2015, BTS went from being one of many promising, hip-hop-oriented boy bands in the Korean music scene to one with its own distinct, wholly separate identity. Though other K-pop acts had incorporated creative narratives into their audio-visual releases in the past—like EXO and B.A.P debuting with fantastical sci-fi storylines that gave both acts an extraterrestrial spin—*HYYH1* took K-pop's transmedia nature to a new level and, paired with the captivating sound of their single "I Need U," the launch of BTS's *BU* became a game-changer.

With *HYYH1* and the introduction of the *BU*, BTS and their creative team pushed things further and actually set about creating a fictional narrative that positioned the members of BTS as characters in their own work. Though BTS had already made two tie-in webtoon series, *We On: Be the Shield*, a sci-fi series that turned BTS into heroes, and *Hip Hop Monster*, which featured a series of animated cartoon characters (a precursor to BT21, an animated character collaboration between BTS and Line Friends that would launch in 2017 to major success), things became more closely tied together as BTS moved further into 2015. Over the years since its debut, *The Most Beautiful Moment in Life* storyline, also known as the BTS Universe, or BU, has grown into a plotline full of angst, friendship, tragedy, and time travel, as it's been relayed through music videos, album imagery, a series of notes (which were later turned into a book), social media posts, a comic series, and much, much more.

The launch of the BU came as *HYYH1* saw BTS change up their style, moving away a bit from the hip-hop idol concept that they had previously focused on and instead towards dynamic synth-pop for the first time with the single "I Need U." The song was their first big success in South Korea, and would precede the release of "Dope" in June. "Dope" seemed self-aware in its position as a turning point for BTS's career growth, beginning with the phrase, "Welcome, first time with BTS?," signaling that the act and the team behind it recognized that *HYYH1* was about to grow into so much more and that "Dope" would become the entryway for many new fans.

TRANSMEDIA STORYTELLING & K-POP

Transmedia is a form of multimedia storytelling that tells a narrative across different platforms. And though it's typically utilized for fiction series, like *Star Wars* or *The Avengers* extending their storylines through films, television shows, books, video games, and other media, K-pop has long utilized transmedia as a way to promote its stars across different mediums and to maximize revenue. For instance, the average K-pop star not only releases and performs music, but also appears in advertisements that reflect their image, whether it's youthful school uniforms, tasty snacks, or luxury skin care, as well as South Korean variety and scripted television shows, and even films. Some host radio shows and, in recent years, many have their own livestreaming and/or video channels through which they share parts of their lives. And then there is social media, where the stars have, predominantly, one-way interactions with fans. The goal is to have audiences so invested in the personal brand of a single act or celebrity across different platforms that not only will fans support the artist's musical career, but also their efforts in acting, modeling, and other industries. Essentially, the K-pop industry is only partially about selling music to listeners and more about selling the stars, and the products or content (including music) they represent, to their fans, creating an immersive experience—ideal for musical acts that exist at a time when musical releases typically make very little direct income from music sales and streaming but dedicated fandoms can be relied on to pay for merchandise, physical albums, concert tickets, and more.

But just about every entertainer in the digital age does cross-media promotions, so how is K-pop different? It's not, except that the commodification is openly acknowledged; fans know that the performer's music video and television show appearances don't necessarily reflect the person themselves but their publicly marketed personas, though of course there is no separating the part from its whole, and these personas typically embody the ideal traits of a specific K-pop idol. Like the religious images that the terminology comes from, K-pop idols are often posed as a breed apart from general humanity, and the standards imposed on them, both by entertainment industry expectations and fans alike, are fantastical emulations of what it means to be beloved stars who are pursuing their dreams bolstered by their fans.

At its essence, this transmedia-style positioning of K-pop stars fleshes out their celebrity personas across platforms, while maintaining a distinct separation from their private lives, which are rarely acknowledged. Though that's been changing in recent years as artists become more frank about their personal lives and their opinions, the aura of idoldom is wrapped tightly around many K-pop stars, with a clear boundary between their personal lives and the fiction of their public image. Romantic relationships can affect careers—particularly for female stars—and idols are expected to display a certain sense of decorum in public. As the industry grows, and fandom matures, the line between stars' public and private personas is blurring, but K-pop stars are still expected to be a cut above the average teen or 20-something.

SOARING INTO SUCCESS WITH A BEAUTIFUL MOMENT

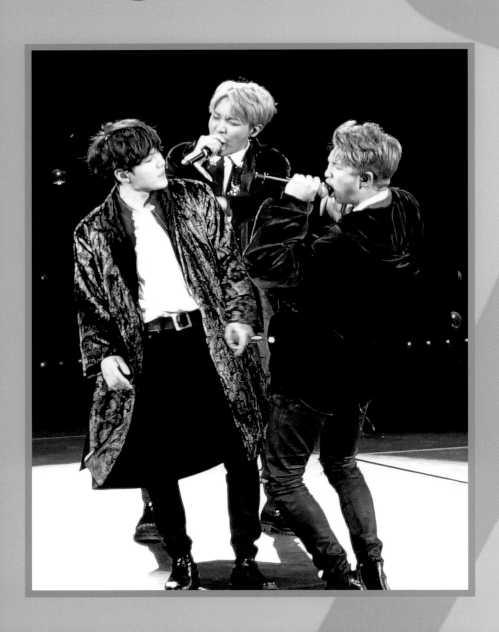

**Chapter
Two**

In the days following their debut, BTS had relayed powerful messages through their *Skool* trio and explored rebellious romance on *Dark & Wild.* But K-pop boy bands often hit their stride in the second and third year, either solidifying their identity and furthering their career with a runaway hit, or failing to form a distinct identity, with releases that please fans but rarely make it big otherwise. While there are some exceptions and a few acts have found more widespread success in their third or fourth year—or even later—the second-year anniversary is when it's truly time to reflect on whether a K-pop boy band has gained enough traction to propel longevity. When BTS released *The Most Beautiful Moment in Life, Pt. 1* just a few months before their second anniversary, they had received a lot of interest internationally, but had yet to make a true impact in their local South Korean market. They were also facing increased pressure as Big Hit's most active group.

Before the release of "I Need U" changed all that, RM, while still known as Rap Monster, released his mixtape *RM* on March 15. First he released a music video for the combative "Awakening" on March 12, in which he confirmed his status as an idol and decried the claims of haters using vitriolic wordplay. He followed up by releasing the music video for lead track "Do You" on March 19, where he once again explored his identity and other people's perceptions of him. Like many of BTS's early non-album releases, songs on the mixtape sample tracks from other artists, with RM drawing on hip-hop's legacy for a creative infusion. The mixtape, and a bonus Chinese version of "Boy In Luv," was released a few days before the BTS Live Trilogy Episode I: BTS Begins show, which was held in Seoul on March 28 and 29, and which truly did mark a new beginning for BTS, as it was the last concert the group held before releasing *HYYH1* on April 29, 2015, which changed things up forever.

Up until that point, the group had found moderate success, with limited international tours and a bit of charting to show for it. But no single song had yet become their breakout hit, the song that every store in Seoul would be playing as customers walked by, tantamount in that market to having a song played once every hour on American radio stations. The melodic, frantic desperation of "I Need U" would provide that, bringing anguished EDM, R&B, and trap together while emphasizing the abilities of the group's rappers and vocalists through its sleek, soaring production. While their earlier singles had been more message-based, oriented around their identity as protectors of youth and leaning more heavily into their own experiences, "I Need U" was more universal, though creatively a follow-up to the youthful, evocative romantic narrative begun with "Boy In Luv" and "Danger." It clicked with audiences, and eventually debuted within the Top 10, at No. 5 on Gaon's weekly digital song chart.

But in putting out a song that was more commercially oriented, the group didn't do away with their distinct sense of identity. Instead they took the opportunity to reorient themselves creatively: with the music video for "I Need U," BTS began the BU, their long-running narrative focusing on the troubles associated with life and growing up, themes they had previously explored directly through their lyrics. As Big Hit describes it, the theme was about "the start of one's young adulthood in which beauty coexists with uncertainty, and focuses on the uncertain future more than the glamour of youth. Love that burns as if it will last forever, but eventually cools down; blooming, yet withering youth—these two overlapping in the song best portray the album's theme."[5]

The video for the song was BTS's most popular yet, rapidly gaining views upon its release and hitting one million views within a reported 16 hours. The first depiction of their BU storyline, it showed a series of seemingly unconnected scenes in which each of the BTS members appeared individually before coming together as a group, introducing their BU personas and interpersonal relationship dynamics for the first time. The music video originally received a 19+ rating from South Korean censors because it featured violence, attempted suicide, and murder, but ended up getting downgraded to a 15+ after a shortened version was released. Only later was the original, extended version of "I Need U" shared. A dramatic, expressive video, it set up the fictive *The Most Beautiful Moment in Life* narrative that would be woven into the majority of BTS's group releases over the next few years.

Cuts of members in varying states of depression, danger, and solitude were contrasted with those of the seven men—the characters of the BU as played by BTS—enjoying their time with one another. It would take years until the launch of the webtoon *Save Me* in 2019 offered a straightforward narrative that integrated the whole plot, told across different mediums over several years, but from the start the BU storyline captivated audiences by leaning into the anxieties of millennial life and the struggles of loneliness, with a sprinkling of

36

hope and the bonds of friendship to make things better. From its launch, the BU narrative served as a visual portrayal of BTS's aim of representing modern youth culture and its ills.

The combination of a hit song and captivating music video showcased BTS's growth since starting out as rambunctious rookies just under two years earlier, and hinted at their potential. It set them up as one of that year's biggest acts, both in South Korea and beyond: in the U.S. the album landed at No. 2 on the Billboard World Albums chart and No. 6 on its Heatseekers chart.

Locally, recognition for the group began to grow, and "I Need U" landed them their first wins on weekly music shows on South Korean cable and broadcast channels. With five trophies from four shows over a two-week period following the single's release, it was clear that the song had resonated among South Korean listeners, opening up a new chapter of BTS's career.

The group followed up "I Need U" with their 2015 Festa and released their first original Japanese single "For You" on June 17. Their fourth Japanese single overall, it topped the Oricon chart following its release. A few weeks later, a music video for "Dope" arrived.

The new song was unrelated to the "I Need U" music video, and stood apart from the BU. Instead, "Dope" more closely aligned with their earlier singles like "No More Dream" and "N.O," showcasing a roguish electro hip-hop track in which they emphasize how hard work has brought them to where they are, all while pulling off complex, tightly synchronized choreography in professional occupation-inspired costumes. As a sequel to their hit "I Need U," the group could have played it safe and released a track more similar in sound, as they would with the likes of "Run" and "Save Me," but instead they shared another side of themselves with their growing audience.

While less of a commercial success than its predecessor in South Korea—it barely broke into the Top 50 of the Gaon digital singles chart upon its release—the dynamism of "Dope" has made it a fan favorite, and over the years it has become one of the most impactful BTS music videos. "Dope" is often cited as the entry point for many fans into BTS's music, and, fittingly, it would eventually go on to be one of their most-viewed music videos on YouTube. It became BTS's first music video to surpass the 100 million milestone on YouTube in October 2016.

After the one-two punch of "I Need U" and "Dope," the group turned its attention to international regions. They picked up The Red Bullet concert series again with a show in Malaysia, and then ventured out of Asia to cities in Australia, Mexico, Brazil, Chile, and the U.S. Playing to an estimated 80,000 fans throughout the tour, The Red Bullet served as a testament to the group's worldwide appeal, and demonstrated how ARMY were waiting for BTS around the globe. However, the tour was dampened by the first serious threat to BTS; the New York City show held at Best Buy Theater in Times Square on July 16 was cut short, with no fanmeeting interactions as promised, due to an apparent death threat aimed at RM over social media. Luckily, nothing came of it, but the scare showed that the group was gaining attention, not all of it positive. (Future concerts the act held in the U.S. would be threatened over the years, resulting in heightened security but luckily no incidents.)

After the Red Bullet Tour officially ended with its final show in Hong Kong on August 29, BTS barely took a moment's break: they held the Highlight tour in North America in September, and played four other cities in the U.S. and Canada that hadn't hosted the Red Bullet. The sequel tour itself had major issues regarding organization and fan interactions, and the group only performed four songs at each show, so it has become infamous as an example of a badly organized and executed K-pop tour.[6]

Following the end of their extended touring season, things were relatively quiet for BTS until they put out a short "prologue" film in October, featuring their song "Butterfly" as a soundtrack. The video, known formally as HYYH on stage: prologue, was the first hint of November's album The Most Beautiful Moment in Life, Pt. 2, also known as HYYH2. Teased on November 17 with the "Never Mind" comeback trailer, the album and single "Run" were released on November 30. It would end up being the album that changed everything for BTS.

Like much of their music, HYYH2 offered an intimate look at BTS and their worldview, offering up nine immensely relatable tracks that explored their struggles and successes. In comparison to HYYH1, which was a bit brighter and youth-oriented ("Converse High," "Boyz With Fun"), HYYH2 featured weightier tracks that revealed the group's innermost emotions in songs that, for example, explored solitude, like "Whalien 52," or critiqued socio-economic injustice, such as "Silver Spoon." With a narrative drawn directly from the septet's own experiences, it helped solidify BTS's artistry with new audiences—and earned them another hit with the expressive single "Run." The video tied into the BU storyline, this time contrasting moments of fun between the seven men with moments of intense drama, including scenes where some of the characters are seen getting arrested or drowning, picking up where prior scenes from the "I Need U" video had left off.

With the increased interest and growing fanbase they had garnered through their previous releases and touring, *HYYH2* and "Run" broke numerous records for BTS: the album became the act's best-selling release up to that point—and would become the fifth best-selling Korean album of the year—and the single was their first song to top South Korea's Melon Chart. While Gaon tracks sales and streams across the board, Melon is the most popular digital music platform in South Korea and topping its singles chart is a sign of widespread interest. Even more impressively, *HYYH2* became the first album from BTS to break into the Billboard 200 main albums chart, showing the immense traction the group had gained by that point. *HYYH2* debuted at No. 171, the first time BTS truly broke into America's mainstream music consciousness, propelled by the support of local ARMY. This was not only a monumental achievement for the group, but also for the entire world of K-pop: it was the first time an act had appeared on the Billboard 200 chart from any South Korean entertainment company other than SM Entertainment and YG Entertainment, two of the country's "Big 3" K-pop hubs along with JYP Entertainment, a sign of change within South Korea's music industry and its increasing popularity overseas.

Just a little over two years since they had started in June 2013, BTS had broken through the crowded K-pop scene to differentiate itself so exponentially that it had leapfrogged past all the competition to find success in the U.S., the final frontier of K-pop since BoA first brought K-pop to the Billboard 200 with her self-titled English-language album in 2009. It was a huge win for both the group and Big Hit, which had struggled for years to truly grow as a label and be recognized as a competitive player in the Korean music scene. Despite beginning the year by disbanding the first idol group it had ever launched, Big Hit ended 2015 on the first of many highs that paved BTS's way to the top.

But dropping an album and making sizable international waves wasn't all the second half of 2015 had in store for BTS: the group had already spent much of the year touring in a way few other K-pop acts did, bringing themselves directly to fans around the world in a variety of countries. They weren't done yet, and launched The Most Beautiful Moment in Life On Stage Tour on November 27 in Seoul for three nights of concerts. They then headed to Yokohama for a duo of their first Japanese Arena-size shows in December. *The Most Beautiful Moment in Life On Stage* concert series continued in March in Kobe, and then picked up again in May with its *Epilogue* portion, which saw the group performing in several Asian cities throughout the summer

of 2016, after releasing the third *The Most Beautiful Moment in Life* album, *Young Forever*.

The success of BTS is largely due to the act's hard work, their music, their fans, their social media presence, and many other factors. But the septet's dedication to touring, and the role it has played in their international rise, can't be underestimated. Since 2015, BTS have regularly toured around the globe, meeting fans first hand, diligently putting on performances up-close and in-person. Though other acts from the K-pop world regularly tour internationally, none has ever done so on such a scale. There has only been a single year in BTS's career—2016, when they were predominantly Asia-based—in which they didn't bring tours or showcases to multiple continents. This expansive approach to touring would not only become immensely lucrative—it would eventually grow to the point where the 2019 *Love Yourself: Speak Yourself* stadium dates in North and South Americas and Europe alone grossed $78.9 million—but it also made BTS more accessible to many fans around the world. Not only have they created music that can resonate with fans both lyrically and musically, but they have continuously put in the legwork to be more than just 2D entertainment in a faraway country for many thousands of fans, and they have particularly focused on the U.S., dedicating time to the market in a way few K-pop acts had attempted prior.

The Most Beautiful Moment in Life: Young Forever

BTS scaled their busy schedules back a bit at the start of 2016 until the release of the compilation album *The Most Beautiful Moment in Life: Young Forever (HYYH3)*, though they did release a Japanese version of "Run" in March. The ostensible end of *The Most Beautiful Moment in Life* narrative, the *Young Forever* album first arrived on the scene through the "Epilogue: Young Forever" video on April 19, and was followed by the release of "Fire" and the album on May 2. Though it was the end of the *HYYH* era, it didn't bring about the end of the BU storytelling, but did give fans another batch of iconic singles: "Epilogue: Young Forever," a culmination of the emotions of youth and career growth that BTS have explored in the *HYYH* era, the explosive bombast of "Fire," and the dynamic expressiveness of "Save Me," which arrived on May 15.

Like its predecessor, *HYYH3* landed itself on the Billboard 200 at No. 107, jumping nearly 70 spots and falling just short of breaking into the Top 100. In Korea, the album topped the Gaon Album Chart for two weeks following its release, and BTS took home some of the top awards at South Korean year-end shows as a result of the combined success of *HYYH2* and *HYYH3; HYYH3* garnered them their first ever *daesang,* or top award, prize at the 2016 Melon Music Awards, where it was named the album of the year. In other words, *HYYH3* was the undeniable capstone hit of a finale for the trilogy, both at home and abroad. The success of the third *HYYH* album showed that BTS's *HYYH*-era artistic shift had succeeded in carving out BTS's identity: the septet could now appeal to audiences as both the epitome of what a Korean boy band looks and sounds like, and also as counter-culture artists creating their own music, focused on millennial-oriented messaging, while still leaning in to their hip-hop roots for inspiration.

With the release of *HYYH3*, BTS put a close to their *The Most Beautiful Moment in Life* album trilogy, but it was only the start of their journey through 2016. Following the release of "Save Me" in May, the summer was mostly based around touring, and saw the group return to the U.S. for appearances at both the East and West Coast KCON events held every summer, follow-ups to performances at other KCON events the group had attended in Abu Dhabi and Paris in March and June. June also saw them celebrate their anniversary with their third Festa, and July brought the launch of BTS's travelogue show *Bon Voyage* on VLIVE, which they would turn into an ongoing series capturing their travels around the world.[7] On August 16, Suga delivered his first mixtape, the widely acclaimed *Agust D* that featured tracks through which he shared his life experiences and struggles with listeners, particularly "The Last," during which he revealed his struggle with mental illness. And September 7 brought about *Youth*, a Japanese tie-in with the *HYYH* era, though by this time the group had already begun teasing their next era. Beginning on September 4, the group upped the scale of their storytelling with the first teaser video related to their impending release of their second LP *Wings.* But while it was a teaser video, it was also much more.

Wings

In the lead-up to the album's release each member was featured in a short film, with Jungkook's "Begin" the first to arrive, at the start of September. The short films highlighted each individual member's BU storyline and their upcoming solo tracks from *Wings.* The October release turned the focus to each of BTS's seven distinct narratives for the first time. In the past, early albums had emphasized the hip-hop line of Suga, J-Hope, and RM, while the *HYYH* series emphasized the group's joint musical identity throughout. In comparison, *Wings* emphasized each individual part of the whole with songs that reflected both their own personal narratives and paralleled the BU; it's never been wholly confirmed which came first when crafting each release, the fictional storyline or the songs, or whether the songs are wholly meant to represent their personal experiences in life or express their fictive personas. For instance, "Mama," produced by popular Korean musician Primary, appears to be a track about J-Hope's relationship with his own mother but it can also relate to his character's storyline of being abandoned by his mother. Similarly, Suga's "First Love" features a plotline about a piano, an element that plays a prominent role in his counterpart's story in the BU, but the song is seemingly about his own relationship with the instrument. Regardless, BTS's dedication to weaving threads between their lives and music and their BU story is to be applauded.

Following the short films and a comeback trailer, this time featuring J-Hope and the album's introductory track "Boy Meets Evil," *Wings* landed on October 10, 2016. Much like *Dark & Wild* following the *Skool* trio, *Wings* was a standalone album that related to the earlier series, but was self-contained in its thematic leanings. Fronted by the moombahton-laden single "Blood Sweat & Tears," the 15-track LP, or full-length album, was darker and more introspective than BTS's previous LP, and overflowed with a variety of musical styles that combined to express both angst and euphoria throughout. It showcased the most mature, self-aware version of BTS seen to date, and reveled in its artistic perusal of the group's identity and growth through both solo and joint songs.

An artistic high of BTS's career, the music video for "Blood Sweat & Tears" offered up dramatic, luxurious shots full of classical Western art motifs—many relating to sin and tragedy as BTS contemplated good and evil, depicted in the most theatrically captivating ways, such as with Jin kissing a black-winged statue and V appearing as an angel who has lost his wings. With sleek dance moves and a voiceover about temptation courtesy of a line from Hermann Hesse's *Demian*, it was a further sign of the group's maturation, both thematically and artistically, and recalled characterizations featured in the BU music videos, although it was not directly, overtly, connected to these. The song became BTS's first to top Gaon's weekly digital songs chart.

Fresh from the success of *The Most Beautiful Moment in Life* era, it was only a question of how high BTS could soar with the release of *Wings*, and the answer far exceeded any expectations. Not only did it become the best-selling album ever to rank on Korea's Gaon Chart since its inception in 2010, and the best-selling album of 2016 in Korea, it also broke through any limitations Korean music had previously faced in the West. While earlier years had seen an album each from 2NE1 and EXO rank within the Top 100 of the Billboard 200 chart, not a single Korean album had ever broken into the top 50 before. But, with the support of Stateside ARMY and new listeners alike, the October release broke every record for a Korean act on the primary American album chart, and *Wings* landed at No. 26 following its release. It would spend two weeks on the main Stateside album chart after debuting, another first for a Korean album as none had ever sustained traction for longer than a single week.

The October charting also marked the start of a new period for BTS, one that would end up changing the game substantially: the group appeared on *Billboard*'s Social 50 chart for the first time at No. 1, and their continued presence eventually led to their first primetime television appearance in the U.S., at the 2017 Billboard Music Awards, where they took home the Top Social Artist award, an honor only Justin

Bieber had previously achieved, and one that made the uninitiated in the U.S. take note of the seven men from South Korea. They became the first Korean group to ever receive an award at one of the primary three music shows in the U.S.— the Billboard Music Awards (BBMAs), the American Music Awards (AMAs), and the Grammys.

The historic album brought BTS's fame to new heights and changed their career forever, as they had officially done what even the most prominent acts in K-pop had been unable to achieve: carve out a place for themselves in the largest music market in the world. They had succeeded without releasing an English-language song or collaborating with a prominent Western artist, but by leaning into their own identity and musicality, and building a sizable, active following. Following the immediate success of *Wings*'s release, BTS raked in accolades at year-end award shows in South Korea, where they became the first non-Big 3 group to win the Artist of the Year award at Mnet's annual MAMA (Mnet Asian Music Awards). But the era of *Wings* didn't finish with the end of 2016, and the following February saw BTS rise even further in prominence with the release of the extended edition, or repackage, as it's known in K-pop. *You Never Walk Alone* came out on February 13, 2017, and saw the group release two oppositional new singles, the poignant "Spring Day" and "Not Today." It led them to even higher peaks than before: "Spring Day," an electro-rock meets synth pop ode to relationships lost, not only went to No. 1 in South Korea upon its release but rapidly became the group's representative song in the country. In September of 2018, it was acknowledged by Gaon Music Chart for achieving over 100 million streams and 2.5 million downloads in the country. The song also broke into *Billboard*'s Bubbling Under Hot 100 chart at No. 15, the first time a BTS song made it into the precursor chart of the main Hot 100 rankings. Shortly after, a Japanese version of "Blood Sweat & Tears" arrived on May 10, and went to No. 1 on that country's charts.

The *Wings* album was tied into the act's 2017 BTS Live Trilogy Episode III: The Wings Tour, which kicked off in Seoul on February 18 and continued through December 10. They performed 40 shows throughout Asia, North and South America, and Australia, in front of over 550,000 people. The tour became the focal point of a YouTube series *Burn the Stage* and an extended film that came out in theaters across the world, *Burn the Stage: The Movie*, both of which were released in 2018, and revealed the group's dedication to their craft and audience, even highlighting scenes of discord between the members and some heartbreaking moments, most notably when Jungkook needed medical attention after powering through a performance

46

while ill to ensure that fans had a good experience. It was a once-in-a-lifetime moment for many ARMY in attendance at that night's concert and he didn't want to let them down.

The tour saw yet another security incident, with Jimin threatened over social media ahead of the group's two performances in Anaheim, California, in April. The authorities took the threats seriously; there was extra security for the shows and nothing came of it, but it was yet another sign of how powerful the group had become, evoking both great love and intense hate. But the darkness was overpowered by a show of support from ARMY, who cheered on Jimin and did their best, as they always do, to support him and the rest of BTS regardless of the concerns.

Throughout the Wings Tour, which spanned much of the year, BTS released a variety of music. RM collaborated with American rapper Wale on "Change" in March, a song that criticized elements of each artist's respective country's cultures, including police brutality, social media toxicity, and socio-economic divides. The group celebrated their fourth anniversary in June, with the fourth Festa bringing forth "4 O'Clock," a mellow rock ballad from V and RM, as well as an alternative version of Suga's "So Far Away," which was previously released on *Agust D* featuring Suran, but was re-released with features from Jin and Jungkook. BTS then remade Seo Taiji & Boys' classic 1995 hit "Come Back Home," participating in Seo's 25th anniversary remake album, paying homage to the South Korean icon and his legacy as both musical innovator and philosopher, creating a linear path of sorts between the progenitor of the current state of South Korean pop music and BTS, who have picked up the torch.

The *Wings* period brought BTS to new heights, and cemented their reign as the top boy band in the world. They had made history on multiple occasions, breaking just about every record put in front of them, and would continue to do so as they taught the world to love itself during their next creative era.

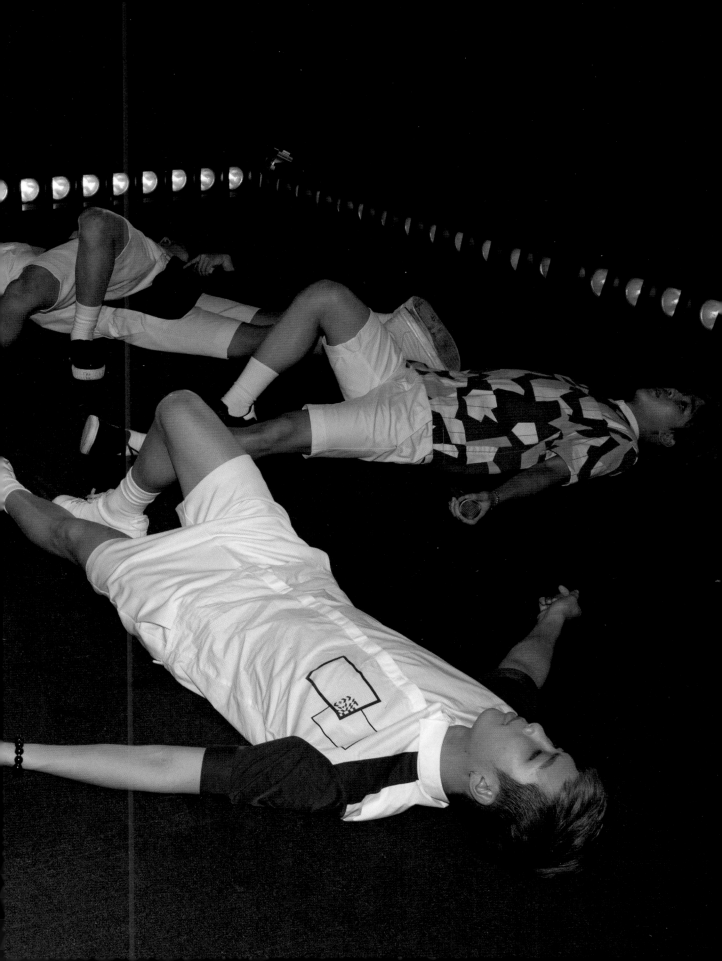

TEACHING
THE WORLD
TO LOVE ITSELF

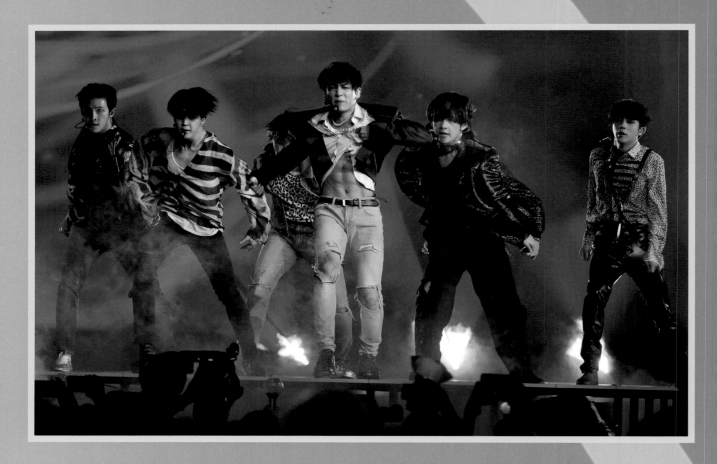

Chapter
Three

Never ones to rest on their laurels, the septet barely slowed down after making history with *Wings*, and instead introduced their new thematic era: *Love Yourself.* With the series' theme directly stated in the title, the three albums that would be released as part of the *Love Yourself* era—*Her*, *Tear*, and *Answer*—would promote the group's lyrical narrative, with each third of the trilogy representing a step on the path to happiness via self-love. Lofty in its goals, *Love Yourself* would go on to become BTS's biggest success to date, raising them to the upper echelons of the global music scene in an unprecedented way, both for the K-pop world and all Asian music markets in general. *Love Yourself* would see the group dubbed the biggest boy band in the world, and result in comparisons to the Beatles leading the British Invasion as BTS became the undeniable representatives of the Korean entertainment world to Western markets.

Beginning in August of 2017, BTS began to kick off the *Love Yourself* era with promotional imagery, a series of highlight reels, and related social media postings—plus a bright teaser video for Jimin's solo "Serendipity," the first of four solo tracks from the group's vocalists that were used in promotions. The material returned to the BU's *Most Beautiful Moment in Life* narrative, which had filtered through the *Wings* era but not quite as overtly as in the *HYYH* trilogy. With references in promotional imagery to the BU storyline, mysterious, fictional smeraldo flowers, and "Save Me," the overt connection to earlier BTS content resulted in widespread interest from ARMY, as fans around the world attempted to decipher the meaning of the teasers and how they connected to the BU's previous elements. The release of *Love Yourself* 承 *Her*, which came out on September 18, offered few immediate answers, but did grace the world with "DNA" and 10 other tracks, two of which were only available on the physical copies of the album.

With an overall light and airy tone, *Her* spent much of its time putting EDM and future bass front and center, especially through "DNA" and "Best of Me," a song co-written by Andrew Taggart of The Chainsmokers. The album was split into two halves. The first focused on the titular *Her* with a romantic slant, which was heard most prominently on the sweet "Dimple," while the second half focused on BTS's worldview. "Pied Piper" addressed fans and the burdens of fandom, while "MIC Drop" reveled in the way BTS had come out on top of the highly competitive Korean music industry, and "Go Go" drew attention to youth spending culture and urged listeners not to worry. It was an album that was all at once intimate and aggressive, and represented what BTS would pursue throughout the entire *Love Yourself* trilogy.

Like *Wings* before it, *Love Yourself* 承 *Her* was an unprecedented success, and continued BTS's global ascent. The album not only topped South Korea's Gaon but also Japan's Oricon, and landed at No. 7 on the Billboard 200, the first time a Korean act had ever broken into the Top 10 of the most established albums chart in the U.S. "DNA" similarly had historic representation: it peaked at No. 67 on *Billboard*'s Hot 100 chart, the first time a Korean male group had ever made its way onto the chart. Only the Wonder Girls, Psy, and CL had landed songs on the ranking in the past.

But that didn't end the success of *Her.* The act released *Crystal Snow* in Japan in December and then came back in full force in November with the remix of anthemic hip-pop track "MIC Drop" by electronic music producer Steve Aoki and featuring rapper Desiigner, he of "Panda" fame." Like "DNA" before it, "MIC Drop (Remix)," which was revealed through a music video on November 24, was a smash success. Released to Stateside radio stations, it became the first song by a K-pop group to reach No. 1 on the U.S. iTunes[8] realtime song chart, and broke into the Top 30 of the Hot 100, landing at No. 28. It would eventually become BTS's first song to be certified Gold by the Recording Industry Association of America (RIAA) the following February; almost a year after its release, it would go platinum in November 2018. No other Korean artist had achieved either feat aside from Psy, whose "Gangnam Style" had been recognized as going multi-platinum by the RIAA.

Her launched a new era of BTS's career Stateside, and was their most dramatic shift into the U.S. market to date as it brought about the group's first performance on a major U.S. award show: the group performed "DNA" at the 2017 American Music Awards (AMAs) in November. No longer relegated to the niche of K-pop fandom, BTS were now so popular that they performed second-to-last during the live telecast, with only Diana Ross following their highly-anticipated performance. The performance led into a media junket that landed BTS on the likes of *The Ellen DeGeneres Show* and *Jimmy Kimmel Live!*, where they also promoted the new version of "MIC Drop." After spending the previous two years solidifying their artistic identity in

BTS having fun on the red carpet at the 2015 Gaon Chart K-pop Awards in Seoul.

South Korea and among their global audience, BTS had truly hit the American mainstream.

As much as the success of BTS and their music spoke for itself, the state of American pop music and social media's integration in 2017 played an important part in their growth. BTS's ascent in the West came at a time when the American pop music scene was stagnating, with the same acts dominating charts for years, even as listeners were looking to new territories for music, such as the Latin and Korean markets. For example, the new artist of the year award at the 2017 AMAs went to Niall Horan, a member of One Direction, who had been nominated with his group for the same award in 2012. Though it recognized the Irish artist's new career path as a soloist, it also emphasized how the American pop music scene had stayed in its comfort zone while hip-hop enjoyed increased popularity in an age of streaming, and increasingly non-English-language music was becoming more prevalent, yet those musical scenes were only slowly being recognized.

Though each year brings new artists to the forefront, the Drakes, Lady Gagas, and Taylor Swifts of the industry remain at the top, and only a handful of young pop acts rise to fame each year. Homegrown boy bands, and bands in general, hadn't been popular in the Stateside industry for around a decade, with only international imports like One Direction and 5 Seconds of Summer truly gaining traction in a scene now dominated predominantly by soloists. BTS arrived at a time when no single male group was prominent in the States; even in the K-pop world, there was a gap as BIGBANG were on hiatus and EXO were dedicated to building their following in Asia.

Amid all of this, BTS picked up a global, intensely interactive fandom, largely in Internet spaces, in the form of the digital-savvy ARMY. BTS was the most buzzed-about artist on both Twitter and Tumblr that year. At a time when television audiences are shrinking, media entities like Dick Clark Productions, which puts on the AMAs, the Billboard Music Awards (BBMAs), and *Dick Clark's New Year's Rockin' Eve*, which all saw BTS either attend or perform in 2017, recognized that tapping into social media's most talked-about musical act of the year would draw in viewers. And it appears to have worked: after dipping to 8.2 million views the previous year, the 2017 AMA event recorded 9.15 million. It's likely that BTS's inclusion had something to do with this; the 2018 AMAs, which did not feature the group though they did win the Favorite Social Artist award that night, only brought in 6.59 million views.

54

The AMAs, and parent company Dick Clark, were far from the only organization to realize that social media traction actually translated into people behind the screens with true spending power, and the year ended with the launch of a collaboration between BTS and Line Friends, the character-oriented brand associated with messenger app Line, which is popular in Japan but associated with South Korea's Naver corporation. The BT21 collaboration, which features characters drawn by BTS's members, reportedly drew over 35,000 shoppers to the Line Friends store in Times Square over the weekend of its launch in December 2017, and later expanded beyond Line Friends stores around the world to bring BT21 merchandise to Amazon, Hot Topic, Uniqlo, and other retailers. Brands like Converse, Hello Kitty, and Anti Social Social Club have also collaborated with the character line.

2017 faded out with BTS and "Spring Day" receiving top honors at multiple South Korean year-end award ceremonies, and also saw them appear for the first time on a Japanese music show, with their performance of "DNA" on *Japan Music Station Super Live* at the end of December. The next year would kick off with their first Double Platinum certification from the Recording Industry Association of Japan for their *MIC Drop/DNA/Crystal Snow* single album, which was followed by "MIC Drop (Remix)" and "DNA" both being recognized by the RIAA for going gold, marking BTS as the only Korean artist to ever receive RIAA certifications for two separate tracks; Psy was awarded the recognition for "Gangnam Style."

February 2018 saw BTS on the cover of *Billboard Magazine*, the first time ever for a Korean group. It also brought about news of J-Hope's upcoming mixtape *Hope World*, which was released on March 2. With retro hip-pop and funk vibes, plus literary inspiration throughout, *Hope World* debuted on the Billboard 200 chart at No. 63, the highest-ever ranking achieved by a solo K-pop artist, even though it was offered for free and only had a day's worth of sales and streams counted for that week's chart. *Hope World* continued to rise over the next week, and the mixtape, fronted by "Daydream" and "Airplane," peaked at No. 38 the following week.

The success of J-Hope's solo efforts set the starting line for one of BTS's busiest years to date. Throughout the rest of 2018, the group would release four albums in Korean and Japanese, and RM would release *mono.*, a solo playlist. They toured the world, spoke in front of the United Nations, and renewed their contracts with Big Hit Entertainment for another seven years, demonstrating the bond between the group and the company. A contract of this sort, signed well before BTS's previous contract had ended, was unheard of in the South Korean music industry.

Throughout, they broke record after record across global music charts. And they did it while promoting the messaging of *Love Yourself* through their musical releases.

First up was April's *Face Yourself*, BTS's third Japanese LP, which dropped on the fourth of that month. Featuring both Japanese remakes of Korean songs released on *Wings* and *Love Yourself 承 Her*, the previously released "Crystal Snow," and four new original Japanese tracks, the album was related to but not directly part of the *Love Yourself* series. Despite few brand-new songs, the album was still propelled to great heights on charts in both Japan and the U.S., even though the latter was not its target market. Before its release, the single "Don't Leave Me" charted on *Billboard*'s Japan Hot 100 chart at No. 25 after a short preview of the song was revealed on March 15, and eventually went to No. 21 on that chart and No. 18 on Oricon's singles chart. In the U.S., the album debuted at No. 43 on the Billboard 200. Despite having no music video, the songs spoke for themselves and with *Face Yourself* BTS proved just how successful they had become in the world's two largest music markets, a true coup for seven men from a country of around 51 million. *Face Yourself* would later be certified platinum by the RIAJ.

Love Yourself 轉 Tear

Almost simultaneously with the Japanese album's arrival, BTS began launching promotions for their next album, *Love Yourself 轉 Tear*. The April 5 release of Jungkook's "Euphoria," via a video dubbed the *Love Yourself: Wonder* theme, raised anticipation about May's *Love Yourself 轉 Tear*. It was later followed by a second new song as a promotional teaser, the dramatic neo-soul solo "Singularity" from V on May 6.

When it was released on May 18, anticipation was high for *Love Yourself 轉 Tear*, and it did not disappoint. Like its predecessor, *Tear* explored the titular phrase in depth, this time through an LP featuring 11 tracks relating to the darker elements of romantic love, exemplified by the single "Fake Love," and self-love, as it applies to BTS and their career through tracks like "Airplane Pt. 2" and "Anpanman." These ruminate on, respectively, the group's success and their position as inspirational heroes of a generation, while songs like "Paradise" take a philosophical turn, exploring what it means to have dreams. Running

Amid all of this, BTS picked up a global, intensely interactive fandom in the form of the digital-savvy ARMY.

the gamut of musical styles, the sleekly produced album made history when it debuted at the top of the Billboard 200, the first ever album by a Korean act to top the main American chart.

In just a few years, BTS had achieved something no K-pop group ever had. An album charting at No. 1 in the U.S. meant that many of their songs were being sold and listened to en masse, repeatedly, by audiences across the country. It was a goal that every K-pop act, particularly those from the "Big 3" K-pop companies, had been aiming for over the past decade. Unlike prior K-pop attempts at crossing over into the West, which typically came in bursts of momentum rather than long-term, active engagement, they did it in a strategic way, focusing on the U.S. market as they had with Japan: sporadically but with intent to build a local audience.

Since filming *American Hustle Life*, BTS had regularly spent time performing in the U.S. and making themselves accessible to local fans and media entities, building up a genuine following from consumers and interest from within the entertainment world. Prior crossover attempts from the K-pop world to break into the mainstream Western music scene had focused on spending extended time in the U.S., often to the detriment of artists' careers in Korea, and/or releasing music in English sporadically, often with prominent Western artists who had little to no connection to the world of K-pop, and few artistic similarities with Korean collaborators. Following Wonder Girls and BoA's initial one-off *Billboard* charting, few acts gained much traction locally even as the audience for Korean pop music continued to grow, driven by engaged fandoms and pop lovers looking for variety beyond the local market. While tours would become increasingly common, especially by K-pop boy bands, only a few South Korean musicians gained true traction in the U.S., such as CL and Psy, both of whom were managed by American entrepreneur Scooter Braun for a time. The U.S. market would occasionally recognize the success of Korea's entertainment industry, but overall K-pop's presence in the U.S. was niched, and seemed to be sitting there for the long run.

But like a perfect storm, BTS had been able to market themselves in a variety of territories without diverging too much from

"At the very heart of BTS's outstanding dancing and singing is sincerity. This magical power turns grief into hope and differences into similarities... Bangtan, which literally means "bulletproof" in Korean, was born out of the will to protect teenagers from prejudice and oppression. The names of each member—Jin, Suga, J-Hope, RM, Jimin, V, and Jungkook—are going to be remembered for a long time." [9]

—President Moon Jae-in

their original sound, gradually integrating into the U.S. scene through subtle, production-based collaborations and one-offs rather than attempting to Americanize the act overnight, while their mixture of social media engagement and regular local performances helped grow their following. With tight bonds apparent in the group, and members who were deeply involved in crafting their songs and style, their hard work and team spirit had served them well, and these new heights were just the beginning of the upcoming era of BTS's career where each week or so saw them making history or launching a new venture.

Their success gained praise from South Korean president Moon Jae-in, who congratulated them on their No. 1 album, one of many occasions when his administration recognized BTS's impact in spreading Korean music and culture across the globe.

The music of *Love Yourself* 轉 *Tear* and its success on the Billboard 200 chart wasn't the only notable element of its release: BTS performed the single "Fake Love" live for the first time at the 2018 Billboard Music Awards, an acknowledgement of their popularity in the country, their prioritization of the Stateside audience, and their global ARMY, which would be watching. (They also won the Top Social Artist award for the second year in a row.) A bold move that could have potentially alienated their fanbase in South Korea, it resonated around the globe, and ignited even more interest in BTS. The song ended up debuting at No. 10 on *Billboard*'s Hot 100 chart, the first-ever song by a Korean group—and the 17th predominantly non-English one overall—to make it into the highest tier of the main song ranking in the U.S. Amid all this, the group also appeared on *The Late Late Show with James Corden,* another sign that they had become a mainstay of American television. With *Love Yourself* 轉 *Tear* and "Fake Love," BTS had broken just about every barrier Korean artists, and non-Anglocentric artists in general, had faced before them, opening up even greater opportunities for those who followed.

Hardly taking a moment's break, the group celebrated their fifth anniversary with remixes, covers, and one brand-new original track, "Ddaeng," out on June 10 as part of that year's Festa. A track dissing haters and featuring the group's rap line, the song was influenced by traditional Korean sounds and used education and game-associated metaphors to address those who had looked down upon them. With an unofficial release through SoundCloud, and no monetary benefits, the song served as a direct message from the group to their followers, as well as the detractors it was addressing, and received wide applause from ARMY across the globe, becoming a fan anthem of sorts.

Love Yourself 結 Answer

The final *Love Yourself* album *Love Yourself 結 Answer* was announced in July, a few weeks before its August release, and was preceded by Jin's solo track "Epiphany." A repackaged album set to summarize and conclude the era, just as *The Most Beautiful Moment in Life: Young Forever* had done for that series, *Answer* was set to reflect the accumulated message of BTS's *Love Yourself*. It wrapped things up neatly in a two-disc album that spends its first half relaying BTS's message about the path to self-love and happiness, and the second featuring other *Her* and *Tear* tracks, including a few remixes. Most surprisingly, the digital edition featured a special version of the single "IDOL" featuring Nicki Minaj, the group's first-ever single to feature another artist upon an album's release.

Like *Tear* before it, *Answer* debuted at No. 1 on the Billboard 200 chart, and "IDOL" dipped just below "Fake Love," landing at No. 11. It went on to become BTS's first song to rank in the U.K.'s Official Singles top 40, peaking at No. 21. The single, which drew on traditional Korean musical styles as well as South African house beats, was simultaneously an anthem about self-love and the group's success, both themes reflected throughout the *Love Yourself* series' prior releases. Its arrival preceded the launch of the Love Yourself World Tour in Seoul on August 25, 2018, which saw the septet perform at 42 shows throughout the world. The tour was accompanied by prominent media appearances featuring the group in the U.S., Europe, and Asia, and it would see BTS play some of Asia's biggest venues, in a glow-up from past tours, as well as major European and Stateside venues, including London's The O2 and New York City's Citi Field, the first-ever stadium-size show by a Korean act in the U.S. All stops of the tour were sold out, and would eventually prompt a second leg, known as *Love Yourself: Speak Yourself*, which launched in 2019, bringing BTS to stadiums across multiple continents.

Amid this tour, BTS had the opportunity to speak in front of the United Nations. While on the east coast of the U.S. for *Love Yourself* shows in New Jersey and New York, the septet were invited to speak at the launch of a new UNICEF initiative, where RM gave what would come to be known as his empowering "Speak Yourself" speech, in which he urged young people to take note of their own internal voice rather than listen to the world around them. A show of self-love, it was impactful and further enhanced BTS's reputation as inspirators for a generation. This was paired with his poignant request at Citi

60

Blood

Field for fans to use him and BTS's music to grow to love themselves, paralleling his own relationship with ARMY: "It was never intended, but it feels like I'm using you guys to love myself. So I'm going to say one thing. Please use me, please use BTS to love yourself. Because you guys help me learn to love myself, every day."

The end of an era, *Answer* and its promotions smoothly brought the *Love Yourself* series to a close, and was eventually certified Gold by the RIAA, the first-ever album by a Korean artist to achieve the feat. But it was far from the last of the group's releases in 2018, which would end with both a new Japanese single in the form of "Airplane Pt. 2" and RM's *mono.* playlist. October 2018 saw BTS continue to thrive, landing them a *Time* magazine cover as one of 2018's "Next Generation Leaders," and seeing them take Europe by storm. During their concert tour there, they not only gained exposure from many of the biggest names in media, including *The Graham Norton Show* on October 12 (sans Jimin, who was injured), but also performed at the Korea-France Friendship concert event in Paris on October 14, during which they took pictures with South Korean president Moon Jae-in.

A few days later, RM announced, and then on October 23 released, his playlist *mono.*, a free, seven-track, digital-only release that expressed melancholy emotions, emphasizing his feelings about cities in the songs "seoul" and "tokyo." Like J-Hope's *Hope World* before it, RM's October release of *mono.* debuted on the Billboard 200, peaking at No. 26, the highest ever for a Korean soloist and jumping past *Hope World*'s peak of No. 38, emphasizing once again how BTS's fanbase had grown even more impactful over the span of 2018, expanding their reach to mainstream listeners worldwide.

The week proved to be a busy one for BTS in an already jam-packed touring schedule: just a handful of hours after the release of *mono.* BTS received orders of cultural merit from the South Korean government on October 24. During the 2018 Korean Popular Culture & Arts Awards ceremony, the seven men were recognized for spreading Korean culture and language throughout the world, and each individually received a fifth-class *Hwagwan* Order of Cultural Merit. The next day, BTS would be represented by RM and Jungkook on Steve Aoki's new song "Waste It On Me," the first all-English song from the group to be directly aimed at Stateside radioplay; it peaked at No. 89 on the Hot 100 chart in November.

But while October was full of successes, the month of November proved to be a trying one for BTS, as the group became embroiled in a mass of tensions surrounding their past actions, especially concerning their upcoming Japanese tour dates.

Difficulties with Japan's pop culture industry had begun earlier in the year for BTS, when they were set to release their new Japanese single "Bird." But an outcry from Korean audiences over the alleged right-wing, pro-Imperial Japan proclivities of its songwriter Yasushi Akimoto, the man behind AKB48 and its associated groups, meant that BTS's team pulled the upcoming single; the group released "Airplane, Pt. 2" in Japanese as a single instead.

The song change coincided with several high-profile conflicts between the Japanese and South Korean governments, relating to the lingering effects of Japan's early 20th-century colonization of South Korea. As the governments parried over lawsuits and naval flags, an image of Jimin began circulating in digital spaces. It showed the BTS vocalist wearing a shirt that celebrated South Korea's liberation from Japan in 1945, but used graphic imagery to equate the country's independence from colonial Imperial Japan to the inhumane actions of the U.S. in dropping nuclear bombs on Hiroshima and Nagasaki. By November, the clip of Jimin wearing the shirt in BTS's 2017 *Bon Voyage* series had become a prominent talking point on social media. On November 8, it led to Japan's TV Asahi cancelling a planned performance by BTS, just days before the group was set to perform two high-profile shows at the Tokyo Dome.

The situation drew widespread attention in Western media, a reflection of BTS's popularity, and resulted in the Simon Wiesenthal Center, a Jewish human rights organization, issuing a statement. In it, the center highlighted three instances: Jimin's shirt, a hat RM once wore in a photoshoot that featured Nazi insignia, and one of the band's performances that appeared to lean into elements of fascism. The center felt the message conveyed by these actions made BTS inappropriate role models for audiences across the world, and claimed that the act was "mocking the past." As the controversy mounted, Big Hit Entertainment released a statement clarifying each of the three situations, explaining that the clothing items were not worn with offensive intent towards the victims of Nazism or atomic bombings, and that the fascist-seeming imagery used in a concert— a cover of Seo Taiji's iconic "Classroom Ideology"—was meant as commentary on the Korean school system. Following the statement, things began to die down and BTS's shows in Tokyo, and the following stops in Osaka and then Taiwan, went ahead unhindered. Things normalized, and RM was featured on yet another collab, this time "Timeless" on Drunken Tiger's final album. Originally a hip-hop crew in South Korea, Drunken Tiger had become synonymous with frontman Tiger JK over the years, and the genre forerunner was ready to put the moniker to rest with his *Drunken Tiger X: Rebirth of Tiger JK* album. After previously teaming up with Seo Taiji, considered the progenitor of K-pop and known as South Korea's "President of Culture," and homing in on BTS's connection to that scene, this collab emphasized BTS's relationship with Korean hip-hop, and showcased their position as torchbearers for many of South Korea's most popular music scenes.

Before the year ended, BTS would also get their first cinematic release thanks to *Burn the Stage: The Movie* heading to theaters worldwide; it premiered on November 15 in the U.S. An extension of the YouTube docuseries about the Wings Tour, it sold 940,000 tickets worldwide ahead of its opening, and reportedly grossed $14 million during its opening week across 79 territories and 2,650 theaters.

BTS, *Tear*, and *Answer* would be awarded multiple times throughout the year-end award show season in South Korea, but *Tear* would warrant one of the highest international nominations of all before the year was out. In December, the Grammys revealed that professional branding company HuskyFox, which worked on the album designs for the entire *Love Yourself* series, was nominated in the Best Recording Package category for its art direction of the physical *Love Yourself* 轉 *Tear* album's elegant packaging. Although the music itself was not recognized, this was still immensely exciting as it was the first time anything BTS-related, and anything associated with the Korean pop music world in general, was nominated for a Grammy.

The Love Yourself Tour would continue into 2019, but the end of 2018 signalled the end of releases associated with this musical period. But before the New Year rang in, Jimin surprised fans in the final hours of the year, releasing his solo, self-composed song "Promise" on December 31. It would go on to overtake Drake's debut-day streaming record on SoundCloud. He later revealed that the song was meant to comfort listeners and had been inspired by his finding solace in the connection between BTS and ARMY during the group's performance at Citi Field, a focal point of the *Love Yourself* era's success. It was with this "Promise" that the group moved on from its biggest year to date.

The new year started off with a busy January in which American toy company Mattel, producer of many popular brands including Barbie and Hot Wheels, produced a line of BTS dolls (though the dolls were unveiled in March and would drop later in the year) and the BU got two new major elements in the form of *The Most Beautiful Moment in Life: The Notes 1* book, a compilation of the notes released on social media throughout the BU's narrative, and also a webtoon series, *Save Me.* Combined, the pair laid forth the BU narrative seen so far, finally making clear the majority of the storyline and its themes that had previously been seen in bits and pieces since its launch in 2015 with "I Need U."

And, if that weren't enough news for ARMY, January also teased the upcoming *BTS World* mobile phone game. This would get its own soundtrack album featuring brand-new music from BTS, including collaborations with Charli XCX, Juice WRLD, and Zara Larsson. The game itself would arrive at the end of June, and simulate a world where players managed BTS's career and members, and interacted with them alternately in other "what if" storylines where the seven men had never become part of BTS. *BTS World* was created by gaming company Netmarble, which was co-founded by Bang Si-hyuk's cousin Bang Joon-hyuk in 2000; Netmarble became the second largest shareholder of Big Hit Entertainment in April 2018.

Members continued to release new music throughout this period: A new song by LeeSoRa featuring Suga. "Song Request," produced by Epik High's Tablo, was also released that month. And at the very end of january, V released his song "Scenery" on SoundCloud, getting one more piece of content out there to set the hearts of fans afire.

February was no less busy for BTS, and saw them become presenters at the 61st Grammy Awards, where they awarded H.E.R.'s self-titled album with R&B album of the year. On February 19, the group announced the *Love Yourself: Speak Yourself* tour dates for upcoming shows at stadiums in Los Angeles, Chicago, Sao Paulo, London, and Paris, while additional ones for each city would be added later on as tickets sold out immediately after going on sale. A few days later, BTS and Big Hit Entertainment teased and then announced the ARMYPEDIA project, a fan-driven archive project that would include an offline element, where fans would find QR codes asking "Hey ARMY! Lost This?" out in the wild, such as on a bus stop in Seoul or a poster in Times Square, and sometimes in digital places like on an old BTS video. Each code would correspond to a date of BTS's career, and whoever encountered them could enter some information about BTS and that date on ARMYPEDIA.

On March 11, 2019, the Suga-produced Epik High song "Eternal Sunshine" was released on the group's *Sleepless in _____* album, an immense show of recognition for Suga's skill as an artist from the group that BTS had looked up to and emulated in their early days. That same day, Big Hit Entertainment announced that the group would release *Map of the Soul: Persona* on April 12, which tied in to all the BU releases of the year, as the day Jin relives in the *Save Me* webtoon storyline is April 11—meaning that both *The Notes 1* and *Save Me*, which ended on April 10, were part of the lead-up to this new stage of BTS's storytelling.

Map of the Soul: Persona

As the month progressed, it became clear that BTS had no plans to slow down, with just about every day bringing something new for their dedicated ARMY to get excited about. With the end of the month came a collaboration between Homme and RM, as the rapper featured on the British electro-soul duo's "Crying Over You" remix along with Beka of the duo These Your Children, while as a whole the group appeared on the cover of *Entertainment Weekly*. Then, on March 28, the first formal hints of BTS's new era arrived.

The *Map of the Soul: Persona* comeback trailer featured RM's "Intro: Persona," through which the rapper recalled the musical styling of the group's "Intro" from *Skool Luv Affair*. With a sampling that appeared in that album's intro ("You give me love"), "Persona," and its video featuring RM, the trailer brought to light the album's contemplative themes of personal exploration, and hinted at the reflective, philosophical concepts on which the *Map of the Soul* era would ruminate.

The following days would see BTS announce their 5th Muster Magic Shop fanmeetings, which would take place in Busan and Seoul in June to coincide with their sixth anniversary, and begin teasing the concept imagery for the *Map of the Soul: Persona* album, which featured dozens of photos expressing slightly different aspects, or personas, of each member. With expectations high for the release, BTS blew audiences out of the water with the announcement on April 7, via a teaser video, that singer Halsey would be joining them on their new single "Boy With Luv" ("A Poem for Small Things" in Korean), which arrived on April 12 along with the *Map of the Soul: Persona* album.

A sequel of sorts to "Boy In Luv," the new single conveyed a sense of maturity and an elated approach towards love, where it no longer causes pain and anxiety but exuberance and excitement. Featuring Halsey, a partnership that had been in the works since they first met the American pop star at the 2017 BBMAs, was a stroke of genius, one that would make the song, already high profile, built for radio play as Halsey is one of the most radio-friendly stars of the past few years. "Boy With Luv" peaked on the Hot 100 at No. 8, and the album, like its immediate BTS predecessors, landed at No. 1 on the Billboard 200 chart.

For many, the *Map of the Soul* era, beginning with the *Persona* EP, is a sequel series to *Love Yourself*. Yet it has an entirely different sense of emotional development from *Love Yourself*. While the entire idea of the *Love Yourself* series is that you cannot love the world and those around you until you have developed self-love, the *Map of the Soul* era is an introspective exploration of identity that grows out of this self-acceptance. Directly related to the idea of loving oneself, *Map of the Soul* is about how self-identity interacts with the world around it, rather than self-worth, as the *Love Yourself* series had emphasized. Both important elements of understanding and loving oneself, they are two sides of a coin.

The *Map of the Soul: Persona* comeback proved to be another major period for BTS. Not only did it precede their immense *Love Yourself: Speak Yourself* stadium world tour, but they also performed on NBC's iconic *Saturday Night Live*, kicked off *Good Morning America*'s summer concert series, and appeared on *The Late Show with Stephen Colbert*, where they performed in the Ed Sullivan Theater in New York City paying homage to the Beatles. They were named one of *Time* magazine's 100 Most Influential People of 2019, with Halsey penning a touching tribute to the act: "Behind those three letters are seven astounding young men who believe that music is stronger than the barriers of language…With positive messages of self-confidence, intricacies of philosophy hidden in their sparkly songs, true synergy and brotherhood in every step of their elaborate choreography, and countless charitable and anthropological endeavors, BTS have put their 14 best feet forward as role models to millions of adoring fans and anyone else who finds themselves drawn to BTS's undeniable allure...For BTS, world domination is just another 8-count in the contemporary dance of life. But if you think that's easy, you haven't seen the love and effort these young men put into each and every step."[10]

BTS and Halsey would perform "Boy In Luv" together for the first time on May 2 at the 2019 Billboard Music Awards, just days after a special "ARMY with Luv" version of the music video dropped on April 26, which featured slightly different visuals and the phrase "ARMY" appearing at one point rather than "LOVE" as in the original music video, a nod to the bond between the fans and the group. The BBMAs that year also saw BTS win not only the Top Social artist award as they had over the past two years, but also the Top Duo/Group award, the first time they had been recognized in an American award show for their artistry rather than their virality.

The album's release would lead in to the Love Yourself: Speak Yourself Tour, kicking off at Los Angeles' Rose Bowl Stadium on May 4 with another show there on May 5; those two dates would

Teaching the World to Love Itself

go on to earn $16.6 million out of the $44 million that BTS's six U.S. dates in May, along with two at Chicago's Soldier Field and two at New Jersey's Metlife Stadium in the Meadowlands, would gross, as reported to *Billboard*'s Boxscore.

Before the first half of 2019 was over, the group would celebrate their sixth anniversary on June 13. As the year went on, BTS would not slow down between touring; ad and product campaigns; media appearances; performing on *The Voice* finale and *Britain's Got Talent*; and a whole slew of Muster releases, ranging from photos to fun videos and a new song "Tonight" from Jin dedicated to his pets. They were also commemorated at the Empire State Building with effects being played on the hour to celebrate their sold-out shows at the New York-area MetLife Stadium; as well as being invited to join the Record Academy, which votes for the Grammys. In July, they released their original Japanese song "Lights."

The following six months were full of awards and accolades for BTS, including acknowledgement that Map of the Soul: Persona had become the best-selling South Korean album of all time, and the second-most best-selling physical album of the year in the United States, second only to Taylor Swift's Lover. They also brought their Love Yourself: Speak Yourself tour to Saudi Arabia; overall, the tour sold 1.6 million tickets and brought in $196.4 million.

December began with Halsey releasing "Suga's Interlude," and ended with BTS performing in Times Square at the iconic Dick Clark's New Year's Rockin' Eve with Ryan Seacrest event, a fitting celebration for a year that saw them win awards at a multitude of events, including the BBMAs, the AMAs, and the MAMA and Melon awards in Korea. They became the first-ever Korean act to win the grand prizes in both physical and digital categories at the 34th Golden Disc Awards, acknowledgement from the industry that the group had grown beyond any act before them.

Map of the Soul: 7

As they entered their seventh year, things only got bigger and bet-ter for BTS and there was no sign that they would be slowing down anytime soon. Although South Korea's compulsory military enlistments hung over their future, BTS had signaled that they were together for the long run with their contract renewals in 2018, and in February 2020 they released *Map of the Soul: 7*, a love song to their career together as seven men over seven years. For *Map of the Soul: 7* the septet returned to the same style of LP release as *Wings* and *Love Yourself: Answer*, with solo and unit tracks focusing on the dynamics among the members of the group, as well as ruminating on their career through the release of singles "Black Swan" and "ON," the latter a parallel to "N.O," which was also released in an alternate version featuring Sia. It preceded their Map of the Soul world tour, which had performances scheduled at many of the world's stadiums and arenas in a major follow-up to the Speak Yourself Tour, though it would be impacted by cancellations due to the spread of the COVID-19 coronavirus.

The *Map of the Soul: 7* album as a whole explored what it means to be BTS, both on an individual level, as a group, and in public spaces, and its release featured some of the act's highest-profile moments yet, with numerous televised appearances in the U.S., including a "Carpool Karaoke" appearance on *The Late Late Show with James Corden*, and an appearance on *The Tonight Show Starring Jimmy Fallon,* during which they took over Grand Central Terminal in the heart of New York City to premiere the first televised performance of "ON." A symbolic hub of America's golden age, Grand Central became BTS's stage and highlighted how the act from South Korea has continued to overcome immense barriers in an entertainment world typically partitioned by geographic and linguistic boundaries. *Map of the Soul: 7* became the act's fourth No. 1 on the Billboard 200, and topped charts in numerous other countries with over four million sales worldwide, and "ON" became BTS's first Top 5 on the Hot 100 chart, debuting at No. 4 on the chart dated March 7, 2020.

With one hit after another, and more and more content released as their career progresses, BTS continue to show the people of the world how to love themselves and explore their psychological depths. The Bangtan Boys from South Korea have truly put their blood, sweat, and tears into their career, and have come out on top, leaving a changed world in their wake.

BTS AND THEIR CO

Chapter Four

LLABORATORS

ENTER THE WORLD OF

KIM SEOK-JIN
DECEMBER 4, 1992

OFFICIAL ROLES
VOCALIST, ACTOR

AGE AT BTS'S DEBUT
20 YEARS OLD

HOMETOWN
GWACHEON, SOUTH KOREA

POST-DEBUT, NON-BTS ALBUM SOLO RELEASES (EXCLUDING COVERS):

2016

"IT'S DEFINITELY YOU" WITH V
HWARANG: THE POET WARRIOR YOUTH
SOUNDTRACK

2019, SOUNDCLOUD

"TONIGHT"

김석진

Born in Gwacheon, which is in Gyeonggi-do province just outside of Seoul, Jin is known as a hard worker and the most improved member of BTS both vocally and as a performer. Before joining the group, he was pursuing acting and had no formal training as a dancer or singer until Big Hit scouted him.

The eldest member of BTS, Jin is considered the "visual" of the group, and his nickname "worldwide handsome" refers to images and videos of him going viral on multiple occasions due to his good looks. He has a degree in theater and film from Konkuk University, where he graduated in 2017, and is now pursuing a graduate degree from Hanyang Cyber University. Known for his high, sweet, singing tone, he has revealed that a Big Hit Entertainment street casting agent approached him when he was on his way to university, intertwining his fate as a member of BTS with his degree.

Jin is known for his sense of humor, particularly his dad jokes and puns, and for being a true foodie who loves eating and cooking. He has his own web series on BTS's BANGTANTV channel known as "Eat Jin," which launched on May 20, 2015. In each episode, he shows off the food he is eating, a common video broadcast format in South Korea known as *mukbang* or *mokbang*, which literally translates into "eat(ing) broad(cast)." He has continued to make the videos over the years, giving ARMY their own culinary connoisseur.

He released his first non-album solo song amid BTS's 2019 sixth-anniversary Festa event, the evocative "Tonight." Jin has often shared his love of his sugar gliders and dog with ARMY over the years and "Tonight," dedicated to his pets, paid homage to them in the most heartfelt way.

Jin plays a key role in the BU narrative, and has showed off his talent as an actor while appearing as the primary character in many of the group's music videos, and his Seokjin counterpart is the main protagonist in the *Save Me* webtoon series.

ENTER THE WORLD OF

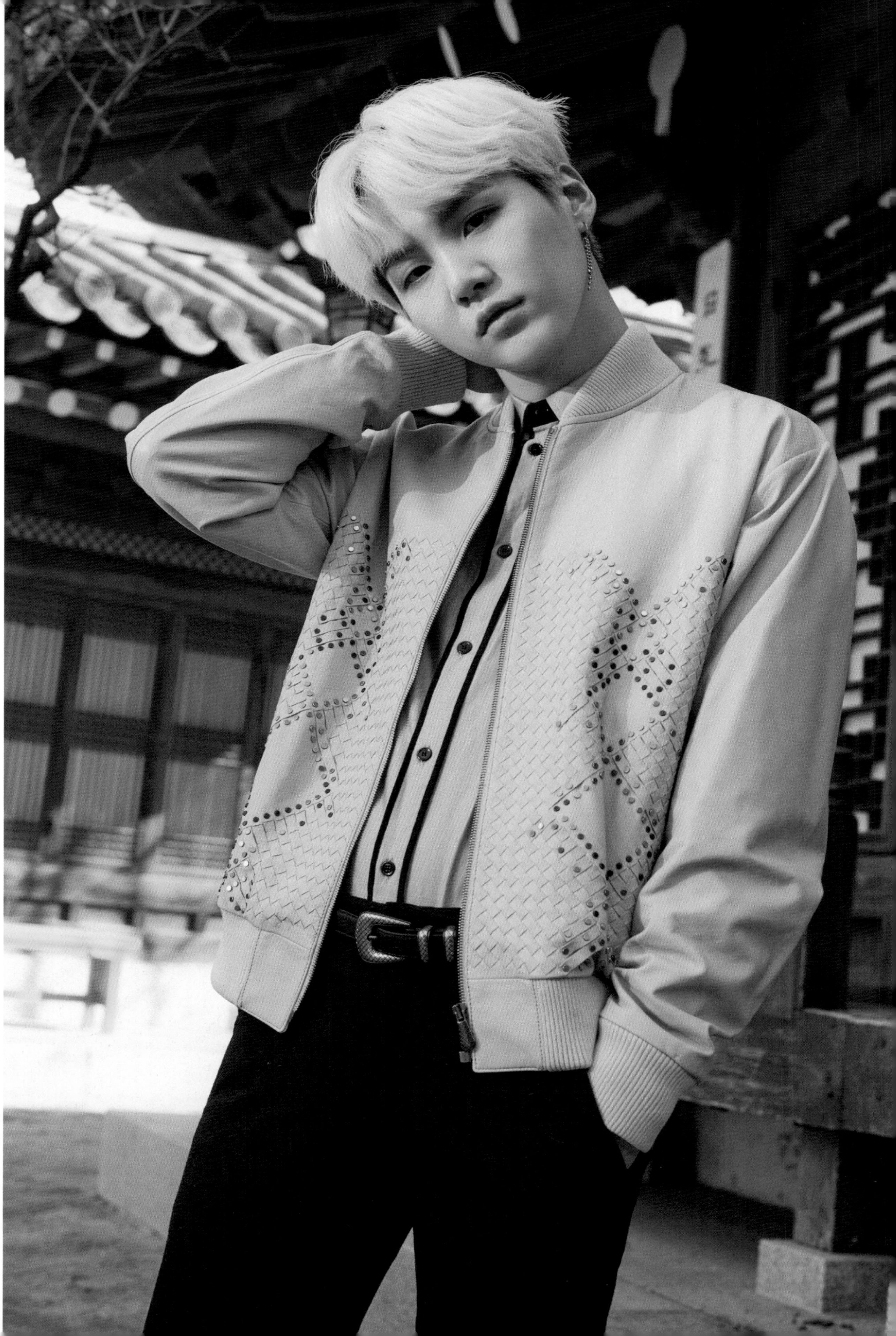

MIN YOON-GI
MARCH 9, 1993

ALSO KNOWN AS
AGUST D AND GLOSS

OFFICIAL ROLES
RAPPER, COMPOSER,
PRODUCER

AGE AT BTS'S DEBUT
20 YEARS OLD

HOMETOWN
DAEGU, SOUTH KOREA

민윤기

Hailing from South Korea's fourth-largest city, Daegu, the quick-witted and quick-tongued Suga became interested in rap after hearing music from Korean reggae artists Stony Skunk. Prior to joining Big Hit, he was originally an underground rapper known as Gloss in the crew D-Town. He competed in Big Hit Entertainment's 2010 "Hit It" auditions, initially aiming to be a producer after struggling to make a living as a songwriter in his hometown. He came in second place, and ended up joining what would become BTS; in the song "724148" from his solo mixtape *Agust D*, he alluded to the fact that Bang's reputation as a songwriter led him to pursue the audition. His current stage name is a reference to an abbreviated version of the basketball term "shooting guard" as he is a fan of the sport and his name is pronounced "Shoo-ga" in Korean, as well as his sugar-pale skin tone.

Known for his gruff but affectionate attitude, Suga is the group's second-eldest member and the most outspoken. Throughout his career as a songwriter, he's written about South Korean politics, such as on "518-062," a song which he produced for another D-Town member, Naksyeon, addressing the democratic uprising and consequent massacre that took place in 1980 in the South Korean city of Gwangju. He's also delved into personal territory with songs about the state of his mental health, sharing his struggles with anxiety and depression on *Agust D.*

With a strong sense of who he is and his place in the world, Suga has been producing music since before his time in BTS, and has been a key player in directing the group's sound. In recent years, the deep-toned rapper has begun producing for acts outside of BTS, including Epik High, who he has credited in the past as his major inspiration for pursuing a career as a rapper. He gained much recognition and praise for crafting Suran's award-winning 2017 hit "Wine," and in 2018, he was chosen as a full member of the Korea Music Copyright Association (KOMCA) a nod to his role as a songwriter for BTS and others.

SOLO RELEASES:

SONGS HE'S WRITTEN FOR
OTHERS OUTSIDE OF BTS:

2016

AGUST D

2019

"SONG REQUEST"
BY LEESORA
FEAT. SUGA

2017

"WINE" BY SURAN

2019

"ETERNAL SUNSHINE"
BY EPIK HIGH

2020

"SUGA'S INTERLUDE"
BY HALSEY

ENTER THE WORLD OF

OFFICIAL ROLES

RAPPER, DANCER, CHOREOGRAPHER

AGE AT BTS'S DEBUT

19 YEARS OLD

HOMETOWN

GWANGJU, SOUTH KOREA

SOLO RELEASES:

2018

HOPE WORLD

2019

"CHICKEN NOODLE SOUP" FEAT. BECKY G

정호석

J-Hope began street dancing during his first year of junior high and quickly gained a reputation in Gwangju and beyond as an underground dancer. He was known particularly for his breakdancing, especially his popping, krumping, and freestyling. He attended the Joy Dance Academy (also known as the Joy Dance Plugin Music Academy), a Daegu idol training school that many other top K-pop stars have attended and which was once part of a chain owned by former BIGBANG member Seungri. While in the underground scene, J-Hope gained renown as part of a dance team known as Neuron, using the stage name "Smile Hoya." He auditioned for JYP Entertainment in 2009 and, though he placed high in the rankings, he didn't end up with an offer from the company but instead joined Big Hit Entertainment in 2010 when the company was still prepping a hip-hop-oriented team. During *American Hustle Life*, he revealed that out of the seven original members of the original lineup for BTS he was the only one who danced. Prior to BTS's formal debut in 2013, he appeared under the name "Jeong Ho-seok of BTS" on Jo Kwon of 2AM's "Animal," where he rapped alongside the vocalist.

Friendliness and happiness personified, J-Hope has an exuberant, hard-working personality that matches the energy he brings on stage and is considered the moodmaker within the group. Since the group's earliest days he's had a hand in writing his own raps and over the years he's been increasingly involved in writing music for BTS. In 2018, he released his first mixtape, *Hope World*, and became the highest charting Korean artist at the time on the Billboard 200 album chart, when it landed at No. 63, before rising to No. 38 the next week. The following year, he'd make history yet again when he became the first member of BTS to appear on the Hot 100 chart with a solo release, when "Chicken Noodle Soup" with Becky G debuted at No. 81. The song, a trilingual homage to the 2006 viral hit by Webstar & Young B featuring AG aka the Voice of Harlem, was released on September 27, and spurred a viral dance challenge of its own.

ENTER THE WORLD OF

KIM NAM-JOON
SEPTEMBER 12, 1994

김남준

ALSO KNOWN AS

RUNCH RANDA AND
RAP MONSTER

OFFICIAL ROLES

LEADER, RAPPER,
LYRICIST, COMPOSER

AGE AT BTS'S DEBUT

18 YEARS OLD

HOMETOWN

ILSAN, SOUTH KOREA

The first member of BTS, RM, previously known as Rap Monster, was inspired by Eminem to rap his life story and thus pursue a career as an artist. He was brought to Bang Si-hyuk's attention by rapper Sleepy from The Untouchable. Sleepy had been aware of RM as an underground rapper trying to make it in the hip-hop scene, and connected Bang with RM. RM, then using the stage name Runch Randa, was a member of the Daenamhyup crew, or "대남조선힙합협동조합" or the "Great Southern Joseon Hip-Hop Cooperative," which featured many prominent Korean hip-hop artists, including Big Hit producer Supreme Boi, rapper Iron, and Kidoh of Topp Dogg. He also collaborated with Zico, then known as Nakseo and later part of boy band Block B, and throughout it all RM built up a reputation that resulted in his joining Big Hit. As the founding member of BTS, RM is the group's leader, and often represents the group when they head overseas, largely due to his English skills, which he says he learned from watching *Friends*.

RM plays a key role as one of BTS's main songwriters, and has featured on multiple tracks by other prominent Korean and international artists over the years. He has released a mixtape, a playlist, and several singles throughout the group's lifetime, and even prior to working with BTS wrote for former Big Hit labelmate, the girl group GLAM, including the track "Party (XXO)," which many fans have heralded for its lyrics emphasizing LGBTQ+ themes. He has gained a reputation as an intellect within the South Korean entertainment world after appearing on several variety shows where he showed off his logical thinking, and revealed that he received an IQ test score of 148, which is considered as being around or at genius level. He is also affectionately known among BTS and ARMY for his clumsiness and frequent habit of misplacing things. His 2018 playlist *mono.* went to No. 26 on the Billboard 200 album chart upon its release, the highest ever for a Korean soloist until then, breaking J-Hope's prior record.

SOLO RELEASES:

2012

"PARTY (XXO)" WRITTEN FOR GLAM

2013

"I LIKE THAT" WRITTEN FOR GLAM

2015

RM

"P.D.D" WITH WARREN G

"FANTASTIC"
FEAT. MANDY VENTRICE
A TIE-IN TO THE RELEASE OF THE
FANTASTIC 4 FILM IN KOREA

"BUCKUBUCKU" BY MFBTY
FEAT. EE, RM, AND DINO-J

"U" BY PRIMARY
FEAT.
KWON JIN AH AND RM

2017

"ALWAYS"

"CHANGE" WITH WALE

"CHAMPION (REMIX)"
BY FALL OUT BOY FEAT. RM

2018

.MONO

"TIMELESS" BY DRUNKEN
TIGER FEAT. RM

2019

"CRYING OVER YOU (REMIX)"
FEAT. RM & BEKA BY HONNE

ENTER THE WORLD OF

JIMIN

PARK JI-MIN
OCTOBER 13, 1995

박지민

OFFICIAL ROLES

VOCALIST, DANCER, CHOREOGRAPHER

AGE AT BTS'S DEBUT

17 YEARS OLD

HOMETOWN

BUSAN, SOUTH KOREA

Initially a dancer before pursuing a career as a singer, Jimin studied modern dance throughout middle and high school in Busan. While attending Busan High School of Arts, he auditioned for Big Hit Entertainment and moved to Seoul. The final member to join what would go on to become the group's official lineup, he is one of its three youngest members along with V and JungKook, collectively known as the *maknae* line. Known for his bright, endearing personality, he frequently shares updates with fans on social media, and enjoys friendships with several other popular K-pop idols, including SHINee's Taemin, EXO's Kai and Ha Sungwoon, formerly of Wanna One. They are collectively known as the "Padding Squad" due to their matching puffer jackets.

Beloved for his charismatic stage presence, Jimin is acknowledged by the rest of the group as the hardest working member and a consummate perfectionist, traits that he's displayed frequently over the years both on and off camera. Though all members of BTS are dedicated to their craft and career, Jimin's drive for improving himself has helped him grow from a skilled dancer into an extremely talented vocalist known for his expressive, crisp tone. Jimin is also an advocate of education, and has donated the equivalent of over $100,000 USD to schools in the Busan area to help support students.

Though he doesn't yet have a lot of songwriting or solo experience beyond BTS, Jimin shared his first solo track with fans on December 31, 2018 (in Korea) gifting ARMY a sweet farewell to the historic year. A song shared for free on SoundCLoud, it promptly set the site's first-day streaming record, beating the previous record holder, Drake.

SOLO RELEASES:

2018

"PROMISE"

ENTER THE WORLD OF

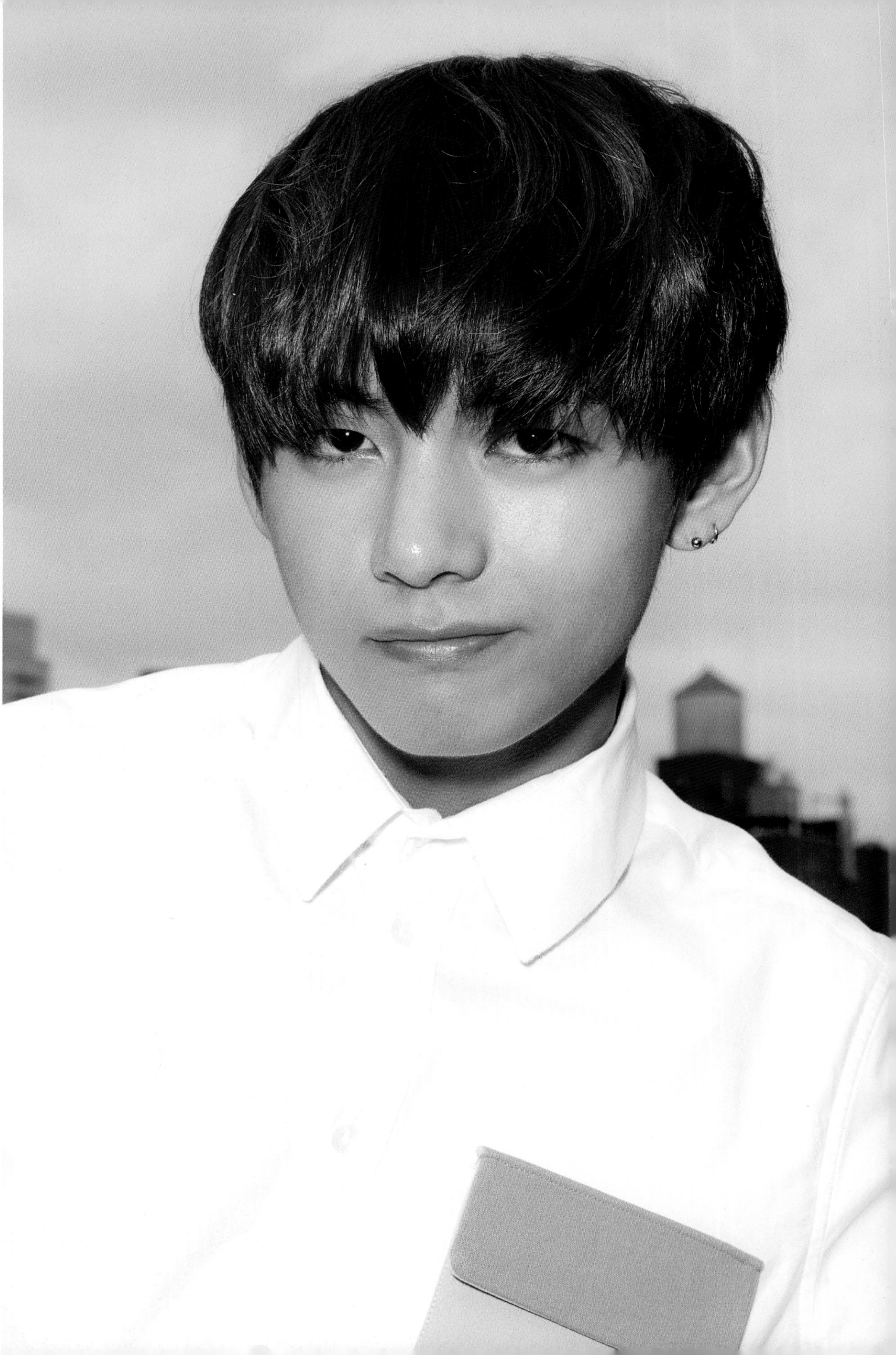

KIM TAE-HYUNG
DECEMBER 30, 1995

OFFICIAL ROLES
VOCALIST, ACTOR

AGE AT BTS'S DEBUT
17 YEARS OLD

HOMETOWN
DAEGU, SOUTH KOREA,
LATER GEOCHANG COUNTY

SOLO RELEASES:

2016

"IT'S DEFINITELY YOU" WITH JIN
HWARANG: THE POET WARRIOR YOUTH
SOUNDTRACK

2017
"4 O'CLOCK" WITH RM

2019
"SCENERY"

"WINTER BEAR"

2020
"SWEET NIGHT"

김태형

Deep-voiced and soulful, Kim Tae-hyung joined Big Hit after auditioning in Daegu in pursuit of a singing career. Unlike the other members of BTS, he was unknown to the public prior to the group's debut and didn't feature in any pre-debut videos or social media content. With the stage name V, ostensibly for the group's "victory," he was positioned as the new act's hidden trump card.

Always musically inclined, with a proclivity for jazzier sounds, V played the saxophone growing up, and has brought this soulful spirit into his career, developing his distinct, husky tone over the years. Known for his eccentric, multi-dimensional personality, he's an artist in the truest sense, and is one of several members that regularly visit museums when the group is touring internationally. A true artistic connoisseur, he also often shares artwork he enjoys and his own photography with fans. Along with his work in BTS, he began to explore a career as an actor in 2016, when he appeared in the Korean historical television drama, *Hwarang: The Poet Warrior Youth.* In 2018, his solo song "Singularity" from the group's *Love Yourself: Tear* was recognized by multiple Western media outlets' year-end lists as a stand-out track for its neo-soul styling and for V's evocative vocals. He released his first non-album solo song "Scenery" in 2019 through the band's SoundCloud account.

V is credited with making purple the color that represents the bond between BTS and ARMY, popularizing the phrase "I purple you" during BTS's third Muster fanmeet in November 2016. To V, and to millions of others around the world, purple now represents trusting and loving one another for a long time. "We will always trust you and step up the stairs [of our lives and careers with you] together," he said. "Don't just support us, everyone, from a distance behind but rather hold our hands and follow us so that we will go to great heights together, and make something wonderful."

ENTER THE WORLD OF

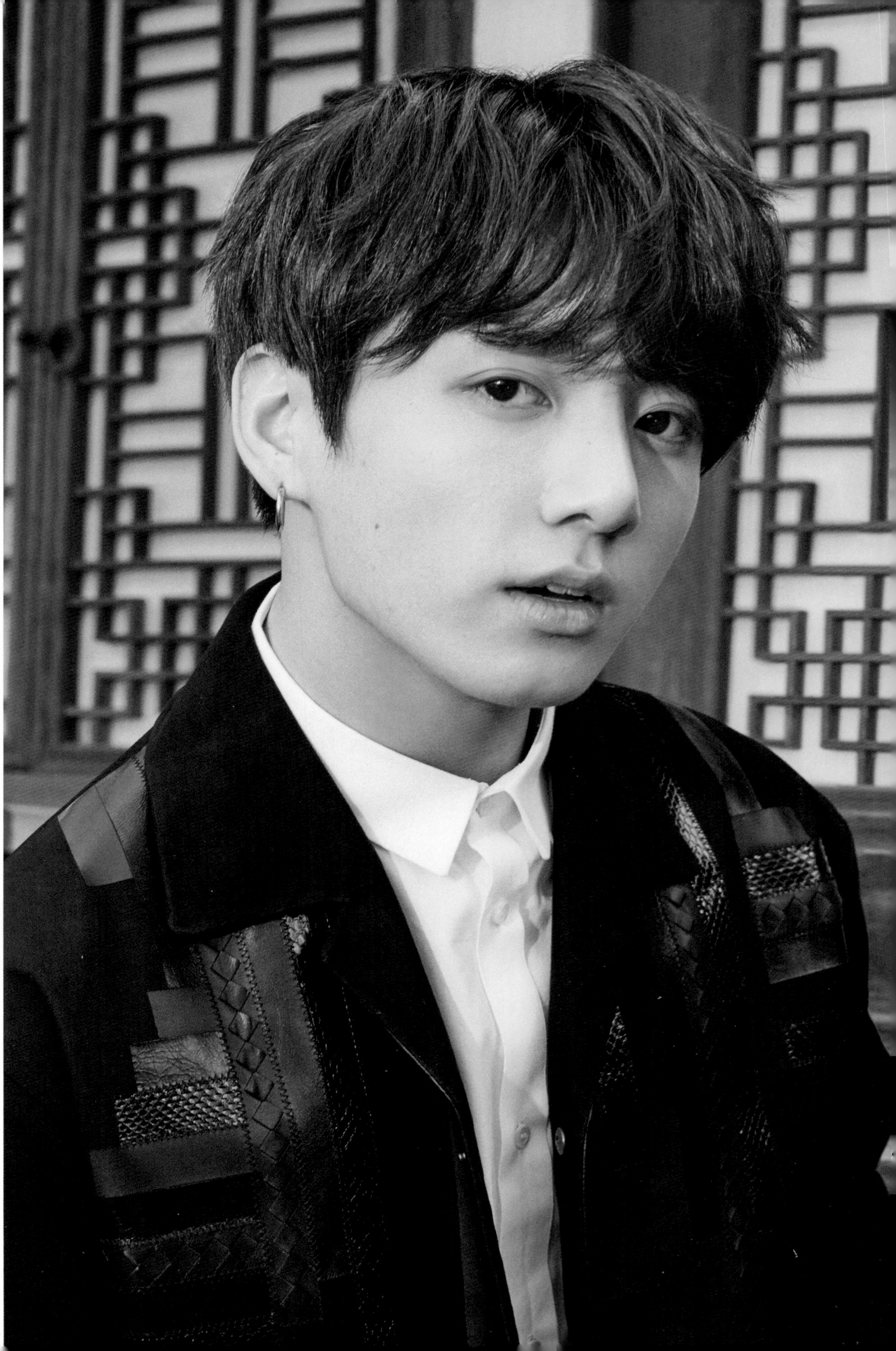

JUNG KOOK

JEON JUNG-KOOK
SEPTEMBER 1, 1997

OFFICIAL ROLES
VOCALIST, RAPPER, DANCER

AGE AT BTS'S DEBUT
15 YEARS OLD

HOMETOWN
BUSAN, SOUTH KOREA

전정국

Jungkook, the band's youngest member, is often referred to as "The Golden Maknae," as *maknae* is the Korean term used to refer to the youngest in a group-oriented relationship, often a familial one. With his talent as a singer, dancer, and rapper evident from a young age, the dynamic performer auditioned for the South Korean star-search television program *Superstar K3* in 2011. Though he didn't make it on to the show, his audition tape, during which he performed soulful renditions of IU's "Lost Child" and 2AM's "This Song," circulated throughout the entertainment industry—and can now be found on YouTube—and he reportedly ended up with offers to join seven different companies.

After accepting an offer at Big Hit Entertainment because he was drawn to RM, Jungkook spent time training, including a period studying dance in Los Angeles, before BTS started out in June 2013. He, along with several other BTS members, has cited BIGBANG, specifically G-Dragon, as his inspiration for pursuing a career as a singer.

Well regarded as a multi-faceted, talented artist, Jungkook has grown up in the spotlight and over the years has continued to develop his already considerable skills. He's known for covering a variety of artists, both Korean and international, on the group's social media channels. Along with his work as a singer, he has been credited on several songs since BTS's early days. In 2017, he began to release his own self-produced short films, documenting the group's career through his studio "G.C.F," or Golden Closet Films.

Jungkook has a magic touch when it comes to sales of products he associates with in his day-to-day life: things like drinking a certain brand of wine or mentioning the fabric softener he uses (Downy) have led to fans buying out the product line.

Jung Kook

MUSIC

Bang Si-hyuk

The founder of Big Hit Entertainment and co-CEO of the company, "Hitman" Bang formed BTS and has been an integral player in the group's career path and music production. Also known as Bang PD (a common abbreviation in the Korean entertainment world meaning "producer,") the man behind BTS—their name isn't *Bang*tan Sonyeondan for nothing—made his name in the K-pop world while working with Park Jin Young, or J.Y. Park, of JYP Entertainment in the '90s and early '00s. Integral in the songwriting of hit acts like g.o.d, Rain, and Wonder Girls, Bang primarily served as a composer and arranger at the time, and wrote music for some of Korea's most prominent artists. He went on to found Big Hit Entertainment in 2005, and put together BTS from 2010 onwards. He has served as executive producer for BTS throughout their career, and has nearly 700 songs registered under his name with the Korea Music Copyright Association (KOMCA) as of August 2019.

Along with the BTS members, there are many important behind-the-scenes figures supporting the group's career. The majority of BTS's songs have been co-produced by either Bang, Supreme Boi, Pdogg, or Slow Rabbit, while Adora has more recently become a frequently credited collaborator. The septet have also worked regularly with Hiss Noise, DOCSKIM, Brother Su, and many others who have occasional credits throughout their discography. From the *Love Yourself* era and on, BTS have increasingly worked with Western songwriters, such as Jordan "DJ Swivel" Young, Candace Nicole Sosa, Melanie Joy Fontana, Ali Tamposi, and Roman Compalo.

Supreme Boi

Shin Donghyuk nearly became a member of BTS, and now produces for the group. A rapper and underground hip-hop artist, he was part of the original line-up before Big Hit opted to reorganize the group into a more typical idol group than an entirely hip-hop-focused team. He has written many of BTS's more blatantly hip-hop-oriented songs, including many of their early singles including "No More Dream" and "N.O" as well as the "Cypher" tracks, featuring on the latter.

Pdogg

A songwriter who has worked with BTS since before their debut, Kang Hyo-won (aka Pdogg) has played a major role in BTS's career as one of the people most integral to their sound. He began writing formally for artists like vocal group 8Eight and Lim Jeong-Hee, also known as J-Lim; both acts eventually were managed by Big Hit. Ahead of BTS's launch, Pdogg wrote for artists including 2AM, 8Eight, Jo Kwon, Teen Top, Lee Hyun, Kan Mi-youn, Seo In-guk, and GLAM. He has written much of BTS's discography since 2 Cool 4 Skool was released in 2013, and has toplined many of the group's singles. Through his work with BTS, he has won several awards during South Korean year-end award show seasons, and in early 2019 he was revealed to have been the songwriter who earned the most from royalties through KOMCA in 2018.

Slow Rabbit

Kwon Dohyung, aka Slow Rabbit, is another producer who has been around since BTS's earliest days. He is credited with writing many of the group's more romantic and softer sounding singles and b-sides, and his artistry is felt throughout their entire discography. Unlike Bang and Pdogg, Slow Rabbit was a relatively new songwriter at the start of BTS's career. The majority of his career has been spent alongside BTS writing songs for their albums and, in recent years, working with members on solo songwriting. He is credited alongside Suga as a songwriter on Suran's "Wine" and he worked on Jimin's "Promise" and Jin's "Tonight." He had a major role in creating the debut album of TOMORROW X TOGETHER, the first new group from Big Hit since BTS, which launched in March 2019, and produced their debut single "Crown."

Adora

The only female Korean producer BTS frequently works with, Adora is one of the newer songwriters working with the act, though her first KOMCA copyright, registered under her given name of Soo-hyun Park, was on Topp Dogg's 2013 debut album.[11] Little is known about her, but her first songwriting credit on BTS's discography, as recorded with KOMCA, is "Interlude: Wings" from Wings in 2016. The sweet, mellow tone of her backing vocals can be heard on several BTS tracks, most notably during the Love Yourself era, during which she played a leading role as a songwriter.

Hiss Noise

A Big Hit songwriter with only a minimal public presence, Hiss Noise has primarily produced songs with BTS since the Love Yourself era. He has co-written several solo tracks, including Soundcloud one-offs from the act's vocalists and mixtape tracks for the rappers, along with album releases, such as "Magic Shop" and "Intro: Persona." As of the end of 2019, he has nine BTS songs and one TXT song credited to him formally on KOMCA, while he is also credited on various BTS tracks as a digital editor and for providing additional production support.

VISUALS

Son Sung-deuk

The key person behind the dance element of BTS's performances, Son is the performance director of Big Hit Entertainment. He has been with BTS since their pre-debut days, and has created the choreography for many of BTS's singles and performances. He teaches dance workshops, and has even toured in the U.S. to instruct dancers. He has also won multiple awards in South Korea for his work with BTS.

Lumpens

With a slogan of "Pursue The Fantasy of The Visual And Auditory Senses," the Lumpens video team, which consists of Yongseok Choi, HyeJeong Park, Guzza, and Jihye Yoon, has walked alongside BTS throughout much of the group's time together. The creatives of Lumpens began to work with the septet on their batch of 2014 music videos, including "Boy In Luv" and "Just One Day," and several Japanese variants, including BTS's debut single "No More Dream." Lumpens has crafted much of BTS's audiovisual storytelling, and has brought to life much of the visual experience associated with the BU creative narrative. Along with working with BTS on both the group's and solo members' music videos, Lumpens has worked on some of the group's promotional campaigns, and created videography for many other prominent Korean artists, including Sunmi, HyunA, Wonder Girls, Lee Hyori, Sistar, MFBTY, and Drunken Tiger, and their associated artists, IU, Block B, INFINITE, Rain, Cho Young Pil, and more.

GDW

Like Lumpens, GDW is a Seoul-based creative content production agency and is behind many of BTS's most visually captivating music videos. Director of photography HyunWoo Nam ("Blood Sweat & Tears," "Fire," "Save Me," and many others) and director Woogie Kim ("Mic Drop [Remix]," "Not Today," "Save Me," to give some examples) have played major roles in crafting many of BTS's videos over the years. The GDW team has also been behind many other visually captivating music videos from the likes of Sunmi, TVXQ!, Red Velvet, NCT, Yoonmirae, Taeyang, Crush, HyunA, and many more.

Lenzo Yoon

Made co-CEO of Big Hit Entertainment in 2019, former chief business officer Yoon currently spearheads Big Hit's business group and is credited with much of the financial success of BTS and Big Hit artists in recent years. He is promoted as a "hidden player" behind the company's positive business efforts, and is reputed to have spearheaded the diversification of video-based, fan-oriented content at the company, leading to great success.[12]

Zanybros

One of the most prominent and prolific video production companies in South Korea, Zanybros was founded in 2002 by director Hong Won-ki and videographer Kim Jun-hong. Over the years, the Zanybros team has gone on to produce hundreds of popular videos in the Korean entertainment industry, and also works for other Asian music markets. They were the force behind BTS's debut-era content, with Hong credited as the director of "No More Dream," "We Are Bulletproof Pt. 2," and "N.O." BTS have sporadically worked with Zanybros on videos ever since, such as "War of Hormone" and "Come Back Home."

Jiyoon Lee

The founder behind the creative design company studio-xxx, Lee crafted the vision behind many of BTS's album packagings in collaboration with a variety of other artists associated with the studio. Studio-xxx is most notable for creating the captivating visual imagery associated with the physical packaging of *The Most Beautiful Moment in Life, Pt. 1* and *Pt. 2* albums, known for their romantic, blurred, butterfly effects. The company worked with BTS on all their Korean albums between *2 Cool 4 Skool* (2013) and *You Never Walk Alone* (2017).

HuskyFox

A professional branding company, HuskyFox began working with BTS in more recent years, and are best known as the design team responsible for the packaging of the group's *Love Yourself: Her, Tear*, and *Answer* albums. HuskyFox's Lee Doohee was nominated at the 2019 Grammy Awards for his art direction in the best recording package category. Though Willo Perron took home the award for St. Vincent's *MASSEDUCTION*, the feat was historic as it was the first time a Korean album had ever been nominated in any category at the Grammy Awards.

THE
MUSIC
OF
BTS

2

SOUND
WITH STYLE

Chapter
Five

Central to BTS's music is the idea of acting as protectors for their audience. From day one, they rallied around the ills of modern-day youth culture, and as their career grew, the members and their messaging grew with it. Not every song has a deeper meaning—sometimes a love song is just a love song—but lengthy, multi-album themes pervade the septet's music as they have incorporated their evolving lives and worldviews into their discography.

Whether rallying against societal norms, expressing poetic ideas of romance, or praising self-acceptance in the face of adversity, BTS have woven a thick foundation of meaning throughout their discography. For a group whose music is performed predominantly in Korean, despite much of their global audience not speaking the language, it is an intensely impressive feat that they have been able to transcend the limitations of language through their music.

Good music is universal, and people around the globe can relate to it regardless of who they are, and that's what makes BTS's songs so approachable: the love, the resistance against wrongs, the emotion, and the self-aware reflection are things the average listener finds relatable, and are expressively relayed through musical style and vocal delivery regardless of language. While the lyrics are important and songwriters include words for a reason, BTS's intent—or that of any artist whose language you may not understand—is not lost by simply enjoying the music.

But, luckily, BTS's music is made in the globalized Internet age, and their songs' lyrics have been translated into numerous languages, making their message and poetic turn of phrase accessible to listeners around the world.

Throughout their wide array of releases over the first few years of their career, the backbone of BTS's music has been their dedication to self-affirmation. Whether it's to do with one's path in life, or one's relationship with others or with oneself, the septet's discography is packed with exploratory music that reflects their mission to be everyday voices of this era.

The idea of creating music with messaging interwoven through it is hardly revolutionary, but Big Hit Entertainment's dedication to it is. The company's slogan is "Music & Artist for Healing," and that has come through in BTS's music, whose lyrics emphasize both the realities and fantasies of life. Whether it's intensely biographical tracks

Whether rallying against societal norms, expressing poetic ideas of romance, or praising self-acceptance in the face of adversity, BTS have woven a thick foundation of meaning throughout their discography.

like *HYYH2*'s "Ma City," in which the septet sing about their hometowns, or their debut track "No More Dream" and its forthright, rebellious attitude to the status quo, or the romantic tracks like *Love Yourself 轉 Tear*'s "134340", drawing on poetic references to the dwarf planet Pluto to express the sorrow of an ended relationship, BTS's songs are always intended to resonate within listeners' hearts and minds. Though pop music at its essence needs to be relatable, BTS achieve this with an authentic intimacy that permeates their discography.

K-pop is typically crafted with the aim of being exported beyond South Korea's relatively small local music market—with only 51 million residents, the country's pop scene relies on external interest and fans to remain lucrative. According to Big Hit's founder Bang and BTS's primary choreographer Son Sung-deuk, two key factors have helped BTS communicate their message and music to fans across the globe.[13]

Firstly, Bang has said that fan translations play a key role. Nowadays, with "digital natives" savvy in near-instantaneous communication, far-reaching fandoms take it upon themselves to make their favorite music accessible to others across the world. Among K-pop fandoms, there are many fanbases and websites dedicated to translating lyrics. Increasingly, South Korean music companies are also providing translations, at least into English, of singles via music videos, but Korean music is mostly made accessible through fan efforts. Additionally, Bang has said that the group's dedication to incorporating global music trends into their music, and to reading the signs before trends have even become popular, play a major role in their success.

Secondly, Son emphasized that choreography is integral to relaying BTS's intent. When Suga described K-pop as "integrated content," it wasn't just about the audio-visual aspects of the music and music videos, but also, and perhaps most impactfully, the performance ones; whether it's at a music show or concert, in Korea or outside of it, the choreography and way the song is relayed on stage affect how fans interpret its meaning. BTS, with their finely tuned performances, breathe new meaning into each lyric with each shift of position as they dance, providing non-verbal cues for listeners to interpret. This works particularly well for BTS's music, as the lyrics are often esoteric, with wordplay and hidden meanings abundant throughout their songs, but their nuanced choreography often features interpretive movements to guide the listener's understanding.

Listening to a BTS song doesn't always have to be an all-encompassing experience; the beauty of music is that even a wordless melody can move a person's soul. Whether you listen to BTS's songs with the lyrics in front of you in your own language so you can sing along and analyze every line, or put it on in the car in the morning on the way to work to stir your spirit, each song exudes a distinct emotive color that helps relay its message, and as the members have improved their skills over the years, the group's ability to convey emotion has become even more impactful. For example, *Love Yourself* 結 *Answer*'s "I'm Fine" isn't just an exuberant drum and bass track about being fine; as the song progresses, the members' light, breathy tones shift in accordance with the song's message: that the past has been hard but the future will be a happy one. Of course, the English chorus helps relay the message to non-Korean, English-speaking listeners in the case of "I'm Fine," but that's not true for every song; *Love Yourself* 承 *Her*'s "Pied Piper" sardonically addresses the fervor of passionately stanning BTS, but, unlike "I'm Fine" and its forthright messaging, the group's sonic performance alone doesn't truly convey the depth of the subversive lyrics. Rather than depicting the intense state of fandom they're describing through intense sounds, the song uses the vocalists' sweet falsetto ranges to seduce, as if tempting listeners to succumb to obsession. Straightforward as its lyrics are for Korean-speaking audiences, it's a tantalizing tease for other fans who have to look to translations to understand the song's meaning.

In this regard, BTS's ARMY have gone above and beyond to communicate the lyrics of each and every BTS song to one another. The group's music and general impact have had such a widespread effect on people learning Korean around the world to better understand the group's messaging that the government of South Korea awarded BTS *Hwagwan* medals of honor in 2018 for spreading Korean culture and language.

On a lyrical front, the songs of BTS can be categorized generally into one of two categories: love songs and life songs. Though many overlap, these are the subjects with which the Bangtan Boys are most deeply concerned. Songs about the realities of life were quite popular during the '90s and early 2000s in South Korea but have since fallen out of favor in K-pop. They are now seeing a bit of a revival, in part due to BTS's success. It's also possible that political dissent among the current generation has made the music more topical as millennials are facing some of life's realities in a way the previous generation did not. By authentically putting a real sense of meaning into their songs derived from their own, distinctly modern experiences, BTS have truly raised themselves above and beyond competitors, and are at least partially, if not entirely, responsible for a rise in new boy bands who self-produce and write their own songs within the K-pop scene.

Whether it's a great love (for example, *2 Cool 4 Skool*'s "Like," *Her*'s "Dimple") or a sad love (*HYYH:YF*'s "Autumn Leaves," *Tear*'s "The Truth Untold"), interpersonal love, both romantic and otherwise (*Skool Luv Affair*'s "Boy In Luv," *Wings*' "Mama") or intrapersonal love (*Answer*'s "Epiphany"), they have a song for it. As for their thoughts on life, BTS have explored everything from socio-economic inequality (*HYYH1*'s "Dope," *HYYH2*'s "Silver Spoon") to mental health struggles (*HYYH:YF*'s "Whalien 52," *Agust D*'s "The Last") to the highs and lows of their career (*Her*'s "MIC Drop," *O!RUL8,2?*'s "Attack on Bangtan," *2 Cool 4 Skool*'s "Road"), their fans (*Wings*' "2!3!," *Her*'s "Pied Piper," *7*'s "Moon") and, of course, finding one's own way in life regardless of social expectations (*2 Cool 4 Skool*'s "No More Dream," *O!RUL8,2?*'s "N.O"). These timeless themes as experienced by BTS have carried through their discography, both as a group and through their solo releases, during the first seven years of their career.

THE SKOOL
YEARS

Chapter
Six

First impressions are everything, and in the music world initial releases often set the stage for an artist's career. For BTS, their 2013 debut single album *2 Cool 4 Skool* laid out very clearly the identity of the brand-new boy band, starting off strong by drawing on the traditions of hip-hop while introducing themselves as a group gearing up to be the voice of teens and twenty-somethings.

2 Cool 4 Skool was not only the first album of BTS's career, but their first of what would go on to be multiple youth-oriented thematic trilogies. The June 2013 release, which featured seven or nine tracks (depending on if you listened to the digital or physical version) was followed by that September's *O!RUL8,2?* and then February's *Skool Luv Affair*, with the span of the entire *Skool* trilogy unveiled between June 2013 and April 2014, when the *Skool Luv Affair* repackaged album was released.

The academic inspiration behind the trio was a fitting topic at the time, considering that Jungkook, the group's *maknae,* was 15 years old at the start of BTS's career while the eldest, Jin, was 20. Throughout the series, the septet would draw on their own experience of putting their musical dreams ahead of scholastic aspirations, while questioning the intense study-based culture for young people in South Korea. Stylistically, the trio of albums was bolstered heavily by BTS's dedication to hip-hop.

2 COOL 4 SKOOL

From the get-go, *2 Cool 4 Skool* makes its own argument for BTS being part of hip-hop's lineage in South Korea: the album is introduced by the exact same phrase as that of the first track "Go" from Epik High's debut album, 2003's *Map of the Human Soul,* an introduction to instruction from K-Tel's 1978 *Let's Disco*. To listeners familiar with the widely acclaimed hip-hop trio's work, the intro, which also features a beat from Epik High collaborator DJ Friz, instantly positions BTS as the newest members of the greater Korean hip-hop community.

The *2 Cool 4 Skool* "Intro" track is brief, less than two minutes long, but it's impactful: along with leaning into Korean hip-hop history, it is a full-fledged introduction to BTS as a "Big Hit Exclusive" group and emphasizes the group's name, spelling out "B-A-N-G-T-A-N" as RM introduces the group's full Korean name, *Bangtan Sonyeondan,* all the while declaring them "2 cool, 2 cool 4 skool" representatives who can easily speak on behalf of teens and twentysomethings. The only member who appears on the track is RM, kicking off their career with what appears to be an acknowledgement of his role as the first member of BTS; it would set a precedent for BTS's albums, with a specific member typically serving as the guide for an album or album era through an introductory song.

2 We Are Bulletproof, Pt. 2

3 Skit: Circle Room Talk

As it progresses, *2 Cool 4 Skool* spends its time introducing the then-new group. Following the "Intro" is "We Are Bulletproof, Pt. 2," a follow-up to the pre-debut "We Are Bulletproof, Pt. 1" which was originally recorded featuring RM with Supreme Boi and Iron (Jung Hun-chul), two former potential group members, then known by the acronym B.P.B for "Bulletproof Boys"; it was later remade with BTS's current line-up and shared on the group's official SoundCloud in 2015 as part of their second Festa celebrations.

"We Are Bulletproof, Pt. 2" was released as the second single from *2 Cool 4 Skool*, with the music video for the track out on July 16, over a month after the song's initial release on June 13. The theme of working hard while pursuing the dream of their musical career as their peers toil away at draining schoolwork is overt here as the members rap and sing over a tinny hip-hop beat laced with sirens, gun-shots, and quirky synth plinks. It is aggressive in its intent to express that BTS are in a class of their own, and though it could have easily been their first single, launching their career with a hard-hitting intro to the members and the group's intent, it would actually be "No More Dream" that gave BTS their start.

During "Skit: Circle Room Talk", the members of BTS decide to ditch class and talk about their dreams. RM and Suga discuss how Epik High's inspirational track "Fly" inspired them to start songwriting and producing. Along with another nod to listeners that the group is drawing on the legacy of those who came before them as they start off their career, other members join in to discuss their dreams growing up, like Jin wanting to have a 7 AM–6 PM lifestyle, leaving his house early in the AM and coming home in time for dinner cooked by his wife, or V learning to play the saxophone. The conversation concludes with Jungkook, the youngest, saying he couldn't remember his dream well. Ending with a teacher interrupting the conversation, the album's third track shows the group's playful group dynamic and positions them as thought-provoking, school-aged artists.

4 No More Dream

5 Interlude

Following the aforementioned "Skit" is BTS's boisterous debut single, "No More Dream." Similar to "We Are Bulletproof, Pt. 2," "No More Dream" expresses BTS's intent through hip-hop, this time with a more melodic element, with rhythmic bass guiding the track's development into a swaggering rap track calling out youth who don't have dreams but just go through the motions. Hypercritical of South Korea's intense student lifestyle, references to study rooms, or *dokseoshil* (독서실) as they're known in Korean, and the aim to become a government worker, seen as a premium career path in Korea, the song ends with RM urging people to pursue their dreams. "No More Dream" is an ambitious debut single, to say the least, and impactfully brought BTS onto the scene as they let the world know what they stood for.

A groovy, echoing instrumental track bisects BTS's first album, serving as a melodic lead-in to the following track, "Like."

6 Like

The third full-length song on *2 Cool 4 Skool*, "Like" arrives after the duo of "We Are Bulletproof, Pt. 2" and "No More Dream," and it's a bit of a sonic gear-shift. The emotive R&B track, also known as "I Like It," is a touch of sweetness after the harsh reality of the two other full-length songs on the album, all the while displaying more of the group's skillset, blending melodic raps with appealing harmonies from the group's vocalists. Lyrically, the song is one of several in BTS's discography to address this generation's reliance on technology, using the term "Like" to refer to both affection and to social media, with "Like" expressing sorrow and the desire to "like" photos of a former girlfriend who has become even prettier after a break-up, yearning to still be able to do so without thinking twice about it.

7 Outro: Circle Room Cypher

8 Skit: On The Start Line
(HIDDEN TRACK)

The first-ever cypher, or a ongoing freestyle rap that flits between individuals, from BTS, *2 Cool 4 Skool*'s outro track features the seven members vibing off of one another over a mellow beat as they introduce themselves comically with freestyle raps. Beginning with the septet discussing food after finishing lessons for the day, the cypher starts with Suga after he plays a beat that he's created. Each member picks up the rhythm, bouncing off one another as they lightheartedly heckle each other and hype up their individual identities, with several mentions of each man's hometown and dialects, known as *satoori* in Korean, which they would frequently reference in BTS's early days. Like the skit, it's a fun intro to the individual members of BTS, though this time with more of a musical feel.

A spoken-word monologue by RM, "On The Start Line," also known as "Talk," is the first hidden track featured in BTS's discography and features the rapper ruminating on the term "trainee," and his life as one. An in-between state where he was pursuing something but not yet actively grasping it, the brief song featured RM expressing his frustrations and anxieties about putting in three years' worth of preparation and standing on the precipice of a career that would inevitably feature highs and lows. Featuring allegories and metaphors that would appear frequently throughout BTS's tracks, such as the desert and sea, which would later be heard prominently on *Love Yourself: Her*'s hidden track "Sea," and showcasing his determination to conquer the industry, "On The Start Line" was a poignant self-reflection from RM just as the group kicked off their career.

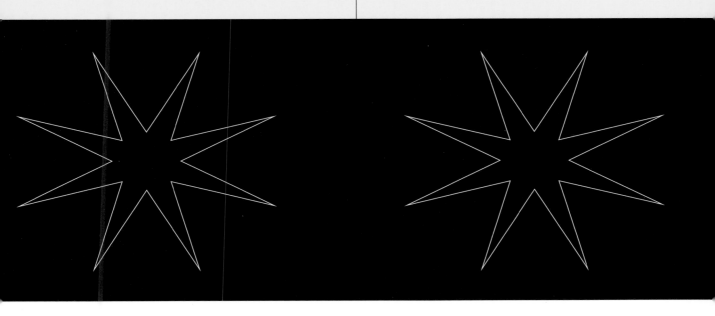

9 Path

(HIDDEN TRACK)

An old-school, relaxed hip-hop track laid out over an addictive boom bap beat, "Path," also known as "Road," picks up the theme from "On The Start Line." As the second and final hidden track on BTS's debut album, it featured the entire group ruminating on the hardships of their career path. The title comes from the repeated choral query of wondering where they would be if they had diverged from their chosen path, which has led them to where they are, living a life where they can pursue the art that they want to be doing.

BTS designed *2 Cool 4 Skool*, their first release, as an introduction to the group. The album made it quite clear who and what exactly they were aiming to be: a hip-hop-leaning boy band with a dedicated message, while simultaneously introducing the members individually on multiple tracks as they repeated the group's name and identity throughout. By referencing South Korean musical legacies, plus drawing on age-old hip-hop elements like cyphers and skits, the group asserted their intention to claim their place as aspiring artistic hip-hop legends, while showing that they have what it takes to be sweet crooners at the same time. Though the album is compact, this intent is finely woven through each moment of *2 Cool 4 Skool*, and it's a fitting starting point for a group that would eventually rise to the top of their game.

BTS igniting their career at the showcase for their debut album *2 Cool 4 Skool.*

RM partying it up with ARMY during a *Wings* tour performance in 2017.

The start of BTS's debut-era trio, *2 Cool 4 Skool* was followed up by the septet's first EP (extended play), or mini-album as they're typically known in Korean music. Released on September 11, 2013, *O!RUL8,2?* was a 10-track release, once again drawing on hip-hop trappings by beginning with an intro, ending with an outro, and including both a skit and cypher, all of which would become regular features throughout BTS's early discography. Like its predecessor, BTS's second album also focused on youth-oriented struggles and questioned societal dedication to education as the only way to achieve success. There were multiple references to the group's members and the act's name, with a special emphasis on its "Bulletproof" nature.

During an interview with LOEN TV,[14] later known as 1theK, RM introduced "N.O" and stated the group's *raison d'etre* through a brief, on-the-spot rap about filling their lyrics with truth. As it progresses, *O!RUL8,2?* lives up to this, as does all of BTS's discography, running through a wide range of styles and emotions, all with one message permeating: that BTS is here to serve up earnest music that is based on their own lives and emotions, and the world they see around them.

This holds true throughout the album, whether they're criticizing society as in "N.O," or bolstering their own career, as on the chanty anthem "Attack on Bangtan" (also known as "The Rise of Bangtan"), or when J-Hope and Suga let loose in their wordplay-heavy native Korean dialects on "Paldogangsan," or "Satoori Rap." Even the romantic, post-breakup track "Coffee" is full of expressive earnestness that showcases BTS's emotions and thoughts.

O!RUL8,2?

O!RUL8,2?

① **Intro: O!RUL8,2?**

Like *Skool*, *O!RUL8,2?* kicks off with an RM-focused intro track featuring the album's name. With twinkling synths and ambient melodies, the group's leader urges listeners (in English) to live their best life, and pursue their future and their "someday" dreams, all the while emphasizing the importance of YOLO (you only live once) and not having regrets by putting things off, before launching into an impassioned rap about living life for yourself. He describes how his heart metaphorically stopped beating when he was a child burdened by expectations, even after his father told him to try and enjoy life. He would later refer to this element of "Intro: O,!RUL8,2?" in his historic speech in front of the United Nations in 2018.

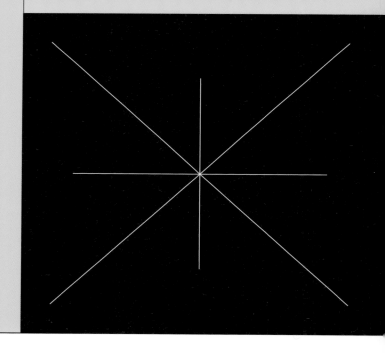

Sweat

O!RUL8,2? doesn't pull any punches, following the impactful intro track with "N.O," an anti-establishment, trap-fueled dance tune which questions why the ultimate goal for South Korean students is to work hard and land at one of the country's prestigious SKY schools: Seoul National University, Korea University, or Yonsei University. The song's title refers to both the choral hook urging everybody to say no to academic pressures, and also "no offense," expressing sensitivity to the feelings of those who might be pursuing that life. The song was released through a subversive music video that features the seven men as students who are force-fed pills and study materials under the tutelage of a futuristic, fascistic instructor. BTS's members ultimately rebel, going up against armed guards, and the fight turns into a dramatically choreographed battle.

(Throughout BTS's career, the group's music has regularly been compared to that of Seo Taiji, who is credited as the progenitor of Korea's idol scene, after Seo Taiji and Boys made waves with their 1992 song "Nan Arayo (I Know)," bringing hip-hop-based, youth-oriented dance music to prominence, and continually addressing societal problems until breaking up in 1996. BTS remade the group's "Come Back Home" in 2017, but "N.O" and "No More Dream" are perhaps most similar in messaging to Seo Taiji & Boys' 1994 hit "Classroom Ideology," a metal-influenced track that also confronts the impact of societal expectations about studying.)

A song for the haters, particularly the "keyboard warriors," or Internet commenters (commonly known as netizens, or "Internet citizens" in Korea), who think an authentic hip-hop idol is impossible, "We On" is chilling in its lilting melody and RM's coolly composed opening rap. With sweet falsetto moments woven into the more caustic rap verses and atop the tinny, clapping beat, the song is an under-the-radar anthem of everything that BTS stands for, and the group states that quite clearly with RM's repeated assertion that, regardless of the naysayers, they're here for their music.

"We On" served as the titular inspiration for BTS's 2014–15 *We On: Be the Shield* webtoon, in which BTS-inspired characters served as protectors of the world.

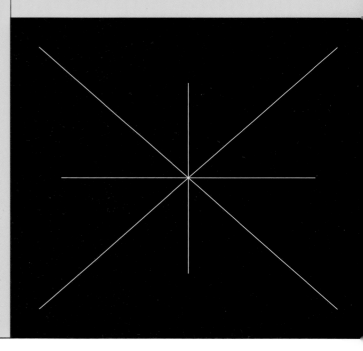

4 Skit: R U Happy Now?

Picking up where the hidden skit of *2 Cool 4 Skool* left off, "R U Happy Now?" features BTS talking about how they're happy where they are now after the time and effort they've put in. Recorded in a car on their way from a fansign event —as they chat about needing a rest and how they can't wait to arrive at a stop so some members can use the bathroom— the discussion and affirmation from members that they're happy with their present in the immediate moment is both humbling and aspirational.

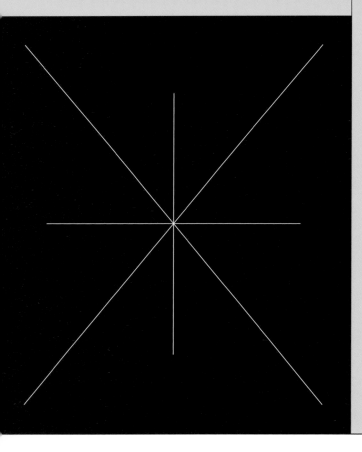

5 If I Ruled the World

A '90s hip-hop rhythm heard in passing during "Skit: R U Happy Now?" was turned into the main G-funk-inspired tune of "If I Ruled the World" with its mechanical scratches and groovy beats. Inspired by West Coast rap, the laidback, chant-fueled song is all about what the members of BTS would do if they were in charge, exuding a sense of confidence as the septet melodically swagger about getting with girls, starting fashion brands, their dreams, and making music. All the while, "If I Ruled the World" mocks itself, reflecting on how these dreams may be far-fetched, but they're still worth singing—and dreaming—about. The track's referential melody and tonal shifts are matched by the vocal displays from the members, with each rapper showing off a distinct flow style, while the vocalists modulate their tones a bit more deeply and gruffly than usual, matching the tune's groovy funk.

The song features the repetition of the phrase "westside," a nod to the west coast roots of gangster rap. RM expressed regret in an interview with Korean outlet *Hiphopplaya* in 2015 over using the term "Westside till I die," acknowledging that he does not share the history and relationship with hip-hop of many of the people who've inspired him, and that his learning process is always evolving. Though the idea of hip-hop as a musical style itself is not limited to a specific location or race, understanding its roots (and your own) is important, and RM's recognition of this is laudable.

A remake of the 2009 song "Café Latte" by soft pop meets R&B balladeers Urban Zakapa, "Coffee" alternates between the original, jazzy melody and hip-hop and rock elements, blending upbeat raps and guitar riffs with the romantic track, which uses different types of caffeinated beverages to depict a relationship that eventually ends in a breakup. Though it's ostensibly a love song, RM begins his verse with a reference to a debut, which could be interpreted to mean the song is not only about a romantic relationship but also perhaps a metaphor for the group's relationship with their careers, with the sweet caramel macchiato moments paired with the more bitter Americano ones reflecting the highs and lows of life.

While a group cypher was featured in the outro track of *2 Cool 4 Skool*, "BTS Cypher, Pt. 1" is the first of several throughout BTS's discography that features the rap line relaying their emotions and viewpoints. The track is pointed, vengeful, and circuitous, with RM, Suga, and J-Hope expressing their outrage over criticism. In this first official cypher, the trio both taunt their haters and assert their own skill through the verses. Each member's third of the cypher is intensely his own, as they reference their own life experiences, past stage names, hometowns, and even historic figures, such as the traditional Korean folk hero Hong Gil-dong, Cassius (the instigator behind the assassination of Julius Caesar) and Chopin, with Suga describing himself as the "Chopin of beats." No minor league—or underground—rappers, they're in the major league, proclaims J-Hope, drawing on a sports metaphor, and they're going to surpass the fakers.

Appearing on their second album after a year of both ups and downs as they faced criticism from South Korea's underground scene for seemingly betraying their hip-hop roots and selling out, while simultaneously facing the highly competivite K-pop scene, this first cypher set the tone for BTS's approach to dealing with opposition through sharp-witted, often caustic lyrics. This sort of sonic inspiration would be featured on several other cyphers and in the rap line's iconic 2018 song "Ddaeng," all of which took those who doubted BTS's prowess to task.

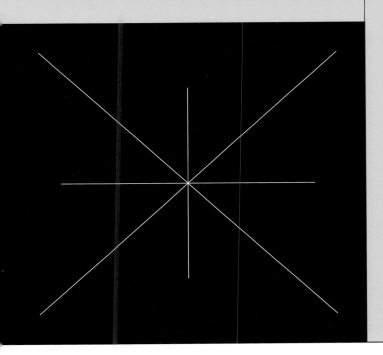

Attack on Bangtan

Paldogangsan

Also known as "Rise of Bangtan," this jocular, brassy rock/hip-hop hybrid track is a sequel of sorts to the previous cypher, picking up the theme of hyping up BTS in comparison to their rivals in the industry. But whereas "Cypher" was about the hip-hop haters, "Rise of Bangtan" is more lyrically focused on the act's ascent in the K-pop scene, hyping up the septet and their success as a rising rookie group that is sinking their shots and gearing up to dominate the industry. Throughout the song, the chorus returns to two parallel statements, the first telling people to get ready, and the second a query of "Who are we?" which they answer with the group's name. Full of impish swagger and laden with exaggerated but earnest hopes and desired goals, "Attack on Bangtan" was BTS's playful message to the world to stay tuned for what was to come.

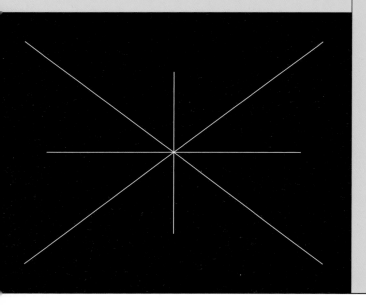

The original version of "Paldogangsan," also known as "Satoori Rap," was first created prior to BTS's debut, and RM, Suga, and J-Hope performed the track in 2011 to much success, even garnering a televised news segment, which some see as the group's first television appearance. It was so popular that V even credited the song as a reason he joined Big Hit. "Paldogangsan," a term used to describe Korea as a whole with specific reference to the country's regions, diverges from most of BTS's discography, and Korean pop music in general, as it features the members performing, and battling it out, in their own regional dialects, or *satoori*.

As they proclaim their regional differences via vocal inflections over a playful, groovy instrumental melody, the ultimate result of the back-and-forth between the BTS members, even as they brag about their hometowns and local slang, icons, foods, and historic legacies, is that all of Korea still speaks the same language despite their differences. This makes "Paldogangsan" not only a humorous show of BTS members' personal life experiences beyond the group—a group made up of those from beyond Seoul's centralized locale—but also an intensely patriotic experience full of BTS's pride in being Korean, a reoccurring theme throughout their discography.

Outro: LUV in Skool

A sentimental R&B tune full of echoing, woozy synths and snapping percussion, "LUV in Skool" is a track wholly performed by BTS's vocal line, and is stylized like peak '90s boy band balladry. It features the quartet smoothly harmonizing and relaying a variety of emotions through evocative ad-libs and falsetto belts as they sing about love, drawing on the titles of previous tracks, like "Coffee" and "If I Ruled the World," to express their desires. The song ends with a query asking the listener whether they want to date—using *satoori* to address a woman—serving as a lead-in to the next album, which is referenced in the title of this outro.

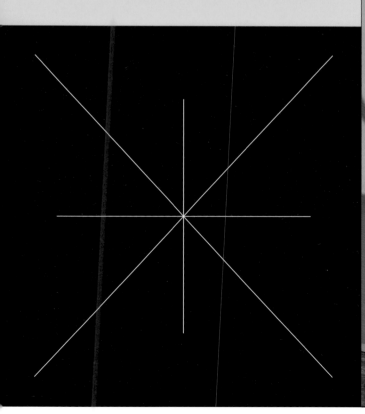

With their first two albums introducing BTS as a forward-thinking act aiming to put forth thought-provoking music, by the time they released *Skool Luv Affair* the following year, the group's identity was already entrenched in their autobiographical messaging. This album took things in a different direction. It was time to talk about the age-old inspiration for music, love, which the group had only minimally addressed in their first two albums. Though their third Korean album still had meaningful communiques spread throughout its lyrics, BTS put out their first romantically slanted single in the form of that February's "Boy In Luv" (aka "manly man" or "real man" ["상남자"] in Korean).

But even as the group moved away from full-fledged hip-hop to incorporate more pop and rock elements and brought more emotive lyrics to the forefront, they still had important things to say, with the album's tracks full of their typical melodic criticism of the world around them: "Tomorrow" addressed the frustrations of not having control of one's own life and so not being able to take steps in the present to make dreams of the future a reality, while "Spine Breaker" criticized young people who spend their parents' hard-earned money on expensive clothes to keep up with trends and their peers, and "Jump" cheered on those who chased their dreams, equating that with being a real-life superhero—a narrative they'd pick up again, most notably in 2018 with *Love Yourself 轉 Tear*'s "Anpanman."

SKOOL LUV AFFAIR

Intro:
Skool Luv Affair

Built around three distinct styles of music featured throughout BTS's *Skool* trilogy, the intro track on *Skool Luv Affair* picks up from the outro of *O!RUL8,2?*, and sets the tone for the new album by relaying the rap line's takes on how they would each confess love. First up is a mellow, lovelorn alt R&B rap from Suga as he ruminates on milestones and promises before J-Hope interrupts to say it's not the right feel, and instead something more hopeful would be better. This results in a funky, bouncing beat over which J-Hope brightly professes his love, only for RM to interrupt him in turn, saying that *that*'s not BTS's style, which is in fact boisterous hip-hop. It ends with the declaration by RM that, when in love, BTS are passionate but when it comes to music, they are sharp. The other two then join in on that vibrant beat, repeating the declaration and then declaring all together "this is Bangtan Style."

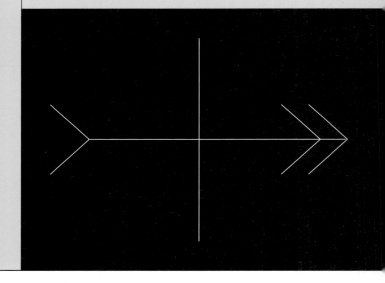

Sweat

② Boy In Luv

③ Skit: Soulmate

A rock-tinged hip-pop track, this youthful song puts more of an emphasis on the act's vocalists than their prior singles. The upbeat track is both domineering and witty, expressing the sort of powerful, frustrated emotions that accompany many a youthful crush. It's tinged with a sense of confidence even while expressing the exact opposite, emulating the confusing emotions of youth when one is stuck between the confidence of adulthood and the callowness of childhood.

The music video for "Boy In Luv" makes it clear that the track is meant to relay the desire of a high school love affair, putting the group in school uniforms as they pop and lock their way through figuring out how to make the object of their affection like them. From the exaggerated nature of the lyrics and the K-drama-style music video, it's unclear whether "Boy In Luv" is meant to mock or to revel in youthful love—or perhaps both—but whatever its intent, it's a whole lot of fun.

During a YouTube video where he shared his thoughts on the album, Suga revealed that they had opted to focus on a style that would appeal to the public ear for their single, in contrast to their previous releases, and the song would become BTS's first single to break into the Top 50 of the Gaon Chart's weekly digital songs ranking. (In the same video, he also revealed he wrote some of the album while hospitalized after his appendix burst in December 2013.)

A return to the skit format featured on previous albums, "Soulmate" features the members teasing one another as they discuss what they should do for the skit. As the members try to find a topic of discussion, their joking around produces a comical threat from RM about downsizing BTS. As the group chats, V and J-Hope play around together, talking about their ideal lovers or "soulmates." J-Hope jokes that he wants a girl like V, resulting in RM saying the group will be down two members, and Suga jumps in to threaten to kill them because of the cringe factor. Lighthearted and a show of their hard work and dedication, and BTS's good relationship with one another, "Soulmate" is brief but full of fun.

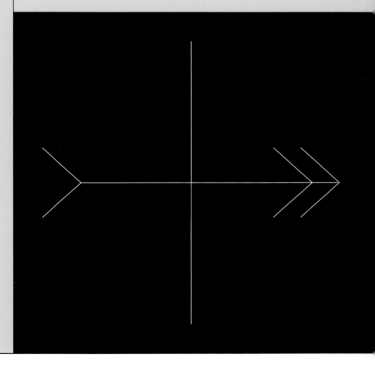

4 Where You From

Another *satoori*-infused track from BTS, this song, also known as "Where Do You Come From," is a sweeter take on dialectal differences among the members, putting Suga and J-Hope and their regional allegiances front-and-center as they try to win over the same woman with their respective Gyeongsang and Jeolla dialects. With a funky bassline and squelching beats driving the track, "Where You From" is both fun and sweet, with the vocal-line members arriving during the chorus and at the end to harmoniously inquire more about the object of affection, only to end with the optimistic acknowledgement that regardless of where people are from, they're all human, essentially BTS's version of "love is love."

5 Just One Day

After the release of "Boy In Luv," BTS returned with "Just One Day", the second romantic single from the third *Skool* album. While its predecessor was boisterous and leaned into the group's youthful image, the septet took a more sentimental, old-school R&B and hip-hop ballad approach to youthful romance with the new track. Throughout it, the seven express a desire to have "Just One Day" with the one they love over a jazzy melody. Like the previous single, the music video for the new song featured the seven members of the group in preppier, uniform-inspired looks than their previous hard-hitting hip-hop imagery full of brand names and bling, a subtle shift for the act towards a more realistic representation of the members—many of whom were still in or around high school age in Korea—as they moved further into their career.

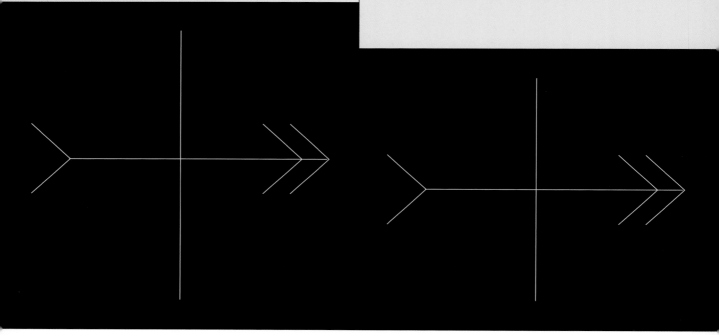

6　Tomorrow

7　BTS Cypher, Pt. 2: Triptych

A philosophical high of BTS's early discography, this track, co-written with Suga while he was still a trainee, slinks along a pounding beat as the rapper gruffly ruminates on the ambiguity of time and the desire to have a different "Tomorrow," or future, from today—the present. Hypnotic, muffled vocal effects split the song between Suga's earlier moroseness and RM's similarly anxiety-infused raps, before ending with a sense of optimism courtesy of J-Hope and the vocalists, as sharp guitar riffs, and sweet, almost seductive, promises of tomorrow blend together.

The tonal and instrumental fluctuations throughout the track reflect the philosophical weightiness of "Tomorrow," all at once infused with hope of a brighter future but also stumbling under the knowledge that the future is happening at every moment, and that to change "Tomorrow" a person has to change today.

The album's cypher, "BTS Cypher, Pt. 2: Triptych" was a swaggering hype track that directly addressed any underground hip-hop artists who might feel superior to the group, who are operating in the mainstream, or ground, level of the music world. Like all of the group's cyphers, it's impactful and intimidating, a show of their fiery response to the world around them. The song, which is split into different rhythms and flows from each rapper, ended with J-Hope incorporating the call-and-response question of "Because of who?" into his verse, which later featured prominently in "War of Hormone," a single from the group's forthcoming *Dark & Wild* album.

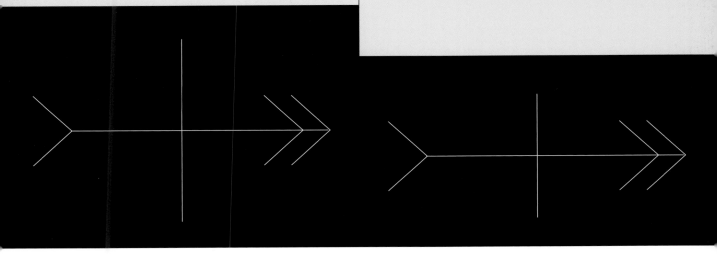

⑧ Spine Breaker

⑨ Jump

Beginning with a sample referencing the title of Song Chang-sik's "Why Do You Call Me?"—Song is considered one of South Korea's most influential folk rockers of the 1960s and '70s—"Spine Breaker" is a mid-tempo hip-hop track with a west coast feel that takes on generational and socio-economic class discord. Based around the "spine breaking"—excessively expensive—North Face long, padded jackets that were trendy in South Korea for several years, especially among teenagers, the members address children who feel entitled to ask their parents to buy these garments with their hard-earned money, critiquing the tendency for things like fashion and food trends to become rampant among consumers in South Korea. With deeper tonal registers than they typically sing in, something which is seen on other tracks of the album as they continue to explore their musical direction, the members of BTS condemn the youth who selfishly engage in this behavior as well as the consumerist society that enables them, all the while grooving along to the funky melody.

An inspirational track for all the dreamers in the world that was likely created in homage to Kris Kross's 1992 hit song of the same name, "Jump" is an enthusiastic foil to the gloom of "Tomorrow," bringing, in the first half, upbeat '90s-feeling hip-hop beats and, later, whirring dubstep rhythms to hype up listeners through the cheer-like track. "Let's jump," BTS declare repeatedly, rapping and singing about how they're moving towards the future, jumping towards their dreams even if reality is hard and nothing like the childhood dreams they had of adulthood and success. Energizing and invigorating, "Jump" is a tune that inspires activity rather than passivity, all the while getting listeners to dance and jump along to the addictive tune.

In his album overview video of *Skool Luv Affair*, Suga said that "Jump" was written years before the album was released, and features some of RM and his vocals recorded originally in November 2011.

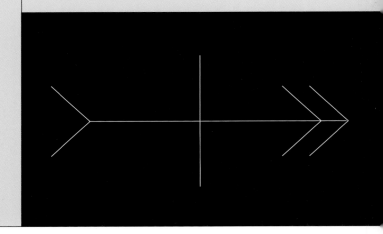

10 Outro: Propose

Honeyed R&B balladry meets groove on the closing track of *Skool Luv Affair*, where the group's vocalists sing of their promise to give their all to the object of their affection. It's a fitting close for an album about school-age romance, with the sweet vocals, breathy harmonies, and affirmations of loyalty putting a warmhearted finish on the *Skool* era, all the while putting the focus on each of the singers' distinct vocal tones, allowing each member to shine in his own right.

The duo of "Boy In Luv" and "Just One Day" showed a softer side to BTS's singles than fans had previously seen, and was a step back from the more aggressive first two parts of the *Skool* trilogy. By emphasizing romance a bit more, the group made themselves more approachable in an industry where love songs conquer all. It also gave the group's vocalists more opportunity to display their skills, though BTS's discography was still heavily dominated by the presence of RM, Suga, and J-Hope in its early days. But though it was a new approach to their promotional tracks, and the album emphasized the topic of romance, *Skool Luv Affair* continued to lean into hip-hop-heavy music with a message for their generation.

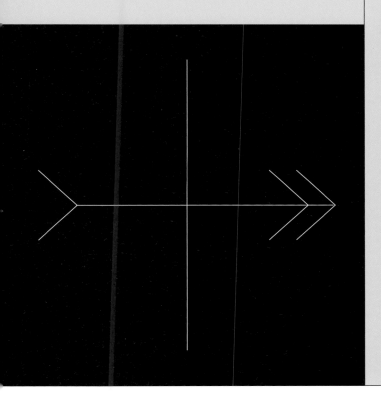

SKOOL LUV AFFAIR

Special Edition

Though *Skool Luv Affair* closed out BTS's *Skool* era, the trilogy was not quite done yet: in May, the group released a repackage, or special extended edition, version of *Skool Luv Affair*, with the addition of two more tracks: the laidback, seductive hip-hop vibes of "Miss Right" and a "Slow Jam Remix" version of "Like," originally released on *2 Cool 4 Skool*. Six additional instrumental versions of their songs were also featured, but only available on physical editions of the album. Though "Miss Right" was never released as a promotional single as might be expected, the song was an ultimate blend of the group's sentimental side with its hip-hop leanings, giving the world a romantic, bouncing slow jam full of groovy strings and horns that sweetly displayed the vocalists' tones as well as featuring sleek rhymes from the rappers. It was a gift for anyone looking for new BTS music, and a sweet farewell to the group's debut era.

BTS on the red carpet at the 100th-episode special of MBC's weekly music show, *Show Champion*.

GETTING DARK & WILD

Chapter
Seven

A full-length, 14-track studio album that arrived in August 2014, *Dark & Wild* showed that BTS and their music were maturing, continuing the lyrical and sonic styling of their first three releases while also dabbling with new ideas as they pursued a tonal shift towards a slightly poppier sound. Following the training BTS undertook during *American Hustle Life* to further explore their relationship with hip-hop and R&B— the album was partially written while the group was in transit and they recorded some of it in Los Angeles— the group's first LP focused on youthful anxieties and romance, and also featured some tracks delivering BTS's perspective on their career and the world around them.

DARK & WILD

DARK & WILD

Intro:
What Am I to You

"Intro: What Am I to You" starts off *Dark & Wild* with the sound of students chatting as the school bell rings, leading into a cheery, orchestral melody while RM sing-raps about turning negatives to positives. But the tune and RM's verse subtly transition, gradually descending into impassioned rage and angst, with the dichotomy of the song's flow previewing the passion and anxiety that prevail throughout much of the album.

Prior to the album's release, the track was revealed through an animated comeback trailer that reflected the song's dueling sentiments, beginning with bright, paradise-like hues before shifting its point of view to a crumbling, black-and-white world, with both the "Intro" and its video emphasizing how the group had shifted away from the youthful exuberance, and perhaps innocence, of their previous eras to something darker, and a bit wilder.

2 Danger

3 War of Hormone

In "Danger" BTS relay their emotions over a vibrant backing track of dramatic beats, guitar riffs, and wailing synths, telling the object of their affection that they're in "Danger" for playing coy and being unresponsive in their relationship. The adolescent feel from "Boy In Luv" is there, but as "Danger" powers through its declarations, BTS express their emotions in a more forthright manner, no longer confessing love but instead actively chasing it while comparing romance to an equation that must be figured out between two people. The music video is equally aggressive, with powerful choreography to match the pounding energy of the song. Stylistically, there's a rocker vibe, with the group in grunge-esque plaid, leather, and jeans, with only a few remnants of their earlier fashion choices, like gold chains, remaining.

The song would later be released with a more ambient vibe for the alternative, "Mo-Blue-Mix" featuring Australian-Vietnamese singer THANH, playing piano and adding an English verse and a new take on the chorus. In his YouTube review of the *Dark & Wild* album, Suga revealed that they had reached out to THANH to write the melody featured in "Danger" after BTS and the Big Hit team struggled to come up with one. A black-and-white music video was also released for the remix collaboration, showing the septet and THANH relaying the emotions expressed in the song more melodically, with orchestral instrumentals ushering in a new sense of vibrancy.

Back-to-back with "Danger" on *Dark & Wild* is "War of Hormone," the second single released. Beginning with a scratching effect and a reference back to the question, "Because of who?" from "BTS, Cypher, Pt. 2: Triptych" on *Skool Luv Affair*, "War of Hormone" is an upbeat track about youthful feelings based on hormones. Like the previous single, there's a rhythmic rock vibe to it all, with gritty guitar riffs vibing off a head-bobbing beat and a variety of sound effects, including a woman moaning and something that comes straight out of a Mario game, similar to the sound when the plumber character jumps to collect coins. Dramatic, chanting raps and verses dominate the song as the seven sing declarations of love, and, more controversially, about how men view women, with one particular line expressing that women are like presents for men. In the blurb on the YouTube page for its music video, which features the group singing to a woman while playing around and showing off exaggerated footwork, the song is described as one that "has a fun lyric where they say the reason a man's heart flutters in front of a beautiful girl is because of hormones."[15] Because of its language positioning women from the perspective of young men, the song has proven contentious.

④ Hip-Hop Phile

⑤ Let Me Know

In "Hip-Hop Phile," the group celebrates the greats of the genre while explaining why they like it. Throughout the track, the rappers lay out their bars over a sprightly beat while the group's vocal line holds their own with R&B-inspired crooning during the chorus. The song isn't just about the group's bond with the genre, but also about each of the rappers' experiences: RM expresses his interest in hip-hop's history and shares how it got him to where he is as a songwriter-rapper, J-Hope expresses that he's still learning from it and that dance led him to where he is, and Suga, the only one of the three to not cite any of his inspirations, instead shares his creative route ever since discovering hip-hop and producing in childhood.

Coming out after BTS's experience in the U.S. for *American Hustle Life*, "Hip-Hop Phile" pays homage to its history in America with references to Jay-Z, Nas, Snoop Dogg, Rakim, 2Pac, Mac Miller, Kanye West, and more, and also shares some of the Korean artists RM and J-Hope were inspired by such as Epik High, Dynamic Duo, and Verbal Jint. It also features a reference from RM to the traditional Korean folk story of Shim Cheong, a dutiful daughter who sacrifices herself for her father, as if the rapper is considering his own origin and narrative while ruminating on the roots of the genre that's inspired him so much; the melding of modernity with Korean traditions would continue sporadically throughout BTS's discography over the years.

Next up on *Dark & Wild* is the emotional highlight "Let Me Know," originally released shortly before the rest of the album. An ambient breakup track produced by Suga, it evokes the sorrow and anxiety that accompany the end of a relationship through off-kilter beats and echoing melodies as the vocalists, especially V, mournfully ask to be told when the relationship is over while the rappers reflect on what may have brought about its downfall. Sprinkled throughout the track are a variety of different entrancing string melodies, as if emphasizing various emotional states, before it ends with a final falsetto cry courtesy of Jimin while Jungkook repeatedly repeats the titular query.

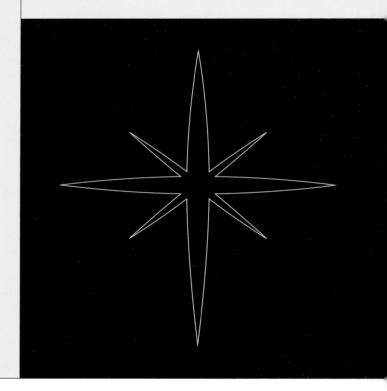

6 Rain

7 BTS Cypher, Pt. 3: Killer feat. Supreme Boi

"Let Me Know" leads into the gloom of "Rain," a jazzy alt R&B tune that blends a scratching hip-hop beat with a lilting piano melody as it relays the feelings of the members about their trainee and post-debut days, what has changed since, and what is bothering them. On a more universal level, the song evokes a sense of depression and anxiety as it reflects on a rainy Seoul day where one feels a sense of loss and loneliness, looking inwards at the internal turmoil that plagues the self. It's melancholic and forlorn, but at the same time its expressiveness offers a bit of comfort: that these feelings are a universal emotion and that the listener is not alone.

After toning down the wild factor for a bit of darkness on the first two tracks, the LP then leads into "BTS Cypher, Pt. 3: Killer," an uproarious cypher featuring producer and near-BTS member Supreme Boi alongside the group's three rappers. Like the previous cyphers, it's all about the trio's frustrations, and this time the threesome are joined by their collaborator to take on stereotypes about their skills and selling out to pursue a career in (or working with, in Supreme Boi's case) a boy band. It's aggressive and full of wordplay, including numerous double entendres, as the four rappers hype themselves and their careers up over a melody built on plucky strings, gunshots, and plinking digital quirk effects. It's a full-blown hype track, and from start to finish is full of the sort of boisterous swagger through which they declare that the group has killed the Korean music world's stereotypes of idol rappers. While a tad premature, "Cypher, Pt. 3: Killer" proved prophetic as the group has since risen to the top of the entire industry, truly showing the world that they have what it takes to transcend genre limitations and stereotyping.

8 Interlude: What Are You Doing Now?

A lead-in to the following track, "What Are You Doing Now?" is a brief, groovy interlude featuring the repeated titular question.

9 Could You Turn Off Your Cell Phone

The funky "Could You Turn Off Your Cell Phone" is a rollicking song through which the members tell listeners to get off their phones, disconnect from the digital world, and just enjoy reality. Throughout their career, BTS have often explored the relationship people have with technology and the track continued this legacy, critically reflecting on the way that people are addicted to their phones in this day and age, seemingly getting dumber as smart phones get smarter.

10 Embarrassed

Things get romantic over the next three tracks, first with the mellow vibes of "Embarrassed," also known as "Blanket Kick." Driven by muted strings, horns, and piano notes, the track has a jazzy throwback feel to it as the members express their embarrassment over being in love; the Korean title refers to a popular K-drama trope of characters expressing romantic frustration by taking out their feelings on their bedding. It's sweet and soft, and a little bit funky, emulating youthful callowness, and projects an endearing image of a young man in love.

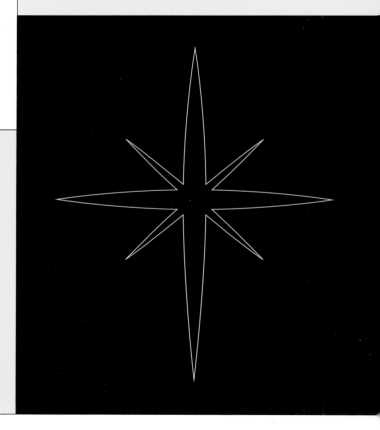

11   24/7=Heaven

12   Look Here

"Embarrassed" leads into the rhythmic feel of "24/7=Heaven," a counterpart that doesn't express anticipation of a relationship but instead moves the relationship along and expresses the desire to spend all one's time with a loved one, making their days together a heavenly experience. Lighthearted and sprightly with its snapping beat and whistling melody, it's a vibrant tune that celebrates love, while it could, like so many of BTS's romantically tinged tracks, also reflect the bond between artists and fans, and how pursuing their path together is a wonderful thing.

Next up is the breezy percussive styling of "Look Here," continuing the radiant approach towards romance of the previous songs with its bouncing beat and washed-out vocals, brassy horns, sweet harmonizing, and smooth raps, all relaying the septet's intention to capture the attention of a person they love. The track's funky instrumentals have an invigorating feel, breathing a new sense of life into love, and the song showcases a different, groovier side to BTS's musicality.

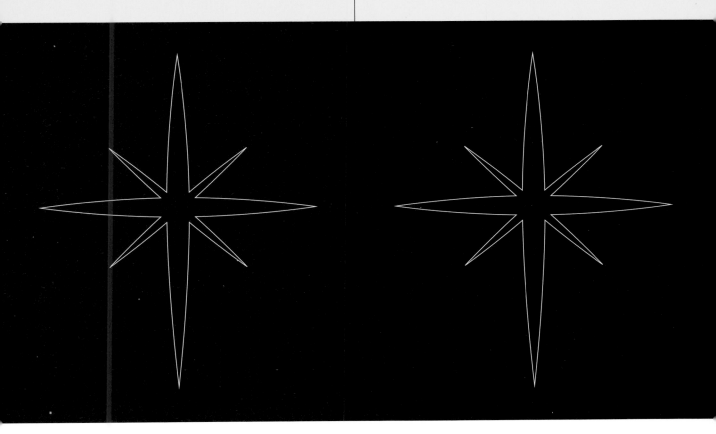

13 Second Grade

14 Outro: Do You Think It Makes Sense?

Things begin to wind down on *Dark & Wild* with "Second Grade," a track commemorating the group's second year with boisterous electro-hip-hop as the seven revel in their achievements throughout that time. The rappers talk about how they got a rookie award the previous year and now have juniors greeting them, yet they still face pressure to live up to what their seniors in the K-pop industry have achieved, as well as stigma for being hip-hop idols. Choruses from the vocalists bouncily express how BTS are working hard every moment, utilizing all 24 hours of the day. It's almost like a resume or report card for BTS in song, all conveyed through an addictive rhythm.

The album closes out with "Outro: Do You Think It Makes Sense?" a romantic R&B slow jam from the vocalists. With their effusive lyrics, plus the haunting auto-tune declarations of the title, bolstered by brass, the four express their desire for time to rewind and for their love to return. Beautifully done, it keeps a bit of the hip-hop edge felt throughout the album, while closing *Dark & Wild* with a reflective, questioning tone, as if trying to make sense of the emotions relayed throughout the LP's tracks.

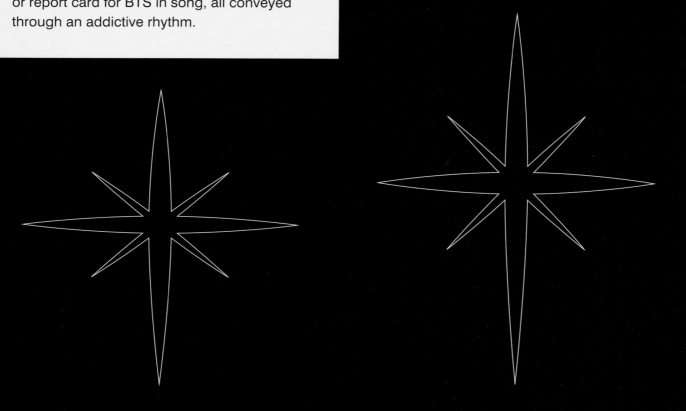

While overall the album is an enjoyable listening experience, it would be remiss to end any discussion about *Dark & Wild* without addressing some of the more problematic aspects of the band's approach to relationships between men and women during their early days. This album is at the center of much of this criticism, with its cover reading, "WARNING! Love hurts, it causes anger, jealousy, obsession, why don't u love me back?" and the singles leaning into these emotions.

In 2016, fans and critics began to question the group's lyrics, raising "War of Hormone," "Miss Right," "Converse High," and RM's solo "Joke" along with several social media posts from the group as examples of potentially misogynistic content. Rather than ignore the situation, the group recognized the severity of the criticism and ultimately Big Hit Entertainment released a statement:

> Big Hit Entertainment recognizes that some BTS songs have stirred heated debate surrounding their misogynistic lyrics. After checking the lyrics, Big Hit Entertainment found that some contents might be misleading and intimidating to the public regardless of what the musician intended. We also found that some posts on BTS' social media accounts might contain misogynistic contents … Big Hit Entertainment and all members of BTS would hereby like to express our dearest apology to those who felt uncomfortable with the lyrics and online posts.[16]

One of RM's acquaintances, MOT's eAeon, who would eventually collaborate on his solo playlist *mono.* in 2018*,* addressed the situation in a series of tweets, sharing that he had spoken with RM about the situation, and that the BTS member had expressed distress. Aeon's response to RM, as translated by *Soompi*, regarding the younger artist's concerns and guilt said a lot about the way artists can handle such accusations: "I said that misogyny is not a label or a stigma that cannot be erased, but rather an obstacle in the right path that can exist within anyone. Rather than feeling like it's unfair or painful, it's a matter of deciding to fix it or not after discovering it within oneself."[17]

Though the songs and music videos in question were not removed from digital albums or websites, the group began to filter them out of their concert performance setlists, and there was a noticeable lyrical shift in their approach to gender dynamics, showing growth from the group. While far from perfect—they are only human, and that's what makes them all the more approachable after all—BTS have proven on multiple occasions that there is a way to mature gracefully as artists in the spotlight, learning from one's mistakes and recognizing criticism. Whether it was owning up to accusations of misogyny, or reflecting on their interpretation of hip-hop, or addressing situations where members wore potentially offensive World War II imagery, BTS have grown up in the spotlight. With all eyes on them, they've taken ownership of their mistakes and learned from them. Not only are they singing about the ideas associated with growing up and youth, but they are living it all in public, and doing so with finesse.

BTS show off their *Dark & Wild* side at the album's showcase in August 2014.

LIVING THE MOST BEAUTIFUL MOMENTS IN LIFE

**Chapter
Eight**

The biggest turning point of BTS's career was, without a doubt, the arrival of *The Most Beautiful Moment in Life* (花樣年華) trilogy. It kicked off with the release of the first album *The Most Beautiful Moment in Life, Pt. 1* (aka *HYYH1*) in April 2015, and continued through May 2016, with the release of the final *HYYH*-associated single, "Save Me." The series title uses the Sino-Korean, also known as *hanja*, characters to express its meaning, and is literally read *Hwayangyeonhwa* (화양연화).

The *HYYH* series revamped BTS's identity, building on the riotous, rebellious schoolboys and young adulthood of their *Skool* trio and *Dark & Wild* eras, putting forward a more refined, artistic approach towards youthful growth and experiences. The stylistic shift put more emphasis on electronic dance music (EDM), R&B, and pop, but still kept the group grounded in hip-hop's sonic elements and its dedication to using music as a way to share their worldview. Incorporating BTS's philosophical approach to determining how the foundations of youth affect adulthood, it was a career-defining era for the act, laying the roots for their global success.

THE MOST
BEAUTIFUL MOMENT
IN LIFE

Intro:
The Most Beautiful
Moment in Life

This time, the album begins with the Suga-fronted "Intro: The Most Beautiful Moment in Life." With a breathy, deep rap about shooting for dreams and happiness, the rapper uses basketball—one inspiration for his stage name—as a metaphor for life's path, its successes, and frustrations, beginning the new era with a sense of introspective philosophizing. It was the first time an "Intro" had been fronted entirely by an individual member other than RM, with Suga's gravitas setting the tone for the mingling sense of desperation and hope felt in the album's first single, "I Need U."

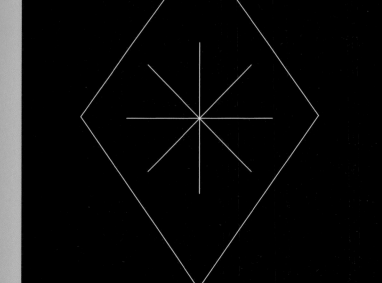

2 I NEED U

3 Hold Me Tight

The second track on *HYYH1*, "I Need U" marked the start of a new period for BTS, positioning the septet as maturing lovers who recognize the pitfalls of more serious relationships rather than sophomoric youths trying to make their way in the world. The frenzied synths, building crescendo, scattered hi-hat beats, and explosive titular choral refrain lean into the trendiest of dance music elements. The verses draw on R&B, while the song also incorporates raps courtesy of RM, Suga, and J-Hope. It was the most melodic single the septet put out at that time, sharing the group's more emotional side. It was also, notably, the first single to truly emphasize the harmonizing of the vocal line, serving up a more melody-oriented tune than most of their past singles, which more often than not saw the vocalists' singing dominated by the rap trio's input. The more sensitive approach to emotions reflected the group's growth from the brightness of youth to the impending seriousness of adulthood, which is reflected in the song's music video, and signaled an overall directional shift for the act.

Along with "I Need U", "Hold Me Tight," is one of four love songs on the album to explore the despondent state of a love that is drifting away. Moody and ambient, the angsty alt-R&B groove of "Hold Me Tight" follows along with the vibe of the single "I Need U," similarly reflecting the desire to be with someone they love.

4 Skit: Expectation!

In "Skit: Expectation!," the group relay their hopes and aspirations for the album with a charming detour into the reality of life as a BTS member, chatting about what they would like the reaction to the album to be, such as getting first place on a Korean music show, as they did with "I Need U," all the while trying to manage their expectations so as not to be disappointed. They go on to discuss their expectations for previous tracks, with J-Hope's predictions always being the reverse of what actually happened, so the members cheer him on when he says he thinks their new single will fail, as this means it will likely become a success, which it did. Towards the end of the track, Jungkook asks if he'll need to fill out tax forms for his credits on the outro track of the album, based on a conversation he had with his father, resulting in the older members of the group teasingly responding that they're essentially broke, implying that even when they make royalties the music is not truly profitable. It's an amiable, but realistic, look at their career aspirations just as they were about to begin their ascent to previously unfathomable heights. (And one imagines that Jungkook now has an accountant to handle his royalties!)

5 Dope

The whiny horns and seismic beats of the anthemic "Dope" usher in new fans with an introduction to the act and their journey to the top. The group sings about the hard work that has brought them to where they are, despite the societal pressures they face. Recognized as one of the most emblematic songs of BTS's career, the second *HYYH1* single was a major game changer, and its musical style, meshed with its captivating choreography and lyrics, made it clear to anyone who hadn't been paying attention that BTS were, indeed, "Dope." The song has become an anthem for a generation, as BTS take on the media, the government, and adults in general for hindering the future of the current young generation. RM refers to a series of slang-derived generational terms ("Sampo" [3포], "Ohpo" [5포], and "Yookpo" [6포]) used in Korea to express how different generations had to give up different things: the "Sampo" generation had to give up on romance, marriage, and children to succeed in their careers, while the "Ohpo" have given up on those, along with finding proper jobs and owning their own homes, and the "Yookpo" have given up on all of it, along with their own general relationships and social life, all in the pursuit of money to survive in the world. The song is exuberant despite its dark social commentary and hypes up the group's members as hard workers who have given their all to hustle and make it in the world. Its addictive style laced with meaning makes it one of the stand-out moments of BTS's career.

6 Boyz With Fun

Following "Dope" are the old-school feels of "Boyz With Fun," also known as "Fun Boys," or a pun in Korean on the group's name, changing their "Bangtan" to "heungtan" (흥탄), with "heung" meaning fun. Like "Attack on Bangtan" or "Jump," it's a festive pump-up song hyping BTS and what they and their music stand for. The groovy hip-hop track needs to be danced to as it runs through its swaggering raps and sweet, bouncing verses, all the while urging listeners to gather and have fun in order to enjoy life.

7 Converse High

The tongue-in-cheek "Converse High" serves up a flirty funk tune that uses sartorial allegories to describe the ideal relationship. Countering boisterous raps with sweet harmonies, it gives the album a fresh, youthful feel, all the while shunning a variety of designer brands, only to express the band's love of Converse high-tops, the epitome of comfortable, yet stylish and laidback shoes. The song is inspired by RM's ideal type of girl, who he's mentioned wears red Converse, and fittingly features Suga rapping about how he's not into that, showing the way the pair of rappers serve as foils to each other in BTS, both musically and regarding personal taste.

8 Moving On

9 Outro: Love Is Not Over

Never forgetting their roots, the album put forth the weighty "Moving On," a lite-pop and R&B tune reflecting on the group's early days, recalling the old house they used to live in as trainees in Nonhyeon-dong, Seoul. As a lilting beat plays in the background, the rappers deliver rhymes about old homes and how life is full of moving, while the vocalists add sweet melodies reflecting on how moving always brings about a sense of melancholy as people remember the fond memories made in their old home. Throughout it all, the literal act of moving is used to relate to change and moving forward in life, and the track ends on a final, English-language outro from RM, who urges listeners to grow beyond the past and move on to new opportunities and places. It's deep and meaningful, and the perfect way to begin to close out an album that led BTS to such new, exciting places.

The Jungkook-penned vocal line track "Outro: Love Is Not Over," which he wrote with Slow Rabbit, is a precursor to the group's 2017 song "Supplementary Story: You Never Walk Alone." Over a retro synth-driven melody fronted by sweet piano and a plinking R&B beat, the four BTS members sing of a yearning that they're not yet ready to lay to rest. It's sentimental and sensitive, and one of the quartet's best displays of their harmonious vocals in their career up to that point, showing how they have transitioned from the singers with "No More Dreams" to ones who can oh-so-expressively share their desires.

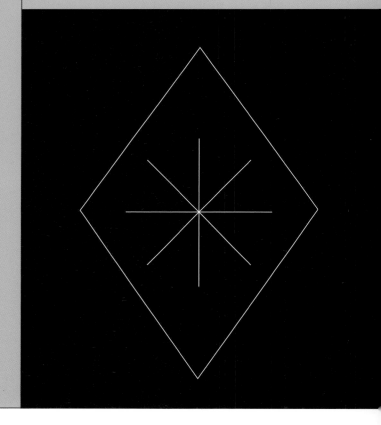

As a whole, *HYYH1* is an elegant, more sleekly produced take on hip-hop and electropop than their earlier releases, a fully fleshed-out showcase of the diverse styles the group is able to pull off with such ease. As the entry point into *The Most Beautiful Moment in Life* series, it marked a new era in BTS's career with the success of "I Need U," which garnered BTS their first win on one of South Korea's weekly music shows, and "Dope," which went on to become one of their first viral music videos and an introduction for many new audiences. It was the start of something new for the group, as their momentum grew and they raced towards the future heights of their career.

Before 2015 was out, BTS would release *The Most Beautiful Moment in Life, Pt. 2*, offering up some of the emotional highs of their career to date. The album begins strongly with the intro track, moves into the soaring heights of "Run," explores the fleeting emotions of love in "Butterfly" and those of loneliness in "Whalien 52," before hyping up the members in "Ma City" and attacking Korean society in "Silver Spoon." During "Skit: One Night in a Strange City," the group would chat about their success and pressures while in Chile during The Red Bullet Tour in 2015—on the verge of success with *The Most Beautiful Moment in Life* series but not quite there yet—and still eons away from the unimaginable success they'd achieve over the next three years. The album, which exuded a sense of poetry throughout, would conclude with "Autumn Leaves" and "Outro: House of Cards," closing with a sense of darkness and sorrow.

This emotional depth filtered throughout the album would come to define the group's next few releases. The youths of the *Skool* and *Dark & Wild* eras were gone. Instead, these were men contemplating the realities of life. And it stuck, with *HYYH2* and its sequel, *The Most Beautiful Moment in Life: Young Forever* each rising in popularity thanks in part to their introspective nature, foreshadowing BTS's upcoming ascent to the top of Western music charts.

If *HYYH1* reflects on who BTS are and how the members perceive the world, with songs that express the group's desires and feelings and look towards the future, the tracks on *HYYH2* are about becoming agents of one's own fate, running towards that same future, and relaying what they want to see in the world around them. From the resistance to antipathy

and animosity relayed in "Intro: Never Mind" to the obstinance of "Outro: House of Cards", there is an overwhelming sense of the perseverance that has driven BTS's career and success.

At its essence, *HYYH2* is about, as it says, "the most beautiful moments in life," but conveys this rather differently from the way *HYYH1* did. During the second album's release press conference, the group expressed the differences between the two connected albums: "Part one explained how youth is tiring and difficult, and it also touched on how we feel like we're always on edge. Part two will have a more adventurous and daring feel to it. That's why our title song is 'Run.'"[18]

THE MOST

BEAUTIFUL MOMENT

IN LIFE, PT. 2

**Intro:
Never Mind**

HYYH2 begins with another Suga-fronted intro track, the gritty "Intro: Never Mind" during which the rapper, with a few additions from RM, aggressively confronts and spurns negativity, and promotes pushing through failures towards the future. With a mellow beat and intense instrumentals fronted by fierce guitar riffs, as well as the sound of a cheering crowd demanding an encore as Suga bares his soul, it's an assertive start to the album, grabbing listeners' attention and taking hold of it.

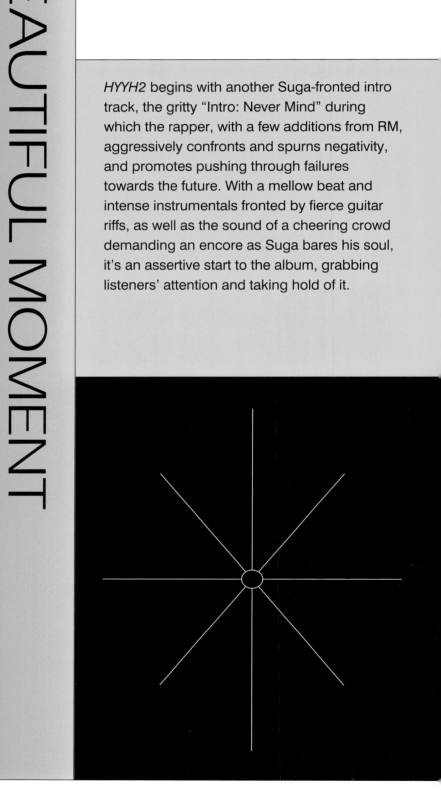

② Run

The *HYYH2* EP is fronted by "Run," and is the only album from the *HYYH* trilogy to feature a solitary promotional single. But even standing alone, "Run" is intensely impactful with its vibrant EDM styling, as it continues the group's divergence from hip-hop-focused singles with a dramatic flair. Wailing synths permeate the angst, as the septet effusively express their desperation about a love that is soon to leave, a fleeting romance akin to "chasing butterflies." Though intense, there's a sense of acceptance littered throughout, as if the lyrical narrator is reluctantly acknowledging that the passion they feel is unrequited and it's better to feel the pain now, even though they don't want it to end. With layered harmonies and distorted, autotuned cries of repeated refrains ("lie/lie," "bye/bye," "cry/cry"), there's a sense of tension throughout as the song explores these very understandable emotions of wanting something you know is detrimental for you. It's intensely poetic, and its accessible sound and relatable nature fittingly led the album to great heights; *HYYH2* was BTS's first release to break into *Billboard* U.S.'s main albums chart, peaking at No. 171 on the Billboard 200 upon its release.

③ Butterfly

A sweeping ballad built on airy instrumentals, hazy synths, and a lilting trap beat, in this song the group turns to the metaphor of a butterfly, a recurring theme throughout much of the era's promotional imagery. In contrast to the despondency of "Run," it's filled with tentative hope, wondering if the "Butterfly" of love that is currently within their grasp will remain there. Used as the soundtrack of the "Prologue" video for the era, a video that connects the plot of "I Need U" and "Run," the song reflects not only the whirlwind of emotions related to love, but is also a homage to youth, as if they're asking, "Can I keep these fleeting beautiful moments alive as I grow older?" The song, which alludes to both the butterfly effect theory, where the smallest incident affects everything that follows, and novelist Haruki Murakami's *Kafka on the Shore*, a fantastical book partly about a teenager trying to change his fate, is an example of what BTS does best: weaving depth and meaning into ideas that seem simple at first and adding emotional weight to sounds that are all at once familiar and utterly captivating in their arrangement.

Following "Butterfly" is "Whalien 52," a deceptively lighthearted-sounding track that leans into old-school hip-hop aesthetics as it explores themes relating to depression and loneliness. The hybrid title is derived from both the word "alien" and the 52-hertz whale, also known as the loneliest whale in the world due to its unique, high-pitched whale song, which allegedly keeps it from interacting with other whales. Both are apparent references to the alienation individuals feel when they're swimming alone in the world. While serving as a metaphorical reference to everyday, individual loneliness, "Whalien 52" also blatantly refers to the group's status as celebrities who sing, but who don't feel they're always heard. But despite its sad nature, "Whalien 52" is far from hopeless; just as the 52-hertz whale can be heard each year as it keeps persisting, making its way through the depths of the oceans, so too can others experience periods of isolation that result in promising moments of being heard.

The album takes a seismic shift in the next track, moving forward into the cheeky "Ma City," a rockish ode to members' hometowns, with references to Ilsan (RM), Busan (Jimin, Jungkook), Daegu (Suga), and Gwangju (J-Hope) making their way into the lyrics. Like other tracks from BTS that take pride in the group's local roots, *satoori* is used sporadically throughout the track. The song is subtly political as it declares their pride in their regional roots, but also because J-Hope references the numbers "062–518." While rapped as if part of a phone number, they are in fact two separate numbers: the first refers to Gwangju's area code "062," while the latter three refer to the date May 18, a nod to the 1980 Gwangju Uprising, also known as the May 18 Democratic Uprising, that was integral to South Korea's shift from authoritarian governments to a legitimate democracy. (Before BTS formed, Suga wrote a song titled "518–062" during his days as part of the D-Town crew, which similarly addressed the topic, which remains a contentious issue in South Korea today due to the way leadership under general and later president Chun Doo-hwan responded to the calls for democracy.) Like their other songs reflecting BTS's South Korean-ness, "Ma City" expresses pride in who they are and where they come from.

6 Silver Spoon

After taking a moment to revel in their roots, BTS spun things upside down with the confrontational "Silver Spoon," perhaps the most radical song of the group's career in its presentation of contemporary young adult experiences and frustrations. Also known as "*Baepsae*" or "Crow-Tit," the song's rollicking, swaggering rhythm and gritty horns and bassline emphasize its mocking intent as the group takes South Korean society to task, referencing a proverb about try-hards: "뱁새가 황새 걸음을 걸으면 가랑이가 찢어진다," which means, "If a crow-tit tries to walk like a stork, its legs will break." A warning against trying to act like others, the petite bird, which The Academy of Korean Studies identifies as the *Paradoxornis webbiana fulvicauda*, or a vinous-throated parrotbill, is told to stay in its lane and not try to act like something it's not. Though it could be interpreted positively, as "be yourself," the meaning is more along the lines of "stay in your lane and don't try to get ahead of yourself." As such, the title of the song could also be translated to mean "Try-Hard", as BTS reviles—using informal speech rather than the more polite phrasing younger Koreans typically use when addressing their elders—the criticism aimed at both themselves and their generation. They have created a millennial anthem in "Baepsae" that confronts the general idea that youth in the 21st century are lazy and not working as hard as past generations did, despite the socio-economic and political state of the world creating widespread economic disparity and job insecurity across the globe.

The song's title in English, "Silver Spoon," is similarly themed, referring to the idiom of being born with a silver spoon in one's mouth, touching on both economic disparity, and the different economic and cultural states in which the previous and current generation of young adults grew up. South Korea has a similar concept, with RM referring to "금수저," a golden spoon rather than a silver one, as in Korean society economic classes are often compared to four levels of material used for cutlery: gold (금), silver (은), bronze (동) and dirt (흙). The rapper calls out the teachers of this generation specifically, as they were born in a "golden spoon" era when their path towards success and happiness is perceived as having been much easier. They are constrasted with the youth of today, who are required to labor over school obsessively and have little job security because of prior generations' influence on the present state of the world. The song is overwhelmingly angry in its millennial artistry, and a fan favorite because it resonates with the feelings of so many people today, as life in the 21st century is far from easy for anyone, and the future doesn't look like it will get much better, with climate change and financial anxiety increasingly becoming bigger issues.

7 Skit: One Night in a Strange City

Following the intensity of "Silver Spoon," *HYYH2* takes a moment to reflect on the success of BTS's career with the "Skit: One Night in a Strange City." Like all their skits, the group humorously entertains listeners with their dynamic, in this case beginning with the members berating RM for his constant lateness, and then easing into a discussion about their singles, before taking Suga to task for his ability to kill a good mood. It's fun, it's cute, and it gives insight into their experience with their rising fame on the album that would go on to be an undeniable gamechanger.

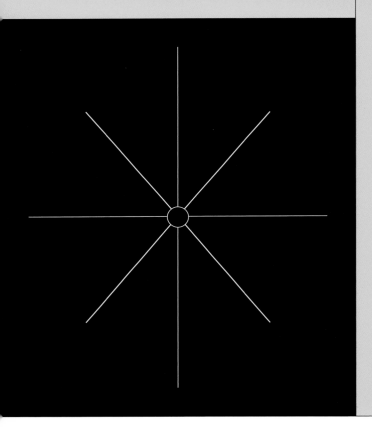

8 Autumn Leaves

The album turns to its close on a gloomy note with the poetic "Autumn Leaves," also known as "Dead Leaves" and "Fallen Leaves," based on the idea of things that fall apart with the gentlest of motions. An airy song, it is full of refined, layered harmonies, reverberating beats, and cool-toned synths. Throughout, it displays the group's growth from their early days as it revels in the members' palette of singing and rapping tones, blending together to create a chilled, ambient, literary song expressing heartbreak, telling a story from start to finish as they mournfully reflect on the effervescent nature of love.

At first glance a song about the fragile state of romance, it can also be interpreted to represent the fragile state of a career (particularly that of BTS in their early days, as the track follows the skit where they discuss their career), where each and every movement feels like it could make everything fall apart. It's poignant, it's poetic, and it's devastating.

(The song also notably gained attention and raised awareness of producers' now-common practice of drawing on sound libraries full of premade beats, instrumentals, synth effects, and so on; another Korean boy band, EXO, used the same sampled elements featured in "Autumn Leaves," in their 2016 song "They Never Know"—as did American rapper BlackBear, on his 2015 song "Deadroses"—causing a minor controversy as BTS and EXO are considered rivals.)

⑨ Outro: House of Cards

HYYH2 ends with the haunting sensuality of the vocal line's "Outro: House of Cards." A creeping alt-R&B track with breathy verses, there's an edge of danger to the song as Jin, V, Jimin, and Jungkook sing about a "House of Cards" within each person and a romance that's ready to collapse every day, but continues due to people's dreams and efforts. The track was released in a longer version on *The Most Beautiful Moment in Life: Young Forever*, bringing it to new heights with additional verses that featured the four building towards a pulsating, soaring finale as they sang of both futility and hope.

The Most Beautiful Moment in Life, Pt. 2 brought BTS to new audiences, both in Korea and internationally, with the captivating music and related creative narrative capturing attention around the globe. The album became their first to break into the Stateside Billboard 200 albums chart, peaking at No. 171, only the 11th album from a Korean artist to ever appear on it, and the first from a company other than SM or YG Entertainments, signaling a shift in the winds as to what international audiences, Stateside audiences in particular, were interacting with.

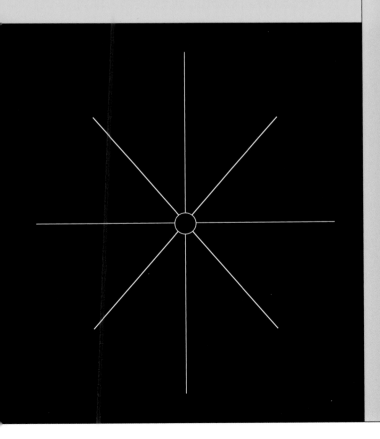

Red-carpet-ready RM in April 2019 at
The Fact Music Awards.

The Most Beautiful Moment of BTS's career was far from over, with the group's momentum building with each passing day, but the era finished with the capstone release of compilation album *The Most Beautiful Moment in Life: Young Forever* in May 2016. The two-disc album came out amid the group's global touring schedule, and featured a total of 23 songs, including the content from *HYYH1* and *HYYH2*, several remixes and extended versions of both "House of Cards" and "Love Is Not Over," plus three brand-new songs. The first, the titular "Epilogue: Young Forever" served as the series' finale theme, but came out ahead of *HYYH:YF*'s release, arriving with a music video that connected music videos from the era. The video began with a black screen that featured the Sino-Korean characters meaning *The Most Beautiful Moment in Life* and the phrase "2015.04.29~Forever," alluding to the idea that every moment of life is not only beautiful, but one that grows out of youthful experiences.

THE MOST BEAUTIFUL MOMENT IN LIFE: YOUNG FOREVER

(1) **Epilogue: Young Forever**

Produced by RM, this is an alluring ballad that starts with lilting beats and increasingly incensed raps before turning into an echoing, sweeping tune with the phrase "Forever we are young" laced into lyrics about dreams and hopes. It ends with a final, chanting declaration by the members that they'll run towards their dreams regardless of any pain that comes their way. An anthem for youth across the board, at the time of release it stirred powerful emotions for a group who had just proven that they could make the transition from hardships to the top of the music game.

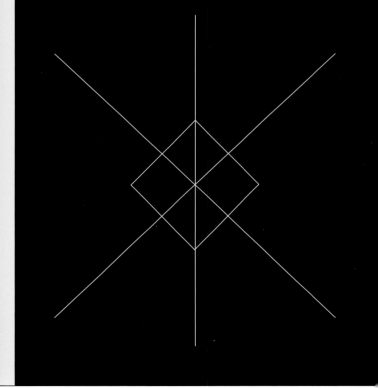

Sweat

② Fire

Shortly after the release of "Epilogue: Young Forever," BTS returned with "Fire," also known as "Burning Up," igniting things once more. Featuring a powerful bark of a beat and chants, it was a dynamic, charismatic flourish to end the youth-oriented HHYH era with. A follow-up thematically to both "Dope" and "Silver Spoon," "Fire" blended explosive trap, electropop, and hip-hop elements to provide a powerful backdrop over which the septet rallied against the oppression of youth and those who think young people need to spend the most beautiful moments of their lives—adolescence—burdened by expectations of what they'll achieve in the future. It was released through a similarly explosive music video, where the members riotously rebel and set the world aflame. It ends with them partying as they perform the song's impacful choreography, only to end with Suga saying "I'll forgive you," as if addressing those who are burdening youth by making the world a harder place to live in.

③ Save Me

While "Fire" exuded immense confidence, the final single of *The Most Beautiful Moment in Life* series, "Save Me," offered something else. Sweeping desperation in the form of a gloriously expressive dance track that soars on tick-tocking beats and frenetic synths, "Save Me" served as the foil to "I Need U" as "Fire" paralleled "Dope," bringing the entire era to a close by paralleling its beginning.

Powerful in its anguish as BTS cry out for salvation, "Save Me" was released through a gracefully choreographed single-shot video. It was deceptively simple, panning in and out on shots capturing the expressiveness of the members' performances. Like "Epilogue: Young Forever," it had a literal message, ending with the phrase "Boy Meets"—hinting at the Wings era to come, a nod to that album's intro song "Boy Meets Evil." But "Save Me" also has what appears to be a reference to *Wings* itself with RM thanking the listener for giving him wings to fly. The moment stands out against the rest of the lyrics, as if he's addressing not a lover to whom he is crying out for help but instead directly talking to fans who have helped bring BTS to such great heights, a theme of the *Wings* era and beyond. The importance of "Save Me" would resonate for years to come, and would be revisited during the *Love Yourself* era through its foil track, "I'm Fine."

THE BTS UNIVERSE NARRATIVE, OR THE MOST BEAUTIFUL MOMENT IN LIFE: THE STORY

Known as the alternative reality of *The BTS Universe* or *The Bangtan Universe* (aka the BU), the fictive story that BTS first shared during *The Most Beautiful Moment in Life* era was about how to enjoy, respect, and reflect on what it means to be living *The Most Beautiful Moment in Life,* adolescence, while growing up in a harsh world.

Writing this retrospectively, it is easy to theorize about the storyline BTS and their team put forth through their music videos and other media. Not only is there more content from which to decipher clues, but the group even released the tie-in webtoon series *Save Me* and *The Notes 1* book to make things more clear. But nothing is ever quite that straightforward in the world of Bangtan, and between the start of *The Most Beautiful Moment in Life* era in 2015 and through the *Love Yourself* period and beyond, the group shared a narrative divided between music videos, songs, and various related social media content—including an extensive series of writing known as *The Most Beautiful Moment in Life Notes*, which weaved together the threads of a plot about friendship based on fictionalized versions of BTS members. For years, fans would analyze each and every element of BTS's career that could potentially be a part of the BU, with numerous blog and social media posts, videos, websites, and essays created as ARMY tried to determine what exactly BTS was conveying. With the release of the *Save Me* webtoon in January 2019, things started to fall into place, with creator Lico working in collaboration with Big Hit Entertainment to tell the tale they'd been hinting at over the past few years, finally shedding light on the dramatic plot built around seven friends and their struggles, fantastically based on time travel and the impact, or butterfly effect, of each minute action.

At its heart, the story of *Save Me*, and the story told through BTS's creative content over the years, is based in a world of magical surrealism. Each member of the septet has a corresponding character, which they portray in their music videos as they act out their fictive persona. Over the years, and through the webtoon, it was revealed that Seokjin, played by Jin, is at the center of the plot to bring the group of friends together after they have separated since they were in school together and individually faced hardships of extreme proportions, ranging from mental health issues, to abuse, to death.

Dramatic and impactful as a narrative tool through which BTS's youth-oriented messaging could be delivered, the music videos comprised intense stories featuring the seven characters—Seokjin, Suga's Yoongi, RM's Namjoon, J-Hope's Hoseok, V's Taehyung, Jungkook, and Jimin—in alternating hellish and heavenly settings and circumstances. Time spent together, sometimes at school, but occasionally at the beach or amid greenery or even partying, were typically awash in brightness, while individually or in pairs (as many characters serve as foils to one another) life was anything but easy for the seven young men. While a variety of storylines play out, the plot focuses on Seokjin trying to save his friends in a variety of traumatic situations. He is outside of things in a time loop, repeating his days. The music videos regularly featured Jin on his own or taking photos or videos of the others, as if looking in on their lives—or post-lives depending on the theory, with some suspecting *HYYH* is based on a concept of one life rather than day-to-day reality—from afar. The conceit raises the question of whether he is in limbo and being forced to relive life and mistakes he's made in each timeline, and whether he'll truly be able to fix the terrible ills that have affected the other characters.

Without a clearly linear structure, it was hard to assuredly lay out the plot of BTS's *The Most Beautiful Moment in Life* narrative before *Save Me* concluded, but several threads carry through the different eras of the group's videography and imagery, most prominently the paired friendships. While Jin stands on his own, Yoongi and Jungkook are seen to have a tight bond and related storylines, as do Hoseok and Jimin, and Namjoon with Taehyung. Though they each appear individually on occasions, the pairings remain consistent throughout numerous videos and related BU content, whether they are together in moments of happiness or of tragedy.

While the BU's protagonists are at their best and happiest together, each character has his own distinct narrative: Seokjin, an outsider aiming to turn back time after being at least partly responsible for the group drifting apart; Yoongi, a mentally unstable arsonist and talented musician who favors the piano, and whose mother died in a fire when he was younger. He dies on multiple occasions by suicide. Hoseok was abandoned by his mother and struggles with what seems to be narcolepsy but may be Munchausen syndrome, resulting in hospitalization. Namjoon faces poverty due to his family's difficulties and bigotry, and lands in jail. Jimin, like Yoongi and Hoseok, struggles with his mental health, and is apparently suicidal. Taehyung has a difficult family life, and ultimately faces a future in prison after killing his abusive father in a rage following his mother leaving the family. Jungkook, the youngest, battles loneliness and a bad situation in his stressful home life, and in different scenes faces either a car accident or choosing to die by suicide.

It is with the last point, where Jungkook is one of several of the characters reaching the end of his life—either literally through suicide or by causing irreparable damage to their lives through their actions—that *Save Me* begins, with Jin returning to Korea after time overseas and finding each of his friends' lives in a state of devastation. He is offered a chance to try and change things, with his life resetting to April 11 again and again as he attempts to alter the future, only to discover that ultimately it is not something he can do alone, no matter how hard he tries, because the bonds of friendship and brotherhood do not rest solely in the hands of one person but instead with everyone.

Both as a fictional narrative and as a creative work meant to reflect the music of the act and its themes of youth, struggles, and self-love, *Save Me,* or the BTS Universe, took its time to craft a story that is both distinctly based in BTS's identity and, like its discography, also intensely universal, reflecting the struggle of individuals with interpersonal relationships and society at large.

The entire story is best experienced firsthand, so I recommend putting this book down, watching every BTS music video, and reading *Save Me*, perhaps taking a look at the *Notes* and fan theories, and then seeking out some of the secret Twitter and Instagram accounts the BU has used if you still feel like you're missing out on things. But it's worth delving into some of the stylistic elements that were featured throughout *The Most Beautiful Moment in Life* story, as told through the act's *music*.

RECURRING THEMES OF THE BU

Butterflies

As a symbol of freedom and the fleeting span of life and relationships, butterflies have appeared throughout much of BTS's cinematography and music, most prominently with *The Most Beautiful Moment in Life, Pt. 2* song "Butterfly." The delicate creature serves as a metaphor for how precious and beautiful life is. One of the first instances where butterflies were featured was during the "Just One Day" music video trailer, where Jungkook was seen performing a dance that emulated the movements of a butterfly. Butterflies played a role throughout the BU, drawing attention to both the limited amount of time the characters would have together, and also the way time passes so quickly that it's hard to appreciate it as it flies by. In the plot itself, the butterfly symbolizes the butterfly effect theory, in which even the smallest detail can affect situations. This is one reason why each time Jin wakes up again on April 11 and does something different, something changes.

Fall from grace

Most closely associated with the *Wings* era, which is fronted by the "Intro: Boy Meets Evil" and features a music video for "Blood Sweat & Tears" that is all about the descent into temptation, much of the BU's plot focuses on the descent from good to bad, with a particular focus on Taehyung, who is an all-around good kid but ultimately ends up killing his father. For the rest of the characters, their respective falls are more personal, as each man is brought to psychological lows where they're unable to help themselves—which is where their friendship comes in.

Changing fate

The idea that people can change their own fate, and that of others, is a major element of the BU plotline. The group's musical messaging similarly suggests that finding self-love and forming tight bonds of friendship will help a person cope with the world's hardships.

Wings

Related to the butterfly motif, wings are symbolically significant to BTS's musicality and narrative, and it's notable that their second LP is titled *Wings*. A nod to the way that the group has soared upon wings, which could either be interpreted as both their hard work and talents or their ARMY—in Nov. 2016, RM tweeted that "BTS+ARMY=Wings,"—the image of wings appears most prominently in "Blood Sweat & Tears." In that video, Jin caresses and kisses a statue with black wings, and V appears as a grinning, fallen angel whose wings have been torn out, a metaphor for the loss of innocence as one ages and faces the cruel world, as well as possibly a reference to Taehyung's character in the BU.

Mental health

Less a theme and more a plot device or narrative element, the mental health struggles characters face throughout the BU narrative are some of the most heart-wrenching, with some of the men suffering from deep depression (Yoongi and Jungkook), anxiety (Namjoon), Munchausen syndrome (Hoseok), and stress-related seizures (Jimin). The members of BTS have touched on their own personal struggles with mental health over the years in their music, through both subtle and overt references, but the BU relays these common struggles as major points of the story, emphasizing how mental health issues are so difficult for those suffering them, especially in a country like South Korea where they are rarely talked about or treated, and are often stigmatized.

The clash between generations

A pervasive theme throughout BTS's discography, this struggle is a focal element of the BU narrative, although it mostly appears in the background. Many of the characters have to face the older generation, whether it's parents, teachers, or strangers, who talk down to them and treat them poorly, in part because of their youth and in part because of the hubris of adulthood. Sometimes it is by direct action, such as the driver who threw money at Namjoon as a way to express a power dynamic, and sometimes inaction, such as Jungkook's parents and Jimin's mother not looking after their sons' mental wellbeing, but just about every single interaction between the seven young men and adults is destructive.

The impact of parents

The actions, or inactions, of parents play a major role in determining the path of each of the BU character's lives. Each of their relationships with their parents determines their storyline to some degree, with this fundamental dynamic being the root cause of much of the trauma they each experience: Namjoon's father is ill, and this results in their family's impoverished state; Yoongi's mother dies by fire; Jungkook's mother remarries and creates an inhospitable environment for him; Hoseok's mother abandons him; Taehyung's mother leaves and his father is an abusive alcoholic; Jimin's parents force him into hospitalization; and Jin's father is perhaps the most subtly vile of them all, as his demands on Jin have led to multiple situations in the BU that have resulted in bad incidents for the seven and the group's friendship dynamic.

RECURRING THEMES OF THE BU

Literature and film

BTS regularly reference outside literary influences in their music, and featured some throughout the BU. *Demian: The Story of Emil Sinclair's Youth* by German author Hermann Hesse, in which a young man grapples with meaning in the world and good versus evil as he grows through his school life and beyond, is perhaps the most prominent book, gaining the spotlight during the *Wings* era, most notably when it is quoted in the middle of the "Blood Sweat & Tears" music video, while the song "Butterfly" references *Kafka on the Shore* by Japanese novelist Haruki Murakami, a book about a 15-year-old running away from an Oedipal prophecy that he would kill his father and sleep with his mother and in doing so ends up kicking off a chain of surreal events through which he may have inadvertently done, or caused, both. Meanwhile, a neon sign in "Spring Day" hints that that video and its role in the BU is inspired by the short story "The Ones Who Walk Away from Omelas" by iconic fantasy writer Ursula K. Le Guin. It tells the tale of the titular utopian city, in which people discover that its peace and serenity are in part built on suffering, and so some opt to walk away from the false promise of utopia.

BTS also may have drawn on films like *Inception* and *Snowpiercer* for inspiration, as each movie revolves around themes that question not only societal roles but also how individuals view reality; the title of the *HYYH* era itself evokes the 2000 Hong Kong film directed by Wong Kar-wai *In the Mood for Love*, which features the same Chinese characters meaning "The Most Beautiful Moment in Life." This itself is a famous Chinese idiom meaning "the flower years."

A variety of artworks featured in their music videos also play a role, such as *The Fall of the Rebel Angels* by Dutch Renaissance artist Pieter Bruegel in "Blood Sweat & Tears", adding to the hidden subtleties of the BU, with images of wings, angels, mothers, celestial bodies, etc. making appearances.

TAKING TO NEW HEIGHTS WITH WINGS

Chapter Nine

After the success of *The Most Beautiful Moment in Life* era, expectations were high for *Wings.* Just as the *Skool* trilogy had been followed by the thematic tie-in of the full-length album *Dark & Wild*, the act's 2015–2016 *HYYH* trio was followed by an LP release. But between the *Skool – Dark & Wild* and *HYYH–Wings* eras, things had changed exponentially for BTS: the question was no longer, "Can they make it?" but had become, "How far can they go?"

Perhaps their most intimate album to date, *Wings* arrived on October 10, 2016, just under a year since the group's first Billboard 200-charting album, *HYYH2*, was released in November. In that time, BTS had gone from being rebellious, rising stars within the world of K-pop to the most prominent Korean act in the world since Psy's "Gangnam Style" became a viral sensation in 2012. And unlike the satirical artist's short-lived relationship with the global music scene, BTS weren't bolstered by viral throngs but instead maintained their relevance in the U.S. with a very active, hyper-dedicated fan ARMY that was growing with each and every day. BTS have described ARMY as being the wings upon which their career has taken flight, and it is from this idea that the album poignantly takes its title. Drawing inspiration from their fans, the album showed a new side to the act and to each member as individual artists, sharing seven expressive solo tracks that tied into the BU narrative and were released through short films.

Overall, Wings deals predominantly with a singular overarching theme, inspired by Hermann Hesse's bildungsroman *Demian*, about how young people struggle with the concept of good vs. evil.

WINGS

Intro: Boy Meets Evil

Wings begins, as do all BTS albums, with an introductory track, this time signaling a new shift with J-Hope fronting the haunting dubstep lull of "Intro: Boy Meets Evil." The song title was teased at the end of the music video for "Save Me," connecting the two eras, and can be seen as an overall theme for *The Most Beautiful Moment in Life* storylines, as each of the seven BU characters encounter a sense of evil in their everyday lives while growing from boyhood to adulthood. The comeback trailer for "Boy Meets Evil" begins not with RM or Suga as had past eras, but with J-Hope reciting a line from Hermann Hesse's *Demian*: "My sin was not specifically this or that, but consisted of having shaken hands with the devil. The devil held me in his clutches, the enemy was behind me." The tone shifts, showing J-Hope as he performs frenzied, theatrical dancing, full of isolations and popping, in a gloomy, purple-hazed warehouse. As the beat drops and the tempting refrain of "Too bad/But it's too sweet" is sung, black light comes on, changing the mood, and the figure of a man, seemingly J-Hope, appears, with a shadow of wings behind him. It was on this sinister note that the *Wings* era kicked off in earnest.

2 Blood Sweat & Tears

Following the introductory track, *Wings* led into its single, "Blood Sweat & Tears." With a moombahton rhythm, tantalizing hooks, and lush, tropical synths, the song was a new sound for BTS, but one that grew out of the previous sleek electronic dance styling that featured during the *HYYH* era. It was trendy and pristine, and was paired with a music video that not only leaned into the BU storyline, but also emphasized a more luxurious side to BTS than had ever been seen before, surrounding them with classical European art and decor, and even opening with a haunting portion of Bach's "Mass in B minor."

With a sense of danger throughout as chiaroscuro effects capture BTS in alternating bright and dark lighting, the septet tauntingly stare down the camera, and the viewer, during the sensual choreography scenes. As the short film progresses, blood, classical artworks, blindfolds, and smoke become more prevalent themes, and moments alluding to previous music videos appear, such as V jumping downwards from a balcony, almost as if into the ocean, as in the 2015 *HYYH* prologue video. "Blood Sweat & Tears" then pauses, capturing the scenery in bright red and black silhouettes as RM utters another *Demian* quote, before the plot picks up again with the haunting organ notes of Buxtehude's "Passacaglia in D minor."

It is at this point that one of BTS's most memorable artistic sequences appears: as the members run towards a bright doorway, V covers Jin's eyes; when he opens them Jin sees a marble statue with black feathered wings, an angel that he caresses and leans forward to kiss. As the kiss occurs, V is seen with marks on his shoulder blades, as if wings have been ripped from his back, and a jarring smirk appears on his face. The angel statue begins to weep multicolored tears as J-Hope sits in front of a pieta scene featuring the Virgin Mary, which later shatters, and Jimin pulls off his blindfold to reveal similar tears. The segment, and music video, come to a close with Jin staring into what appears to be a mirror, but the reflection is different, and as he stares his face begins to crumble apart. The phrase "Man muss noch Chaos in sich haben, um einen tanzenden Stern gebären zu können," appears above the mirror, a quote by Friedrich Nietzsche that translates as, "You must have chaos within you to give birth to a dancing star."

There is meaning packed into each and every moment of "Blood Sweat & Tears," but even if you are new to the world of BTS, and to the BU, it comes across as a haunting mini-film about the fall from grace. Simultaneously, it conveys a theme of ascendance from youth to adulthood, and all the pain and darkness that accompanies it, and is a singular work that encompasses so much of what BTS stand for and have explored through their music.

③ Begin

④ Lie

After descending down a dark path in "Boy Meets Evil" and "Blood Sweat & Tears," *Wings* turns to solo narratives, each of which tie in to the themes and/or storyline of the BU, lifting off with Jungkook's mellifluous, tropical R&B melody, "Begin." Featuring tight, layered production, it's a song that showcases Jungkook's tonal versatility. An autobiographical ode to how he's grown up supported by his "brothers" and has been able to fly into success with them, the tune emphasizes the emotions of BTS's youngest member as he reflects on how far he's come after moving from his hometown to start his career at 15 years old. Though seemingly straightforwardly autobiographical, it also reflects the corresponding character he plays in the BU, a younger boy who met friends in adolescence and created a tight bond with them to find happiness, only to face sorrow later.

Jungkook's "Begin" leads into Jimin's "Lie," a powerful alt R&B dance track dominated by dynamic strings, creeping beats, and the singer's stirring voice, which dips and soars throughout, displaying his expressive tone. Tying into the theme of "Boy Meets Evil"—the song includes a biblical reference to a snake—"Lie" is seductive in its delivery, with reverberating beats and sound effects layered over Jimin's alternately confident and despondent delivery. During a V Live[19] review of the album's songs, RM said that Jimin drew on his feelings about his career to write the lyrics, discussing how the vocalist used to feel that he wasn't doing well enough, even when the opposite was true,[20] making the track an anthem for imposter syndrome. As he sings about wanting to be saved from being caught in a "lie," Jimin's heartfelt passion shines, creating a haunting, lyrical testament to how far he's come as a singer.

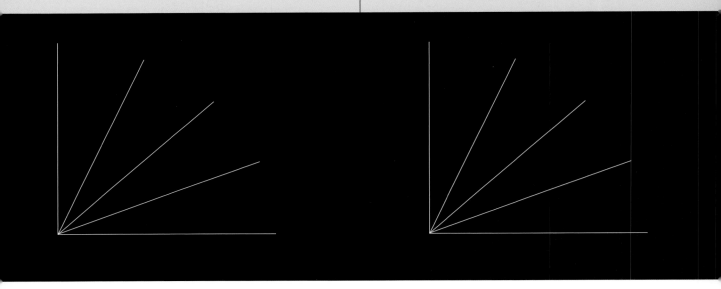

180

5 Stigma

The neo-soul of V's "Stigma" jazzily relays what appears to be a confession of the BU's Taehyung, reflecting on the pain he feels about being unable to protect those he loves, but at the same time wounding someone "like pieces of broken glass that I can't reverse," a blatant reference to the character murdering his father. Both a confession and apology, the song ends with a snapping beat leading into V's alternating deep and sweet tones. A smooth, evocative display of the singer's capabilities as he jumps between breathy, airy moments and sweet falsettos, the songs ends with a request for forgiveness, but no apology is necessary for this impactful tune.

6 First Love

Similar to Jungkook's "Begin," Suga's "First Love" relates both directly to the artist's life and his parallel BU plotline. In a shift from his usual, hard-hitting rap, the song is primarily based on gently intensifying instrumentals fronted by piano notes, a nod to the "First Love" he is talking about in his mellow singsong rap. Rather than a romantic love, the rapper waxes poetic about the instrument in his childhood home that made him fall in love with music, and the sense of loss he feels at leaving it behind to pursue his career. Building in intensity as a metronome ticks reflecting the passing of time, the tune ends with Suga contemplating his career, desperation building and then crashing down with the assurance that the piano—a metaphor for music or loved ones—will always be there.

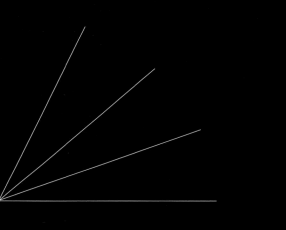

⑦ Reflection

An emotional highlight of *Wings*—one of many—came with RM's "Reflection," an echoing, mellow track in which the rapper ruminates on the pain, loneliness, and fear people feel while trying to understand themselves and their state of happiness. Beginning with audio he recorded alongside the Han River at Ttukseom, the place where he also wrote "Blood Sweat & Tears" and "Begin", the song hones in on the artist's own reflections, and ends with the guttural repeated cry, "I wish I could love myself." A heartbreaking sentiment, "Reflection" set the tone for BTS's following *Love Yourself* series, which was concluded with *Love Yourself* 結 *Answer* expressing the idea that the answer to happiness is self-love.

⑧ MAMA

Following the melancholy of "Reflection," J-Hope arrives with the bright, jazzy, swing sound of "MAMA," a song that, like Suga and Jungkook's solos, refers to the rapper's personal experience pursuing his career path. In this case, J-Hope is addressing how his mother worked hard to support his dream of being a dancer, and tells her to smile now as he has become an adult she can rely on. As connected as it is to J-Hope's real life, it is also artfully tied into the BU narrative: the corresponding character Hoseok is abandoned in his childhood by his mother and pursues dancing afterwards, a narrative opposite to the one J-Hope is telling in his solo.

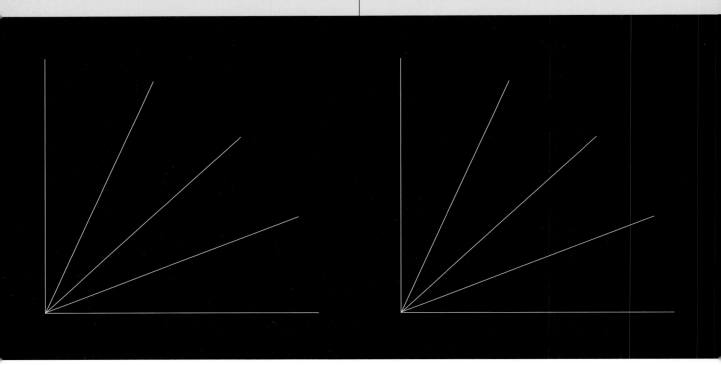

182

⑨ Awake

After the jovial vibes of "MAMA," things turn to a solemn, yet inspiring, statement of self-affirmation from Jin on "Awake." A gentle, sweeping ballad backed by dominant piano and string melodies, the song is a testament to the artist overcoming insecurity as he proudly declares that he is determined to keep moving forward, and is going to keep fighting towards the future he wants. A theme of six flowers, ostensibly referring to the rest of BTS's members but also tied into the BU's storyline and its frequent reference to flowers and flower petals—especially the nonexistent smeraldo—is carried throughout the song; Jin expressively describes himself as keeping the flowers tightly within his grasp as an inspiration to keep running towards new heights. As with RM's "Reflection," "Awake" is an affecting show of openness from the artist as he melodically relays his innermost emotions. This sweetly sung, frank approach to music from the eldest member of BTS ends the solo portion of *Wings* on a tender high.

⑩ Lost

"Lost" features the act's four vocalists as they turn the poppish song imbued with trap and scratchy synths into an anthem for the post-adolescent confusion of early adulthood. Thematically in line with both the solo songs on the album as well as BTS's overarching exploration of what it means to be a young person in this day and age, it's an impactful display of Jin, Jimin, V, and Jungkook's expressive tones. A rare full-length, non-outro song from the vocalists, "Lost" gorgeously demonstrated how the group had surpassed their early days as a hip-hop-focused team and were continuing to spread their wings, and their focus, to the singers as well as the rappers.

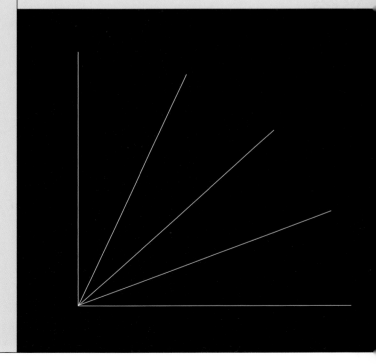

Just as the vocal line got their turn, Suga, RM, and J-Hope arrive with the group's new cypher, called "BTS Cypher 4." With a deceptively simple title, "Cypher 4" is an aggressive nod to BTS's place in the industry in 2016, with the group aggressively shouting down the haters who have spoken out against the group over the years, all while declaring that they love themselves—yet another reference to the theme of their next album series. Wild and rambunctious, it's the perfect reprimand to all those who try to drag BTS down.

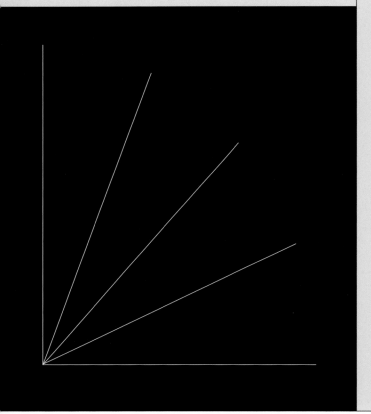

After diverging into solo songs and their respective unit tracks, the act gets back together for the boisterous, Keb' Mo' sampling "Am I Wrong." With a bright, bluesy, almost folksy sound flowing over its tinny percussion and wheezy brass melody, the group sings about the world going crazy. The song serves as a sequel of sorts to "Silver Spoon," with Suga referring to the stork and crow-tit idiom once more. "Am I Wrong" is perhaps even more confrontational in its admonishment of South Korean society, drawing inspiration from ongoing political disputes: Suga's rap "We're all dogs and pigs/we become dogs because we're angry," is likely an allusion to a 2016 scandal[21] during which former Ministry of Education official Na Hyang-wook reportedly referred to the average South Korean people as "dogs and pigs."[22] Given the time of the song's release—*Wings* came out in October and the situation rose to prominence in July—it's one of BTS's most overt commentaries on a modern-era Korean political issue.

"Am I Wrong" doesn't stop with holding a sole, bigoted official to task though: during the first verse RM shouts the words "mayday mayday." A well-known distress call, the phrase may refer to the 2014 South Korean Sewol Ferry tragedy, when over 300 passengers, including 250 middle school students, perished after the crew, several of whom were later brought to court for negligent homocide, failed to properly issue a distress signal, or "mayday." (BTS's "Spring Day" has also been recognized for its potential allusions to the incident, though when asked directly RM did not confirm them.) As weighty as the lyrics are, however, "Am I Wrong" is jovial in nature, taking to task people who see the absurdity of the world and its horrors as normal and acceptable in an age when the Internet has inured us to extreme tragedies or shocks. "Are you ready for this?" the song ends, as if daring listeners to reconsider whether they are truly ready to face the state of the world in the 21st century.

The intensity of "Am I Wrong" leads into the rambunctiousness of "21st Century Girl," a complete about-face from the group's earlier approach to women, showing just how far the group has grown from the missteps of the *Dark & Wild* days. Gone are the lyrics commodifying women in terms of young male ardor, and instead BTS are promoting female empowerment, hyping up women by telling them how wonderful they are. To the group's fanbase, which is largely female, it's an intensely powerful moment to hear the septet not only telling all the "21st Century Girls" that they're worthwhile, beautiful, and strong, regardless of what the world, media, and the people around them may be saying, but also literally calling them to rally, raise their arms and scream at the injustices of the century they're living in.

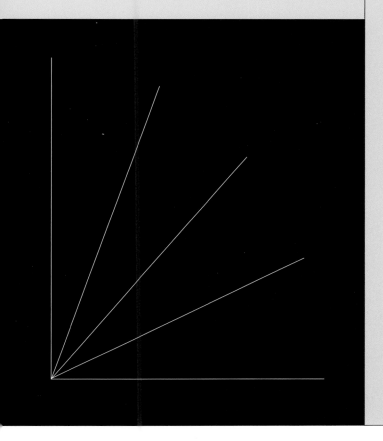

J-Hope and RM interact with the audience
during the U.S. leg of BTS's 2017 *Wings* tour.

After the festive, empowering vibes of "21st Century Girl," BTS takes things to a more laidback place with the celebratory, fan-directed song "2! 3!," also known as "Still Wishing/Hoping for More Good Days." This is the septet's first song directly aimed at ARMY, though of course many of their songs have touched on the relationship between the artists and their supporters over the years. Starting off with lo-fi strings and opening up into a sweet percussion melody, the song reflects on BTS's emotions regarding their fans and their career. There are no false promises of a bright future, only gratitude for support through the hard times and the suggestion to their fans—and themselves it seems—to take a breath, counting "one, two, three" when they encounter hardships, and to look towards the bright days to come. Coming at a career high, the song is poignant in its recognition of the group's ARMY and how they've cheered BTS on over the years, always moving forward.

As a whole, *Wings* is a testament to how far BTS have come since starting their career in 2013, both as a group and as individuals, with the solo tracks in particular highlighting how each man is not only an essential part of the whole, but also able to stand on his own with his personal sense of artistry. Fittingly, *Wings* topped charts in Korea, and ranked on several international charts, including the U.S.'s Billboard 200, where it flew up the ranks to beat its precursor *The Most Beautiful Moment in Life: Young Forever*'s No. 107 to land at the record-breaking No. 26, the highest a Korean album had ever reached at the time.

BTS followed *Wings* with the sequel repackaged album *You Never Walk Alone* the following February, bringing the act into 2017 with its biggest hit in Korea to date in the form of the single "Spring Day." Like *Wings* before it, the album landed high on the Billboard 200 chart, peaking at No. 61 despite only having three new songs: "Spring Day," "Not Today," and "A Supplementary Story: You Never Walk Alone." It also featured an extended version of "Wings," this time titled "Outro: Wings" rather than "Interlude: Wings," homing in on the fact that the *Wings* era was now closing with the release of *You Never Walk Alone.*

YOU

NEVER

WALK
ALONE

1 Spring Day

One of the two dual singles released, "Spring Day" is a seasonally inspired, sweeping synth pop-rock ballad. Intensely evocative, it draws on natural phenomena as metaphors to describe the sorrow and anguish felt with the loss of a loved one. Rather than a hopeless end, "Spring Day" expresses a separation where hope still remains, with the group forlornly singing "I miss you" with the hope that once spring comes and ushers away the winter of the heart, the one they are longing for will return to them. A touching tune that resonates with anyone who has ever suffered any sort of loss, "Spring Day" became BTS's biggest hit in South Korea upon its release, and the song resurges in popularity at the start of each spring.

The music video for "Spring Day" remains one of BTS's most cinematic, and is full of symbolism that refers to the BU,[23] while simultaneously depicting a variety of captivating scenarios revolving around the members as they come together. Full of imagery, such as shoes that stand in for the loss of someone, and blink-and-you'll-miss-it-moments that allow for a multitude of interpretations, like many of BTS's videos it ties into the struggle of growing from youth to adulthood, with one interpretation being that the song's message of longing is not for another but for the past. A true standout, it is one of the emotional highs of BTS's career.

2 Not Today

As "Fire" balances "Save Me," so too does "Not Today" serve as a counterpart to "Spring Day" on *You Never Walk Alone.* Shunning the soft emotiveness of its parallel track, "Not Today" is a propulsive track aimed at all the "underdogs of the world." Full of pounding beats and grating synths, the group uses the opportunity to declare their intent to keep fighting in the world they live in. Throughout, they rally those around them to keep fighting, declaring that their end *might* come but "Not Today." Survival is at the forefront of the song as it serves up a stomping beat over which the septet gutturally take aim at the future and inspire their listeners. The song met with some controversy[24] upon its release for the use of the term "glass ceiling," which is typically used to refer to women's struggle for equality in workplaces, but the group expressed regret over the confusion when they'd intended to refer to the restrictions placed on all those who are struggling in society, with the song frequently referencing BTS's recurring crow-tits, much like "Baepsae."

In comparison to the music video for "Spring Day," "Not Today" was released with a choreography-heavy video full of powerful moves from BTS as they're backed by an army of dancers, a fitting visual for the song's anthemic call to arms.

3 Outro: Wings

Along with the two new singles, *You Never Walk Alone* ended the *Wings* period with the aforementioned "Outro: Wings" and "A Supplementary Story: You Never Walk Alone." The former was an extension of its original "Interlude: Wings" variant—which some Korean broadcasters refused to play because of the use of the word "쌔가,"[25] which is typically translated to mean "bastard"—featuring a new rap from J-Hope and taking a shift towards future bass, adding an even more upbeat, positive message.

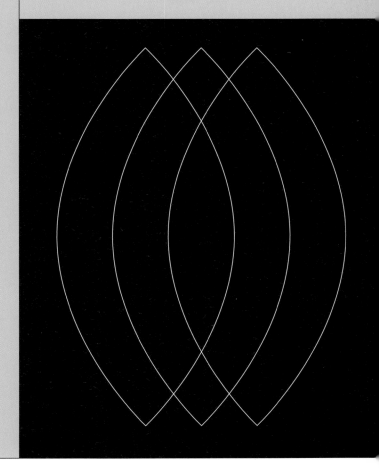

A Supplementary Story: You'll Never Walk Alone

Though last, this song was certainly not least, as it is the one from which the entire extended version of the album takes its name. Beginning with a subtle heartbeat and moving into a twinkling, plinking melody and dulcet hip-hop beat, the tune takes flight and then falls with a drop into a different tempo entirely, vacillating between rhythms and emotions to match the lyrics, which express both pain and hope, loneliness and togetherness. Sentimental in meaning, the song recalls "2! 3!" as a song about how a journey together is always better than a journey alone. References to wings and taking flight recall the group's emphasis on *Wings* being inspired by ARMY, and it's a fitting note for the album's era to end on.

An album that shed light on BTS's shifting, increasingly nuanced artistry, and acknowledged that their successful career has been thanks to their fans' support, *Wings* was the final push before its success sent them soaring to unparalleled heights.

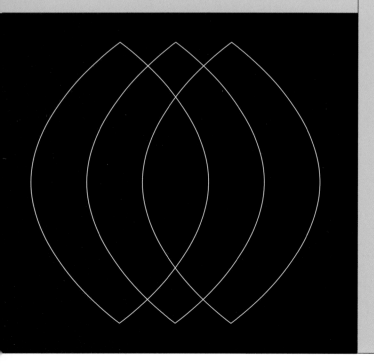

EXPLORING LOVE

Chapter
Ten

YOURSELF

When *Love Yourself 承 Her* arrived in September, it launched a new period of BTS's career. Not only did *Her* represent a shift in production style towards an even more pop- and EDM-focused sound than prior albums, though the act would still regularly emphasize its earlier hip-hop roots, it also introduced the impactful *Love Yourself* trilogy theme that was something new for BTS. Though the trio still explored youth-oriented concepts on the album, it was a more mature, philosophical version, an exploration of what it means to love and be loved in return. But even more than that, *Love Yourself* explored the path of self-realization that a person must tread in order to be able to be loved, a path that is laid out explicitly in the trio's compilation album *Love Yourself 結 Answer*, after different types of love, along with other themes, were explored throughout *Love Yourself 承 Her* and *Love Yourself 結 Tear.* The *hanja* featured in the series refer to a storytelling technique: 起承轉結, or 기승전결 in Korean, *kiseungjeonkyeol*, which describes the composition of a story based on four elements: introduction (*Wonder)*, development (*Her)*, turn (*Tear)*, and conclusion (*Answer)*.

But *Answer* wouldn't arrive to conclude the story until the following August, and *Love Yourself 承 Her* opened things up on a bright note. Teased initially in August 2017 through a series of promotional images that linked into the BU narrative—and drew further fan fervor by focusing attention on long-running themes like the fictitious smeraldo flower—the *Love Yourself* series was announced later that month. *Her* would be its beginning, and it would take global audiences and BTS on a journey unlike any other, bringing the group to heights no Asian act had reached previously.

Whatever label you pinned on the success, one thing was clear: *Love Yourself 承 Her* was the start of something new for BTS, something that would only keep building.

The album itself is a nine-track EP that, like most BTS albums, features an intro, in the form of Jimin's solo "Serendipity," an outro track "Her," and a skit to bookend the rest of the content. In this case, the group utilized the announcement of the group's win and the speech RM gave at the 2017 Billboard Music Awards the previous May for their skit, rather than adding something brand-new, a nod to the importance of the event for the group.

LOVE YOURSELF 承 HER

Love Yourself 承 Her kicked off with the first of four exploratory solos from the group's vocalists that would come out of this series. Jimin had the honor of bringing the *Love Yourself* era to life with his dreamy "Intro: Serendipity." Revealed through a comeback trailer in early September ahead of the album's release, the song's romantic alt-R&B leanings expressed the feeling of destiny, of love being brought together fortuitously, with Jimin lushly, breathily, asking for permission to love in a dreamy, fantastical music video inspired by Antoine de Saint-Exupéry's *The Little Prince*, a novella for children that famously contemplates human nature and reflects on loneliness, adolescence, friendship, love, and more. A fitting start to a series of songs that explored love, the song would later be extended for *Love Yourself 結 Answer*, but in the meantime served as a short but sweet intro to *Her*.

② DNA

③ Best of Me

Next up was "DNA," the group's rhythmic, whistling future bass of a hit single, another forthright vision of romance and destiny. A bright representation of love, it was a bit of a divergence for BTS, whose romantically slanted singles were typically more aggressive or more somber, but "DNA" was a pleasant shift, and might have been motivated by the group's recognition that a global audience needed more radio-friendly pop songs—or that a more upbeat sound reflected the current state of BTS's career.

The song's music video was similarly bright, featuring the members buoyantly performing complex choreography that emulated the double helix of the titular molecule amid a burst of colors. Like the album as a whole, it came across as a refreshing burst of something new and euphoric from the group, whose members seem to have creativity and success written into their genetic makeup.

The next song on the album, "Best of Me," was co-written with Andrew Taggart of The Chainsmokers, whom BTS had met up with when they were in Los Angeles for the 2017 BBMAs. Fittingly, it had a sound akin to the bright EDM pop styling that the pair are known for, creating a shimmering blend of synths against which the group expressed how the object of their affection has the "Best of Me." Alternating between sweeping verses from the vocalists and mellow, rock-inflected raps, the song frequently shifts tempo and vibe, always building to a beat drop that leads into clapping percussion, itself serving as the basis for the song's melody. It's an engaging, gentle dance track about love, and fits perfectly into the album's themes.

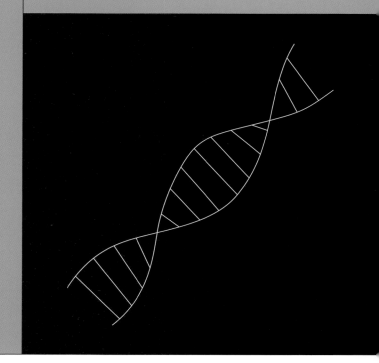

The next track on *Her* follows a similar theme, but while "Best of Me" focuses on the lyrical narrator and how a lover has helped them become the best person they can be, "Dimple (Illegal)" is more about the affection felt for the lover, specifically a facial feature that draws them in (and one that RM is famously noted to have). Ephemeral in its trap-laden future bass styling, the song, sung only by the group's vocalists, is a warm, comforting dreamscape as the four men sing of a facial dimple so sweet it should be illegal. Like the best BTS tracks, wordplay features heavily, with the quartet often altering the word to "ille-girl." It's cute, it's charming, and it's one of BTS's most tender musical moments to date.

Dulcet funk-pop arrives in the form of "Pied Piper," a tongue-in-cheek track in which BTS address the costs of fandom and the effects it has on individuals' lives, especially the group's most dedicated fans. Whereas in the past they had sung about how they appreciate their fans and always want to be with them, "Pied Piper" was a different sort of song entirely. Lulling listeners into a mellow calm through sophisticated bass and drum instrumentals and whirring digital quirks, the group took their fans to task in the most alluring way possible. A cautionary tale, as is the folktale of the Pied Piper of Hamelin that inspired the song, the group draws parallels with the titular character, who kidnapped the children of Hamelin after their parents failed to repay him for ridding their town of rats. Like the Pied Piper, BTS's music is seductive, and can take up hours if not years of time, money, and major dedication from their fans. While in one breath singing about how ARMY's parents and teachers curse them for stealing their time – and youth, much like the Piper did – and in the next asking fans for forgiveness, the song is cautionary and intensely subversive of the typical K-pop fandom, or standom, behaviors. But it doesn't come off as the artists shirking responsibility; "Pied Piper" brings the issue into the open, a commendable act of transparency. Like the best of BTS, it is a realistic take on the world as they see it, and a seductive criticism of fan culture in the modern era.

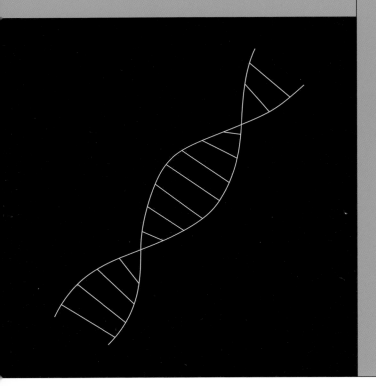

6 Skit: Billboard Music Awards Speech

7 MIC drop

After giving their fans some tough love, the Billboard Music Awards speech skit, taken from RM's historic speech when they won the Top Social Artist at the 2017 BBMAs, arrives to shift the tonal gear of *Her*. If the first half is about external love, both romantic and that between artists and audience, the second part shifts things up to reflect on self-love and the group's success.

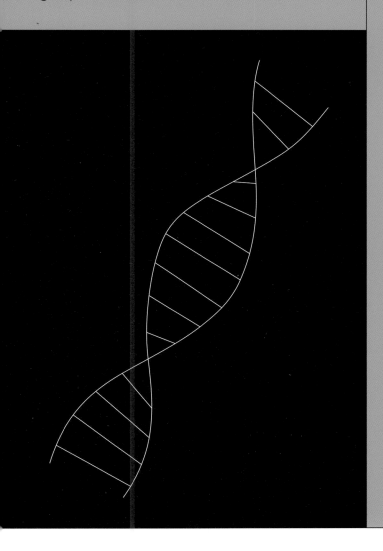

The drawling, boisterous "MIC Drop," full of reverberating string melodies and tinny beats, has the group swaggering about their win at the BBMAs and how far they've come. RM compares the story of BTS's success with one of Aesop's fables, where a character who works hard and does things the right way comes out on top. Slow and steady wins the race and BTS have done just that, going so far that their peers can't even compete with them. The recurring theme of dirty and golden spoons reappears, but this time BTS aren't suffering from being downtrodden but instead have the golden spoons in their hands—in the form of their mics and trophies, which are beyond counting at this point.

"MIC Drop" is a track full of pride, and they ended up remaking and releasing it as a second single from the album, with the added production of EDM producer Steve Aoki and a feature from rapper Desiigner. The music video for the remix features a rowdy party of sorts; BTS perform as Steve Aoki DJs in a room under surveillance and surrounded by microphones, an apparent nod to their place in the spotlight, until an impactful dance break where the seven perform amid flashing lights, suggesting cameras. The most iconic moments take place as they dance amid a parking lot full of flaming cars and fiery debris, recalling scenes from "Fire" where they similarly set the world ablaze.

The remix went on to become BTS's first song to achieve platinum status in the U.S., later joined by "IDOL" in 2020.

Before *Her* closed out with its outro, BTS served up some of their typical criticism of societal norms in "Go Go" (also known as "고민보다 Go" and "Rather Than Worrying, Go"), this time parodying the YOLO lifestyle, where money isn't seen as a resource to be saved but something to be enjoyed in the moment. While it's sardonic and confronts contemporary consumerism, such as through their recurring use of the Korean slang term *tangjinjaem* ("탕진잼"), which represents the idea of needlessly spending money to feel pleasure in the present rather than saving for the long term, the song fits into the group's view of the current generation as seen through past albums. Although they describe individuals who are spending their own hard-earned money rather than their parents', as in "Spine Breaker," there's an underlying sense that this generation is going to suffer in the future, regardless of whether they save or spend their money, with Jin expressing that there's "already a mortgage on my future."

Despite its bleak message, the song has a bouncing beat and, if taken at face value, it might appear as if BTS are promoting the "treat yourself" mentality that in Korea has spurred the term "시발비용" (*shibal biyong*), essentially "fxxk it, expense it," or spending money for temporary pleasure rather than saving for the future: the world will not be kind to you, so you might as well enjoy it in the here and now. Of course, while every song is open to interpretation, Suga made it quite clear that the song is a critique of society: "The current generation uses phrases like 'YOLO' and *tanjingjaem,* but I don't think people think about why they use such terms so much even while using the terms," he said during the group's press conference upon the album's release.[26] "We tried to interpret [this] through BTS's unique perspective. I think it will be a fun track if people listen and think about it again. It isn't a BTS album if there isn't a track criticizing society."

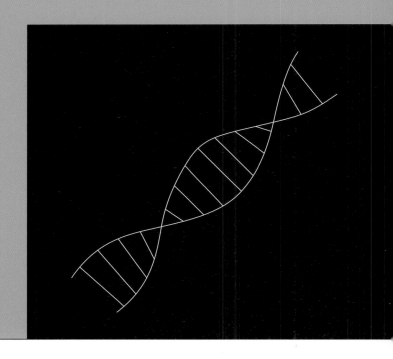

9 Outro: Her

10 Skit: Hesitation & Fear

The album officially closes out on the lo-fi hip-hop feel of "Outro: Her," a song addressing the mixed emotions of love. RM told *Billboard* that he wrote the song quickly, as it "just came, very truthfully, from the bottom of my heart. I thought it was the right outro for this album because it is really a range of emotions—I'm saying I met this person that I really love, this person is the love of my life right now, I'm saying that I was confused and I was looking for love and this world is complex. But I think it's you so, 'I call you her, 'cause you're my tear,' 'I think you're the start and the end of me.' That's what I'm saying: 'you're my wonder, but you're also my answers. You're my her' but you're still the tear." With one brief reference, he touched on all three albums from the *Love Yourself* era, as well as the series' theme of Wonder, which was shared through a video that featured Jungkook's "Euphoria," and was released prior to the release of the *Love Yourself* series.

But while "Outro: Tear" would be the finale of the *Her* album in digital versions, prepping listeners for *Love Yourself* 轉 *Tear*, the physical version of *Love Yourself* 承 *Her* actually featured two additional tracks: another skit, known as "Hestitation and Fear," and "Sea," a somber, yet uplifting, song about the bleak hardships that BTS have been through and the hope that accompanies darkness.

An extended version of the original "Skit: Billboard Music Awards Speech," this time it opens with the members walking in on a producer watching the video from the BBMAs, and then the group themselves talking about their experience. The seven recall how they feel now that they've succeeded at rising so high and talk about their early days—including how several members didn't know what *Billboard* was—as well as what they hope to achieve in the future, rather than staying stagnant and making the BBMAs their only mark on the industry. The group also expresses their earnest desire to put meaning into their music, refuting any accusations of superficiality.

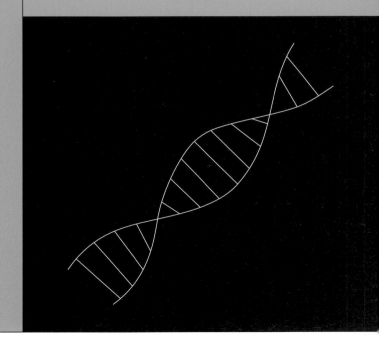

Her's finale, the hidden track "Sea," recalls the frequently occurring allegory of BTS's career with the ocean and the desert, where water represents the thirst for success, imagined at first as an impossible-to-reach desert mirage, with the desolate landscape representing hardship and suffering. The ambient track features the septet ruminating on how they've gone from struggling to gain airtime and living in cramped spaces to the top of the South Korean music industry. Written by RM in 2016, the creeping tone of "Sea" is wary rather than happy, with the rapper comparing life to both an ocean and desert. The song is filled with cautious hope for continued, rather than fleeting, success.

By the time the group's third LP *Love Yourself* 轉 *Tear* was announced in April 2018, it seemed like a whole new world had been opened up to BTS. The group had developed a following no other K-pop act had before, crossing linguistic, geographic, socio-economic, gender, racial, and other boundaries to draw in a diverse ARMY that cheered them on into the Top 10 of the U.S.'s most prominent album chart. Yet, some anticipation and caution were expressed on *Her* in the closing "Skit: Hesitation and Fear" and in "Sea"—although it seemed impossible based on the fervor of their fanbase and increasing recognition among general music listeners. Was *Her* to be BTS's career high point? Had they peaked? Would they be able to go even higher?

The answer to the final question was a resounding "yes" in the form of the Billboard 200 chart-topping album *Love Yourself* 轉 *Tear.* An artistic exploration of the depths of heartbreak and angst, *Tear* was the darker counterpart to the brightness of *Her*, a brooding sequel that positioned the romance of the previous album as counterfeit rather than heartfelt. The group's sprightly styling did a complete about-face as *Tear* came in to address the realities of a "Fake Love." The arrival of the single and album ushered in one of the most groundbreaking moments of all modern music history, opening up the Western music industry to a more diverse future through BTS's chart-topping hits.

LOVE YOURSELF 轉 TEAR

Inspired by Ray Kurzweil's 2005 book on artificial intelligence *The Singularity Is Near: When Humans Transcend Biology*, the neo-soul anguish of V's "Intro: Singularity" utilized the singer's smooth, deep tone to express the gravitas of the theme of losing oneself. Yet again, the song evokes elements of nature, and was released in a dramatic, theatrical video that used passionate red and purple tones, similar to those seen in "Blood Sweat & Tears," as a backdrop to V's exploratory performance, giving new meaning to dancing with oneself while seemingly, through multiple water and mirrored scenes, referring to the Greek myth of Narcissus—a man who fell in love with his reflection, and died by suicide after determining that no love could ever compare.

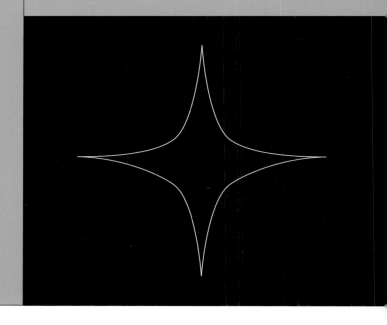

2 Fake Love

3 The Truth Untold

BTS's first song to break into the Top 10 of the *Billboard* Hot 100 singles chart, "Fake Love" is an emotive hip-pop track, weaving trap beats, guitar riffs, and echoing synth effects together to create a soundscape full of anguish as the members relay the devastation of finding out that what they thought was love was anything but.

With tightly modulated, desolate vocal effects wrapping the septet's verses as they sing about how the idea of love doesn't match with reality, the song has an overall off-kilter quality, reflecting the emotions of someone who has come to this realization. Jimin in particular is at the forefront of the song, his crisp vocals expressively driving much of it. "Fake Love" is heartfelt poignancy wrapped in a vibrant dance track, and that's just what the group needed to soar up charts across the globe.

Paired with a haunting music video that not only references the BU, such as through the reappearance of the smeraldo flower and members witnessing devastation while in settings familiar to their corresponding BU characters, and the masks people hide behind, "Fake Love" also incorporates the idiom "See no evil, hear no evil, and speak no evil" into its choreography, creating a captivating performance to relay the song's dispirited meaning.

After the deep despondency of "Fake Love," BTS shifted to an even more sorrowful place in the form of "The Truth Untold," a vocal-line track featuring Steve Aoki. Foregoing the DJ's typical sweeping EDM styling, the song is instead dominated by an impassioned piano melody and Jin, Jimin, V, and Jungkook's tender voices as they sing about feelings of loneliness and sorrow. Telling a story of a person trapped by the limits of his own emotions, who feels as if he has to mask his true self from the object of their desire, "The Truth Untold" is a ballad that ties in to the BU narrative, especially some elements featured in the "Fake Love" video, with the Korean title (전하지 못한 진심) referring to the meaning of the mysterious, fictive, smeraldo flower featured in the BU, "The Truth [literally sincerity] I Couldn't Tell."

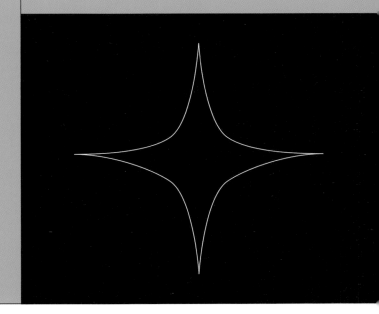

④ 134340

⑤ Paradise

A poignant, flute-imbued song, "134340" literally transposes the alienation of a broken heart to another planet. The title refers to the numeric designation of Pluto, formerly the ninth planet of the Solar System. Through a blend of hip-hop beats and jazz instrumentals, the group adopts the voice of the former planet after its status was downgraded in 2006. The celestial metaphor expresses the feelings that accompany a one-sided, overwhelming heartbreak, where the narrator is still revolving around the intended listener, who has moved on.

With the creeping, snapping beat of "Paradise," BTS serves up a groovy, inspiring alt-R&B track that returns the group to their *raison d'etre* as they counteract the idyllic interpretation of what love and dreams are, and instead determine that simply moving forward and continuing to breathe is true paradise. The song, co-written by British singer-songwriter MNEK, is based around the idea that life is a marathon that each individual is running, and BTS instructs listeners to take things slowly, as this is literally the race of a lifetime. The track draws on motifs the group have previously incorporated into their lyrics, such as it being okay to not have dreams, motivations, or a destination like those around us, because we each have our own pace. These ideas are layered over the song's rhythmic bounce to motivate listeners to recognize that every breath, every love, and every dream is a win, even when things are hard; just living and moving forward is a "Paradise" of sorts.

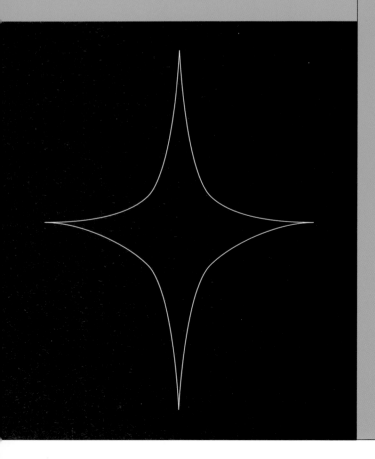

6 Love Maze

7 Magic Shop

The groove of "Love Maze" adds a bit of a bounce to the album with a trap beat and synth-infused R&B elements. A lighthearted moment after the weight of *Tear*'s first few tracks, "Love Maze" is an answer to the previous song's question of what it means to have love, responding that it's walking the "Love Maze" together. It may not be a logical journey, but if it's true love, everything will be okay. While it's ostensibly a song simply about love, it also comes across as a message to BTS's ARMY: as long as we're together, cheering one another on, things will be okay.

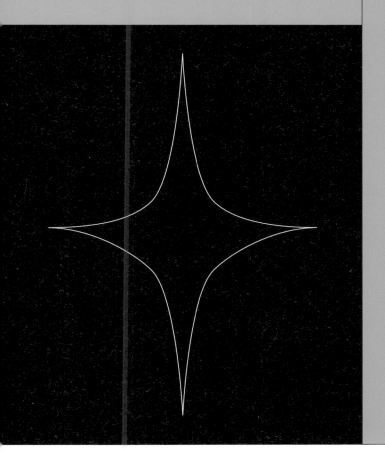

While "Love Maze" may have an extended meaning based on interpretation, it's "Magic Shop" that BTS dedicated to their fans. Co-written by Jungkook, the chill, subtle EDM track sails along sweetly as the act sings, directing fans to form a secret space for themselves full of BTS within their hearts, a place they can look to for moral support when times are rough.

The idea of a "Magic Shop" as a psychological space to make your heart more open came from James Doty's book *Into the Magic Shop: A Neurosurgeon's Quest to Discover the Mysteries of the Brain and the Secrets of the Heart*. As interpreted by BTS, the idea of "Magic Shop" was introduced in the teaser for "Fake Love," which described it as "a psychodramatic technique that exchanges fear for a positive attitude," and the music video for "Fake Love" heavily played up the exchange elements; their fifth Muster fanmeetings in June 2019 would also be titled *Magic Shop*.

According to RM during a V Live review of the album, the song is intended for anyone dealing with moments when they want to be anyone other than themselves. He went on to describe the interiors of each and every person's heart having a unique galaxy inside of them, a space where they can truly be themselves and find the best of themselves. Poetically phrased and especially meaningful to fans, the song is a stand-out expression of the bond between BTS and their ARMY.

⑧ Airplane, Pt. 2

⑨ Anpanman

Things shift into a Latin pop vibe in "Airplane, Pt. 2," a sequel to "Airplane" from J-Hope's *Hope World* mixtape, released earlier in the year. Both tracks, as their titles suggest, revolve around traveling, but are specifically about the worldwide heights to which BTS have soared throughout their career. But while "Airplane" is a mellow hip-hop track and revels in J-Hope's solo success, "Airplane, Pt. 2" sees BTS singing about being modern mariachis. The song possesses a well-deserved, confident strut for a boy band that has forever changed the way the global music game is played, and though it didn't get the single treatment in Korea, it was later re-released as a Japanese single.

It's almost impossible to resist a smile on hearing V's opening "Waiting for you Anpanman" cry as the next track on *Tear* starts. A jovial hip-hop track with an underlying organ melody filtered through its rollicking beats, shrill whistles, and synths, the song is inspired by the Japanese superhero character of the same name. A bread-headed hero, Anpanman, or Anpangman as he's known in Korea, always does whatever he can to save the day. BTS takes on the role of this symbol for justice, saying that they can give listeners sustenance for their hearts and minds even though they're just average guys. They've put in the hard work, fought against countless hardships, and continue to fear for their future but always come out on top to stand as protectors—and oftentimes a conscience—for their listeners.

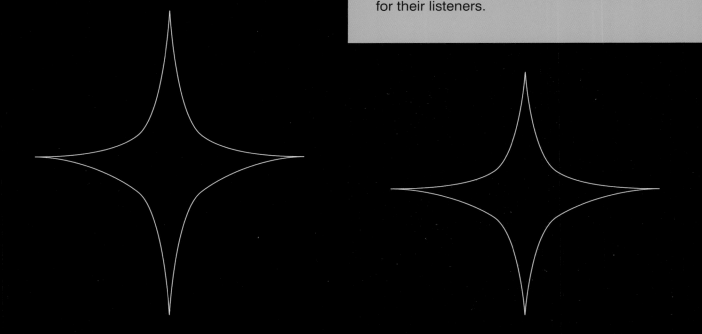

So What

Outro: Tear

The album heads to a close with the sweeping, soaring EDM party track "So What." As fun as it is to get up and dance to, the song is an audible shrug of the shoulders to anyone has ever been filled with fear and self-doubt. "So what?!" BTS sing, wondering why people question themselves and the mistakes they make instead of just moving on, creating an anthemic, upbeat tune that urges a carefree, yet thoughtful, lifestyle.

After exploring the devastation associated with romantic love, then singing about self-love and the love between artist and fans, BTS bring things to a close with the devastation of "Outro: Tear." Starting off with an eerie piano melody and then spectral synths, the song turns into a powerful rap track featuring each member of the rapper trio exploring what "tear" means, where RM's "Tear" refers to those spilled from the eyes, Suga's is the physical act of ripping something apart—like a heart or piece of paper—and J-Hope's is aligned with fear. Emphasized by the choral refrain, each reflects themes explored throughout the album, bringing Love Yourself 轉 Tear to a close with shouting, enraged raps that perfectly encapsulate the album's overarching concepts.

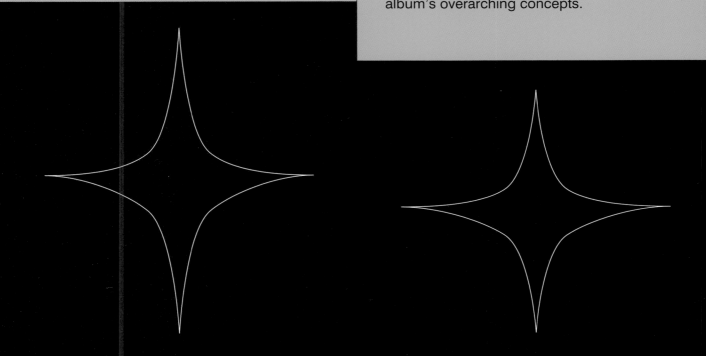

As a work of art, *Love Yourself 轉 Tear* is an impactful exploration of related themes through a variety of sonic sounds and styles. Throughout, it allows time for each member to shine, showing the growth in the vocalists' ranges and the rappers' diversifying styles since their earliest days. The maturity of both the members' performances and the album's lyricism felt like a new high for the group—and fittingly brought them to new levels of success. On May 27, less than 10 days since the album was released on May 18, *Billboard* announced that BTS's *Love Yourself 轉 Tear* had topped the Billboard 200 albums chart, the first Korean artist ever to do so. *Tear* was the first predominantly non-English album of the decade to achieve the feat.

Only a matter of months, but an eternity's worth of career opportunities, had passed between the releases of *Love Yourself* 轉 *Tear* in May and August's *Love Yourself* 結 *Answer,* which arrived to conclude the *Love Yourself* series. Just as *The Most Beautiful Moment in Life: Young Forever* had closed out that era with a compilation album, so too did *Answer*. A composite of new and old songs alike, some remixes and variants, *Love Yourself* 結 *Answer* featured two discs with a total of 25 songs on the physical version, and 26 on digital ones.

The first part of the album's narrative is made clear through a pattern: the 16 tracks can be split into four different sections, each featuring songs that reflect the path of observation and understanding regarding the idea of love as told through *Her*, *Tear*, and *Answer*, based around the storytelling device 起承轉結 previously utilized throughout the series.

Answer featured both old and new songs on its primary disc. Every member but V, whose "Singularity" was featured in full on Tear, saw a new solo song or variant of a solo song previously released, in the form of the "Trivia" solos from the rappers, Jin's "Epiphany," Jungkook's "Euphoria," and the extended version of Jimin's "Serendipity," which previously had been an intro track on *Her*. As a full act, BTS released three new songs, "I'm Fine," "Answer: Love Myself," and the single "IDOL."

Although not confirmed by BTS, it appears that the first disc of the final third of an album trilogy is meant to be seen as a summary of the series' essence, one that creates a narrative path through the series' relationship with love: after feeling the first blush, or introduction (起), of love as in "Euphoria" and "Just

Dance," the *Her* section reflects the development of the relationship (承), before things take a turn (轉) to understanding the essence of what love is through the *Tear* section. And *Answer*'s final quartet of songs act as a conclusion (結) that expresses how things are truly meant to be understood. On March 28, 2019, the "Album Identity"[27] of the *Love Yourself* series was uploaded by HuskyFox to Behance,[28] a platform for designers to share their work and, along with showcasing the nuanced artwork of the series' albums and promotional content, it also revealed the formal meaning of each *Love Yourself* stage.

The meaning of *Love Yourself* was described as "the process of love and youth completed by self-love," and the four steps to this were relayed through each of the subtitles: Wonder, Her, Tear, and Answer. Each corresponded with a specific meaning, with the Wonder theme described as "Crush: Curious and surprising step before love begins," while Her was described as "Love: Step that make[s you] feel that love is all about life." Tear was about "Parting: Step of tearful par[t]ing as love leaves," while Answer was about "Self-Love: Step of self-love that has been developed by looking back on oneself after suffering." Each step was relayed through its own color palette (gray, white, black, and hologram, respectively), and floral graphics that budded, bloomed, fell, and remained with each step of the exploratory era.

BTS, ready to take on the 61st Annual Grammy Awards in Los Angeles in February 2019. Their suits, designed by JayBaek Couture and Kim Seo Ryong, were later put on display at the Grammy Museum.

LOVE YOURSELF 結 ANSWER

The culmination of the *Love Yourself* series, *Answer* begins with the breezy introductory theme of "Euphoria," Jungkook's sweeping future bass track, which features lyrics by RM and was produced by frequent BTS and The Chainsmokers collaborator, DJ Swivel, and was originally unveiled prior to the entire *Love Yourself* era. Also known as the Wonder theme—the fourth part of the storytelling of the *Love Yourself* series—the youngest member of BTS opens the album up with sweet crooning as he sings about an innocent, dream-like love that brings clarity and happiness. The song refers to an idyllic utopia where everything is perfect, defining the emotions as comparable to a sort of paradise. (Unfortunately, "Paradise," along with "134340," "Love Maze," and "So What" from *Tear* as well as *Her*'s "Pied Piper," did not make it on to *Answer*.)

As the introduction to the entire *Love Yourself* era, the music video for the "Wonder" theme, "Euphoria," began with V jumping off a scaffold into water, leading into flashbacks of incidents that took place during previous BU videos. The *Wonder* theme's video poses Jin beyond the other six, looking at them from afar, and features a scene from Jin's finale video "Epiphany," implying that this video theme is the culmination of the overall message of the *Love Yourself* era and the BU.

2. Trivia 起: Just Dance

Following "Euphoria" is J-Hope's solo, the first "Trivia" track on *Answer*, "Trivia 起: Just Dance." A funky future house track reminiscent of the styling of his *Hope World* solo mixtape, J-Hope took the opportunity to emphasize his skill and relationship with dance, and used the song to express how he wants to dance with the object of his affection. Fairly straightforward, it evokes the feeling of a perfect match, two people who groove to the rhythm in time with one another, fitting together in the age-old dance of love. Living up to the BTS member's stage name, "Just Dance" is full of hope for what's to come in a relationship at its very start, full of wide-eyed wonderment as the first feelings are forming and potential is everywhere.

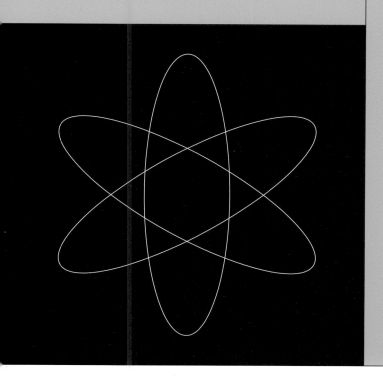

3. Trivia 承: Love

Following the "introduction to love" portion of the album, *Answer* turned into the "beginning to love" section, expanding on Jimin's rich vocals in an extended version of "Serendipity," and then returned to the romantic highs of "DNA" and "Dimple." Before closing the section with "Her," originally *Her*'s outro, the *Her* section of *Answer* leads to its wholly original song, RM's brilliant "Trivia 承: Love."

Much has been made of RM's ability to create poignant lyrics, but it's his turn of phrase throughout BTS's discography that has really shown his personality through the group's joint songs—beyond what he has revealed in his solo content—and "Love" shows him at the height of his gifts. A jazzy alt-hip-hop tune, it's full of wordplay as RM expresses the uncertainty and anxiety that accompanies the early stages of a relationship as a person tries to sort out their feelings.

Throughout the song, RM explores how letters affect the meaning of words in simple ways: only an "i" and "o" separate the words "live" and "love," and because one is alive, one is able to love. Similarly, only a "v" keeps "live" from turning into "lie," and in Korean, by rounding out the squared edges of the word for "human," 사람 (*saram*), it turns into "love," 사랑 (*sarang*), which he points to again as proof that love and the sense of being alive are related, suggesting that people should live by the idea of love. RM also uses the differences of letters to explore how love is like "wind" (바람, *param*) as people (*saram*) pass one another by, and how his mood is blue (파랑, *parang*); though blue is typically associated in art with sadness and depression and may be used here to refer to the forlorn feeling of love ending, it also represents calm, loyalty, and strength, and is often related to the eternal grandeur of the ever-changing sky and sea, and so RM may be referring to the way a pure love could be eternal, just like those two entities, the latter of which recalls prior BTS references to the sea. And from this overall idea of love (사랑, *sarang*), one can develop pride (자랑, *jarang*). The rapper also, comically, curses out the letters of the English alphabet "JKLMNOPQRST," for having the audacity to keep "i" and "u" apart. Sweet and romantic, it's a change from RM's usual fare while still maintaining his sense of musical identity.

After finishing the *Her* section and leading into the turning point (轉) of *Tear*, V's "Singularity," an anthem about masking one's own emotions in favor of pursuing love, leads into "Fake Love" and "The Truth Untold" before arriving at Suga's "Trivia 轉: Seesaw." The first time the rapper had leaned into his skills as a vocalist in earnest in a BTS song, the mellow synth-pop melody and the funky disco feel of the chorus emulate the feeling of being up and down in a relationship. The artist's tonal shifts, pairing sweet singing with his typically husky rap tone, reflect the emotional vacillation, and are enhanced by the airy singing of producer Adora and vocoder-enhanced gruffness. It's evocative and impactful, and has less of an overwhelmingly dark feel than many of *Tear*'s most poignant moments evoke, instead fitting into the corresponding album's overall vibe by adding a bit of a bounce to the dragging back-and-forth feelings that precede the end of a relationship, when both parties know things are done but each are holding on and denying reality because of the idea, and even perhaps the true feelings, of love.

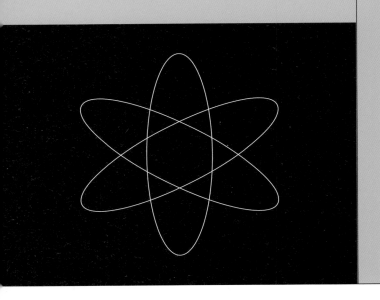

5 Epiphany

With the outro track of *Tear* ending that album's related section, the finale of the *Love Yourself* era's philosophical musings finally arrives, ushered in by Jin's solo song "Epiphany." The group's eldest member spends the whole emotive pop-rock tune tenderly singing as he comes to the realization that love must exist for one's own sake, and that changing for another person won't work. Instead, the *Answer* to finding happiness in external relationships begins with loving oneself. The lyrics poetically guide the listener through this "Epiphany," beginning with Jin expressively recognizing the situation he is in, his realization of what love truly is, and then ending with feelings of trepidation, acceptance, and enlightenment as he declares that he loves himself.

Jin's "Epiphany" was released through a comeback trailer that featured the singer on his own, sitting in a room, only to leave and face the rain before coming back. As both part of the BU storyline and a closer for the *Love Yourself* era, it's a powerful show of acting from the BTS member, who dominates the screen with the slightest of actions. The video ends with a brief paragraph expressing his determination. "At the end of the journey to find myself, I was once again in the same place. At the end, what I have to find is the map to the soul, which is the start and milestone of everything. The thing that everyone can have but not everyone is able to find, I'm setting out to look for it from now on."[29] Powerful and weighty as it describes someone embarking on a period of reflection and soul-searching, "Epiphany" is the perfect finale for *Love Yourself*'s overarching message, and its closing statement hinted at more of what was to come from the group.

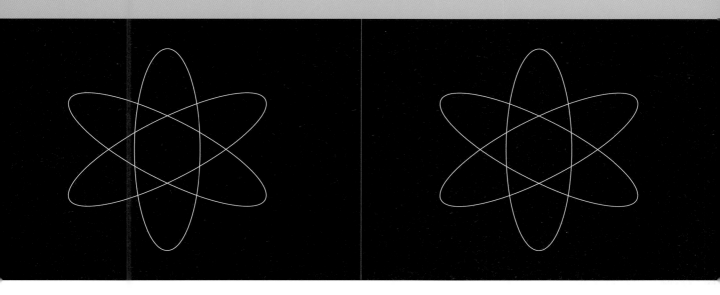

6 I'm Fine

Following this emotive weightiness, *Answer* leads into the uplifting drum and bass styling of "I'm Fine," but not before the track opens up with a brief, ticking sampling of the melody of "Save Me," in a nod to the early *Love Yourself* posters that paired "I'm Fine" and "Save Me" as two halves of one whole.[30] A foil to the 2016 single, BTS no longer need outside salvation, but instead use "I'm Fine" as a mantra of sorts, asserting their independence while declaring that as long as a person has the intent to feel fine, eventually hardships will pass and they actually will feel that way, as if the mantra of "I'm Fine" will create a mental state where it is true. With its infectious melody and verses, "I'm Fine" shifts *Answer*'s tone to its uplifting finale.

7 IDOL

Inspired by South African house music sub-genre Gqom and classical Korean artistic elements, "IDOL" is the group's swaggering, propulsive response to everyone who has ever wondered who or what BTS are, one that exudes the overall theme of *Love Yourself: Answer*. "You can call me artist/you can call me idol," RM starts off, before going on to add that it doesn't really matter what anyone calls him, because as long as he knows and takes pride in who and what he is, outside opinions don't matter. The opening lines are particularly subversive considering BTS's background as a K-pop idol boy band featuring underground hip-hop artists who faced criticism early on for not being authentic enough. By the time the song was released it was impossible to criticize BTS for pretty much anything they had done as a group, as it had led them to such immense success. It was no longer relevant whether they were seen as artists, idols, both, or neither; the song's themes of self-love and self-affirmation, described through the choral shout, "You can't stop me loving myself," are all that matters.

"IDOL" was BTS's first primary album single, rather than a second release like "MIC Drop (Remix)," to feature an outside artist, and it was none other than Nicki Minaj. Featured on a digital-only version of "IDOL," the American rapper served up a fiery extra verse and appeared in a second music video released for the song.

After putting out one album that topped the dominant albums chart in the U.S., BTS could have played it safe and tried to create an airwave-friendly song that would go to No. 1 in America after "Fake Love" went to No. 10. Instead, the seven men opted for something daring, and drew on their artistic history to make a point in the present: that they don't need to lean into other people's standards, in this case American/Western-friendly songs, and instead just do their own thing, live the way they like and be their best selves.

"IDOL" features a variety of outside references, including a shout-out to the comparison of BTS with Anpanman, but its most groundbreaking elements were the traditionally inspired Korean ones that featured in both the song and music video. Like "MIC Drop (Remix)," "IDOL" and its music video explored BTS's success, but rather than focusing on the hip-hop-inspired slant of the group and their success in America, "IDOL" leaned into the group's global success as Koreans. Minaj's inclusion on the alternate single reflected their success, but was preceded by a BTS solo celebration of their own identity.

Elements of traditional South Korean music, known as *pansori*, are featured in the song, with boisterous shouts emulating the *chuimsae*, or encouragement from the audience, playing a prominent role, while other parts of the song relate to other traditional

Korean musical elements, such as the 12 beats of a rhythmic melody known as the *gutgeori jangdan* appearing during the choral chanting. Visually, the music video features BTS drawing on a wide range of traditional Korean elements for inspiration, such as appearing in *hanbok*, traditional Korean clothing, and dancing at a *hanok*-style pavilion. Traditional fan and lion dances also appear, as does a roaming tiger, which has historically represented Korea and its people, and a rabbit in the moon as RM says the Korean name for it, *tokki* (토끼), multiple times. This is a symbol of immortality in East Asian culture, an apparent reference to BTS's name and idoldom surpassing a single lifetime, and a fitting metaphor for the act of unparalleled "IDOL"s.

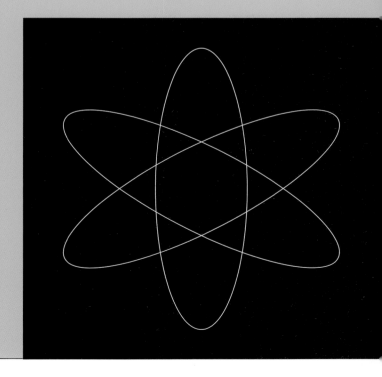

Answer: Love Myself

Coming off the high of "IDOL," the main portion of *Love Yourself: Answer* concludes with the responsive "Answer: Love Myself." The theme not only of the album but also the group's campaign in partnership with United Nations International Children's Emergency Fund (UNICEF), the rockish pop song swoops and soars with positive motivation, revelling in staccato raps, falsetto belting, and mellow declarations of having learned to find and love oneself. It also recognizes that perhaps there is no answer at all; the idea of self-love is just that, an idea, one that can't really be captured. It's insightful, and it's the perfect note on which to end the *Love Yourself* series.

Upon its release, *Love Yourself: Answer* roused widespread attention, and, like its predecessor, landed atop the Billboard 200 chart the first week it was eligible. It also topped charts in South Korea, Japan, and multiple other countries. "IDOL" similarly impressed, and became the act's first song to land in the UK's Top 25 on the Official Charts singles chart, peaking at No. 21. The crowning glory of BTS's work over the past year and a half—both artistically and commercially— it was also the act's first album "post-mainstreaming in the West," following the success of *Tear*. A test of sorts to see if the group could reproduce their previous success or if it all would be downhill from that singular peak, *Answer* passed with flying colors, and within half a year—the following November— it would become the group's first RIAA-certified gold album.

The *Love Yourself* series unrepentantly defined the act's place in history as groundbreaking artists who refused to be limited by geographical boundaries and linguistic limitations.

J-Hope takes center stage while performing "DNA" during the act's historic appearance at the 2017 AMAs.

MAPPING
THE SOUL

**Chapter
Eleven**

While the *Love Yourself* era led BTS, their ARMY, and the world down a musical path to self-love, the act embarked on a different sort of self-affirmation journey when they launched their *Map of the Soul* series. Beginning with *Map of the Soul: Persona*, the seven-track EP was the start of a new period, during which the septet focused not on self-acceptance but instead on understanding the various aspects of the self, as seen within the context of Jungian psychology. Inspired by and pulling its title from Murray Stein's *Jung's Map of the Soul: An Introduction*,[31] the album picked up the conversation where RM's Speak Yourself speech at the U.N. left off, and launched a new period for BTS in which they'd peruse the subject of identity.

Map of the Soul shifted its focus to figuring out who you are, with the Korean title of its lead single "Boy With Luv" referring to the subtle, poetic aspects of the self. Based on Jung's and Stein's ideas about psychoanalysis, three parts of the soul, or self, inspired the *Map of the Soul* series: persona, shadow, and ego. The first part, persona, relates to the identities a person assumes when interacting in different social contexts. The shadow, unlike the public-facing persona, corresponds to a person's innermost desires, both positive and negative. Ego refers to the conscious aspects of the self that feel emotions, and where a person's sense of self and identity reside.

The seven-song *Persona* EP set forth ideas of identity, homing in particularly on what it means to be a member of the group. In a V Live where he discussed the album, RM revealed that he was responsible for around 80–90 percent of the lyrics featured on *Persona*, with other lyrics contributed by J-Hope and Suga.

MAP OF THE SOUL: PERSONA

While expressing the *Persona* of BTS, the first song was a throwback to earlier periods of the group's career, referencing the intro track for *Skool Luv Affair* by sampling the same song that opened up RM's part in that song, and generally emphasizing grungy rock and hip-hop elements that felt more like the BTS of their earlier years rather than the more electropop-influenced songs they had been putting forth ever since *The Most Beautiful Moment in Life* series. Lyrically, there are mentions of themes that have recurred throughout BTS's discography, such as RM repeating the metaphor of pigs and dogs heard in "Am I Wrong," and his expressing a desire to fly, as heard on "Outro: Wings," while his references to being a "superhero" recall "Anpanman."

In addition, RM spends his time in "Intro: Persona" ruminating on the age-old question of "Who am I?", putting his insecurities and concerns front and center. The track primarily explores the disparity between who he is as an individual and as a performer, and how his perspective on his music and his performances has changed over the years, as he questions himself, his musicality, his motivation, and his varied personas all through confident, rhythmic raps. The song is contemplative and impactful in its exploratory self-reflection, and a fitting starting point for the path along which the *Map of the Soul* era led listeners.

② Boy With Luv

③ Mikrokosmos

Bright and breezy, with ample hook phrases, "Boy With Luv" is almost a pastiche of how a boy band should sound: sweet tones, groovy rhythms, and romantic lyricism pervade the track while It Girl Halsey features. All the while, references to the group's previous songs and their relationship with ARMY pervade the track. Although the Korean title, which RM pushed for, translates into "A Poem for Small Things" (작은 것들을 위한시), the English "Boy With Luv" recalls "Boy In Luv" of *Skool Luv Affair*, and the lyrics reflect lines featured in earlier songs by the group and its members—including a shout-out of "Hope World" as J-Hope delivers his lines. With its refreshing, smooth, funky pop-rock styling, the song serves as a testament to the bond between BTS and ARMY, with multiple questions directed at ARMY—which members tweeted in the lead-up to the album to make the connection overt—about their well-being and the overwhelming love the titular Boy (BTS) feels towards the object of his affection (ARMY); a special ARMY-oriented music video was later released, a slightly altered version of the vibrantly colored initial version featuring BTS and Halsey dancing their way through retro-inspired date-night settings.

Overall, the song's ebullient, straightforward attitude is intensely addictive and easy to listen to. While it diverges from the more thought-provoking styles typical of their singles, its blatant dedication to pop comes across as a celebration of everything that the group and their ARMY have achieved.

If "Intro: Persona" served as the launchpad for the album's messaging and "Boy With Love" engaged listeners and took flight with its euphonious styling, the gentle, twinkling sound of the third track "Mikrokosmos" soared straight into the stratosphere. Opening up with a soft, repeated synth melody, the song builds upon itself, adding vocal elements and layering the members' voices before reaching the impactful, sweeping EDM chorus. Leaning into the album's themes of self-exploration and identity, the song is based on the idea of microcosms as understood in philosophy, with BTS drawing inspiration from the way ancient Greek philosophers, including Plato, identified each individual as a small universe. Literally "micros kosmos" in Greek, the septet sweetly spend the single reflecting on how each person shines in this "macros kosmos," or universe. Like many of BTS's songs, it incorporated celestial imagery to relay how brightly the objects of the song—themselves, ARMY, and individual human beings—shine.

④ Make It Right

⑤ Home

The fourth song on *Map of the Soul: Persona* is arguably the most commercially friendly aside from the single, co-written by none other than Ed Sheeran, and later released as a remix featuring Lauv. A groovy, almost sleepy, synth-pop song driven by wind instruments and an R&B beat, "Make It Right" is full of promises and confidence. At first glance "Make It Right" seems aimed at audiences, with the group assuring them that they can make right any hardships their ARMY face, just as ARMY have supported them along the way; J-Hope's rap makes this clear as he talks about becoming a hero (see "Anpanman") and all their successes, and says he's trying to reach "you." But RM's following verse lacks that confidence and instead expresses pain and confusion, with the rapper sharing concern over how "you" no longer recognize him, which leads to the possible interpretation that perhaps the intended listener of "Make It Right" is not only the audience—ARMY—but BTS, as they assure themselves that the path they are walking is hard but the right one. The song also makes reference to the metaphors used in "Sea" and also leans into the BU narrative, with the idea of Seokjin having to correct the storyline of the friends, or "Make It Right." However you interpret the intent of the lyrics, the message remains the same, with a comforting, promissory vibe that things will eventually be made right.

This lush R&B-infused track is all about the longing for "Home," a feeling BTS are familiar with since leaving their homes to start down their career path. Now that they have found success in the spotlight they seek a new "Home" to find solace and rest in. And yet, though they say they're exhausted, they admit that the world itself has become a "Home" for them, that "you," the listener, have become a space for them to make their own. Doubling as both a traditional love song full of longing and a song dedicated to their ARMY, it can also be listened to as a sequel to "Moving On," itself about how the idea of home and moving on relates to their lives. "Home" is, like so many of BTS's songs, about the reality of life at the top. Here, they express the desire for shelter from it all, and how they have found it with "you," turning the whole world into a home where they, BTS, can feel at ease as long as their fans are there.

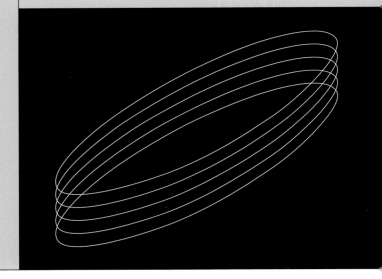

Following the reflection of "Home," *Map of the Soul: Persona* introduces "Jamais Vu," a song that is heavily influenced by the album's psychoanalytical inspirations. The term is used to refer to the opposite of *déjà vu*—rather than feeling as if something new is familiar, it refers to the sensation of not being able to recall something you have familiarity with. Fittingly, the song itself is an echoing bittersweet ballad infused with ambient synths and a trap beat that is immediately recognizable as sorrowful, but which comes across as new and fresh due to its meticulous production, which layers not only the instrumentals but also the voices of the three members featured on the track.

Featuring Jin, J-Hope, and Jungkook, "Jamais Vu" is one of the few tracks throughout BTS's discography that mixes the rap and vocal lines without including either group in its entirety, and with each movement in the song it almost feels as if other voices should join in. But instead, the tender vocals of Jungkook and Jin blend with J-Hope's despondent rapping to come together and create a heartfelt song demanding a remedy for pain. According to RM, the song is supposed to bring about feelings reminiscent of when you're playing a video game where you can die and be reborn via a remedy or cure, applying that theme and emotion to the game humanity calls "life."[32]

The crestfallen vibes of "Jamais Vu" dissipate and lead into the anthemic styling of the album's closer, "Dionysus," a standout moment and a buoyant celebration of BTS's success. A dynamic party rock song, it served as the opening song of their *Speak Yourself: Love Yourself* stadium concert series, and with good reason. Drawing again on Greek mythology for inspiration, the song's title is derived from the Grecian god of wine and acting, perhaps again tying in to the theme of masks or *persona*s. Upbeat and boisterous, "Dionysus" incorporates hard rock and old school hip-hop influences into its liquor-infused lyrics, through which the group paralleled their artistic drive with that of the desire to drink, a pun of sorts considering that in Korean liquor is known as *sul* (술) while art is *yesul* (예술), and the fact that the Korean word for grape, *podo* (포도), is used in slang Korean to refer to available concert seats on ticketing sites, as they are left shaded in purple until sold. (The group featured the phrase in "MIC Drop," saying that their concerts don't have any such grapes, implying they're always sold out.)

An anthemic drinking song, "Dionysus" doubles as a revelatory experience for BTS as they sing of their success, and is thematically similar to "Idol." A complete celebration of who they are as artists, it was a fitting closer for *Persona*.

Overall, *Map of the Soul: Persona* began a new era for BTS as a cerebral answer to the more emotive *Love Yourself* series that preceded it. That, in turn, was built on the provocative, youthful maturation of *The Most Beautiful Moment in Life* series, which found its footing in the dreams and earliest expressions of BTS's message during the *Skool* era. Though each of BTS's thematic works are distinct entities, they relay new emotions, insights, and sounds that the septet want to share with their listeners as they grow as artists and adults. At first glance, *Persona*'s narrative may not appear new: the group has always sung about topics like identity, passion, love, their career, and hardships. But by pursuing each of those elements as individual personas of BTS, the album establishes its self-aware identity, showing different facets of the group and exploring what it means to be BTS and to present yourself to the world.

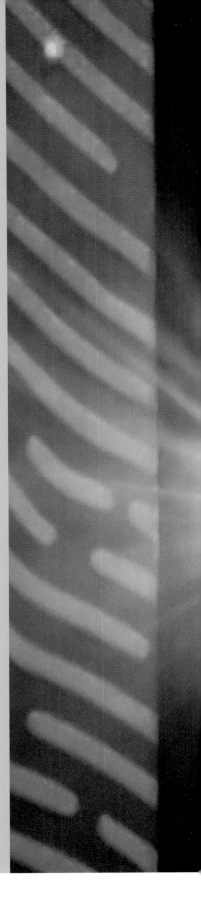

DR. MURRAY STEIN ON MAP OF THE SOUL AND THE PSYCHOANALYTIC NATURE OF BTS'S MUSIC

The author of *Jung's Map of the Soul: An Introduction*, released in 1998, Stein is a Jungian psychoanalyst working at the International School of Analytical Psychology in Zurich, Switzerland. His book was cited by BTS as a source of inspiration for their *Map of the Soul* series.

TAMAR HERMAN: It's not every day a professor is cited as an inspiration for a pop act. How did you first hear about BTS?

DR. MURRAY STEIN: A Japanese student at the school where I teach told me that BTS had posted my book, *Jung's Map of the Soul*, for sale on their website. A few weeks later the same student informed me that the new album being released by BTS, *Map of the Soul: Persona*, was titled after my book and would be on sale shortly. All of this came as a total and very pleasant surprise. Before this I did not know about BTS.

What was your first impression on hearing that an album series had been inspired by your book and work?

STEIN: I felt I needed to quickly learn something about BTS. When I viewed on YouTube the talk RM gave at the United Nations last year, I was impressed by his seriousness of purpose and sincerity. He urged people of the world to take care of their mental health and focus on their value as human beings and not only on what other people think of them, to remember who they are, where they come from. It was a very touching talk he made and I was impressed by it. This gave me a very positive impression of BTS and their message to the fans. As far as I can tell, they're making a positive impact in this generation and bringing some psychological awareness into the world where people aren't reading very much or aren't exposed to a lot of these kinds of perspectives, I'd imagine. To me, it seemed like a good thing.

What were your initial, and later, reactions to the album's release?

STEIN: When I received the English translation of the lyrics and read through the songs' words carefully, I could see that they showed a thoughtful progression moving quietly and steadily from the first to the last. The progression shows a development from questioning persona and asking about "true identity," to stating the uniqueness and precious value of each individual human being on the planet, to the release of intense emotions and joy at the conclusion of this journey. I was shocked by the numbers of sales of the album in so many countries. This convinced me that BTS is carrying a message that the world is responding to and needs. I think BTS is more than entertainment, but, of course, the members of BTS are brilliant performers.

The first number is called "Intro: Persona," in which RM sings about the issue of persona. What "persona" is, is the social identities that we all form at one time or another in our lives, usually in our early years. It's the interface between ourselves and the social world around us. It starts very early in childhood, as we adapt to our family and its values and we take those values into ourselves and we conform to them and we try to please others, our parents, our siblings, our friends. And so we build up a kind of official or social personality with which we confront the world and we try to fit in. This goes through a crisis several times in life and one of the big crisis times is adolescence, which is the group that BTS is addressing. It's a crisis about identity or who I am to other people and who I am in the world around me, so peer groups become very important and being accepted by the peer group and recognized. And, of course, this is an eternal question that people ask themselves all their lives but critically, when they're young, that question: Who am I? And that goes very deep.

What RM talked about in his U.N. talk was this discrepancy between who he is publicly, now a huge celebrity in the world, and who he is in his past, in his history, where he comes from. He didn't grow up in elegant, affluent circumstances and now suddenly he's a world-class celebrity. Wealthy, recognized. Everybody is practically worshipping him and the group. And so this discrepancy is disturbing. "Am I that person that people see when I'm on stage and when I'm presenting myself to the public? Or am I the boy that grew up in a small village in Korea?" [Note: Ilsan, where RM is from, is a suburb within Seoul's metropolitan area.] And he goes back to that and that's very important to remember, who you are by looking to your past and your roots. That's a good insight that he's holding on to himself as a human being, not as a celebrity.

And then I thought further about this as a cultural issue. You know, the whole world's going through a kind of identity crisis now. In America, for instance, you have this question: what are American values? Who represents us? What is America, really? Is it a land of opportunity for immigrants or is it a closed and barricaded fenced-off community for the wealthy? Those kinds of issues trouble a lot of people all over the world, but I think especially in some of these old, traditional cultures like Korea and China and Japan, where their past cultural identity and history is being totally wiped out by globalization, by what's happening in the global world. If you look at Korea, it's based on ancient traditions and philosophies, Confucianism, and Daoism. Do those still have a place? What is Korea today? So the question of who are we has to do not only with these individual young

236

Sweat

men but with their culture as well. If Koreans ask themselves, if Korea asked itself, what are we? Are we just manufacturing automobiles for the world and cell phones and all of that and getting rich, or do we have a deeper identity than just a commercial one? So this question of identity and persona—who are we, to ourselves and to the world, how do we want to present ourselves and how do we feel about ourselves—I think is a big issue. And they, in a strange way, they sing about this.

I looked through their seven songs in the album and I see a very deep message there. For instance, in the song "Mikrokosmos," when they talk about how there are 7 billion stars, and every human being on the planet is a star. Well, that feeling that you are a star, that you have contact with something eternal and permanent, of permanent value, of infinite value, that's an answer to this existential question: what is my value or who am I, what am I worth? So while it looks like they're just an entertainment group, and they're very good at what they do—I mean their dancing performances are fantastic. That's why they've gotten where they are. It isn't because of their deep message. But they're carrying that deep message with them and that's what I find extraordinary, that in addition to filling the Rose Bowl and all these stadiums with tens of thousands of fans, they are also delivering a message in their music that maybe some of the fans will resonate with and pick up, and I'm sure they do.

What exactly is the "map of the soul"?

STEIN: It's a map of the psyche and the psychic world, the inner world. It is very complex. It's layered. It has a personal element, your own personal life history and what has happened to you in your lifetime, but it also has a cultural level to it that you inherit, cultural experiences through your family, through your education. That is all a part of your inner world, you're influenced and formed by it. Then, in Jungian psychology, there is what is called a collective unconscious or the archetypical unconscious that is almost trans-historic. It's universally human so that at some level, we're all human beings, we all inherit the same basic structures of mentality and fantasy and need and desire. So we discover that we are not only individual but we're universal in that sense. We can connect to all human beings. At the center of all that is the star and that is a sense of deep uniqueness that's buried in all the mass of other materials and you want to be able to connect to that, to feel that you're unique and of eternal value and that you are a representative of the human species at the same time.

You're one among 5 billion others. But you're culturally formed, you're individually formed, you have your own experiences. But that isn't all of it. So this map tries to go through all those layers, and persona is the upper layer and you have shadow.

Maybe the next album will be about shadow. That's the human part. The parts of ourselves we don't like to admit. We have certain desires and tendencies and cravings, like the seven deadly sins and that kind of stuff, that we try to hide from ourselves and other people. Competitiveness, selfishness. And then a level below that we have a connection to what Jung called the anima and animus, the soul level that reaches out to the stars and to the deep uniqueness that you are to the self. In my book I describe these different levels, and whether BTS will in future albums go through some of the other levels is an open question.

We won't find out how BTS explore "shadow" and "ego" for a while. [They incorporated both onto *Map of the Soul: 7* following this interview.] But since you already discussed "shadow" a bit, but what exactly would "ego" be ruminating on?

STEIN: What we call ego is the "I," the part of ourselves that we refer to when we say "I." "I want," "I'm going to do this," "I will." That "I" that we put into our sentences. It's a feeling that you have about yourself as an individual, your own individual needs. You know, if you say to yourself "I," you use your name, you can identify yourself. You look in the mirror and you see your body. The "I" and the body are very connected. The "self" is a much bigger concept in Jungian theory. It includes the whole, all the contents of the psyche. It's an all-inclusive concept. So your conscious and your unconscious parts, the shadow, the complexes, all the drives, everything—all of that is referenced by the word "self" and the self also has a center. The ego is intimately connected with that center but when it identifies with it, is gets inflated because the center of the self, it's the center of your creativity. It's the center of all your energy. And if the ego starts feeling that it is the self, it becomes inflated. You feel that sort of god almightiness. "I can do anything." "I'm indestructible." "I'm beyond the law." "I'm beyond restrictions." "I can get away with anything." We see people like that in the world around us and it's a kind of narcissism to be that identified with the self because the self is much bigger than the ego. So finding the right place, the right position for the ego in the world and in one's

238

life has a lot to do again with ethical responsibility, with having a realistic view of your abilities and your limitations, coming to terms with who you are as an individual. You might have great capacities and potentials but those have to be worked out over long periods of time and you probably won't be able to fulfill all of them in a lifetime. So the ego should be relatively humble in relation to the self, while at the same time, taking good care of the body and asserting one's self when one has justifiable needs. So when they sing about the ego, I think it will be connected to the shadow and persona, and to identity issues.

You mentioned "Mikrokosmos" earlier. What is the idea of this personal star?

STEIN: The human being has a capacity for connecting to exceptional states of consciousness and you can identify those as religious, mystical states, transcendence. Something that is eternal or star-like. We think of stars as being eternal. Well, they're not. They also have a time span. They're billions of years old, and our life and our planet are not in that category—certainly not our personal life. So the star, it's a sense of your immortality. It is a feeling, and people who have that have a capacity to endure and to be exceptionally resilient. They have a sense of meaning and a sense of destiny, let's say, and they have a mission in life. This is more in philosophy and religion, where you get to these concepts of the human capacity to consider immortality and to heighten states of being, transcendent being that isn't just something you make up out of ego, out of wish, out of desire, but it comes to you. It calls you. It's a calling.

You don't manufacture it. It's deeper than the shadow. The shadow is what is hidden from the ego. Ego means "I" and when you dig into "I" and down into "I" far enough, you come into something very, you could say, cruel and ruthless and determined. That "I" will survive. "I will make it at any costs." In certain situations, people do terrible things in order to survive but sometimes in relatively calm situations, they also do terrible things out of cold selfishness. Most of us don't act on it but it's there and so to become aware of the shadow is very difficult and taxing moral work. And this is constant work that all serious people, psychologically serious people, engage in throughout their lives to try and stay on top of the shadow and reflect on it and keep it under some level of control if they can.

It struck me that BTS have been exploring that struggle with shadow in some of their earlier content also.

STEIN: They have a song in this series too, called "Jamais Vu." "Jamais Vu" means you're in the place you've been in before but you don't recognize it and it's all new to you. It's a kind of psychopathological phenomenon. We do it all the time when we repeat the same argument with our spouse, let's say. And it's like we hadn't had that argument 100 times already. And now we're going to do it again. We repeat over and over again the same patterns and to see that and recognize it, that's why this song is important. Once you see it and you catch it and you can say "Oh, that's a jamais vu." "Oh, I've been doing this routine for quite a few years." Once you see it, you have a slight chance to change it a little bit and to keep working on it and then it will gradually diminish in its severity at least. And you can pull out of it quicker. So that kind of thing in these songs has struck me. That kind of psychological sophistication is somewhere in the background, of course, when they're singing these songs and performing. I don't know if their fans out there in the Rose Bowl, how much of it they get. But I think some of it sinks in. They certainly enjoy the performance.

I think that's the beauty of music. A good song is all at once universal and also meaningful, and BTS certainly accomplishes that. Did you have any personal favorites on the album?

STEIN: Well, you know I can't say I'm a fan of pop. I'm more a classical music guy, but I watched a couple of times—I guess it's the most popular, "Boy With Luv." I like that one the best as a musical piece. Also, I was struck by the title "Boy With Luv" as opposed to an earlier one, "Boy In Luv." It's a higher level of maturity to come into a relationship *with* love than to be *in* love, and it means you have more control over the emotional. Not that you want to control it, but you are just swept away and you're bringing something. You aren't just needy. If you come with love, you've got something to give. If you go in love, you're just hungry. You want to take. So it's a very different approach to a relationship to come with love than to be in love. Being in love passes you rather quickly usually, a few months. If you really come with love, it can last for a long time in a relationship because it's not just a feeling. It's a capacity. Capacity to consider the other person and to be in a loving relationship with them, to care for them, even if they're nasty to you sometimes. It sustains a relationship, so that struck me, that they're singing about going with love and Halsey comes and appears in the ensemble. It's like they've called her. There she is and they can move forward with love when they have her with them. I think she represents the loved element. Now they're *with* love and when they move into other relationships that comes with them.

> During your episode on the *Speaking of Jung* podcast[33] you mentioned the Jewish idea of *tikkun olam,* repairing the world, and how BTS are using their message to leave the world a better place than they found it. Can you tell me a little bit about why you thought that's what their music represented?

STEIN: This isn't just Jungian, of course. This is in religious traditions, it's in spiritual traditions of all kinds. The idea of *tikkun olam* comes from the kabbalistic idea that there are shards, world pieces of the divine broken and it's our job to put it together and to try to repair what has been damaged or broken. Religious people do it different ways, maybe by prayers and so on, but we psychologists try to do it by actions that contribute to health, mental health, the well-being of people. In a sense, I see that's what BTS is essentially doing, whether they're intending it or not. They're trying to repair something that is broken in the world of their fans, these young people who are suffering or having problems, but also in a wider sense. It isn't just young people that are listening to them. Some of the letters I've received with questions have been adults, people in their 50s and 60s who are enjoying their performances but also paying attention to the message, the words, and studying them, having questions. So it's a kind of intervention, I like to think of it as a calling.

> How do you feel about the message that BTS are imparting to their ARMY, based on your own work?

STEIN: What makes me happy is that BTS is able to carry the ideas in my book to a much wider and younger audience than would ever be reached by my book. They have taken the message of psychological awareness and the importance of mental health to a global level. This of course pleases me very much, and I am happy to be a part of this effort to bring greater consciousness to the world.

Hands up for 7! BTS having fun at *The Today Show* on the release day of *Map of the Soul: 7*.

Though speculation suggested BTS's next releases might be *Map of the Soul: Shadow* and *Map of the Soul: Ego,* the group instead opted to blend their continued perusal of self with a celebration of their seven years together as the seven members of BTS with the release of *Map of the Soul: 7.* Along with five tracks already released on *Map of the Soul: Persona* — all but "Home" and "Mikrokosmos" appear on *7* — the album features 15 new songs, making it BTS's longest single-disc release. Like *Wings* and *Love Yourself: Answer,* it features solo tracks from each member, and also several duets, putting the spotlight on both the group and the seven men individually.

MAP OF THE SOUL:

Interlude: Shadow

Following the opening act of "Intro: Persona," "Boy with Luv," "Make it Right," "Jamais Vu," and "Dionysus," *7* dips into its "Shadow" zone, with Suga's multifaceted "Interlude." Leaning into his Agust D personality, with touches of BTS's Suga, the rapper spends this intermediary track confronting his desires and dreams. Sirens, melodic synths, gritty rock strings, barks, and industrial, distorted vocals play off of one another as he ruminates on his conflated, yet intertwined aims to be a "rap star," a "king," "rich," and, ultimately, "me." All the while, he creates a tune that is both stirring and gripping as Min Yoongi, the man behind Suga, grapples with himself, his artistry, and his fame.

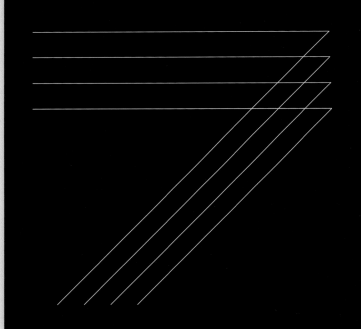

② Black Swan

③ Filter

Drawing inspiration from the 2010 film *Black Swan,* the song first arrived through a choreographed performance by Slovenian modern dance troupe MN Dance Company released weeks prior to the arrival of *Map of the Soul: 7*. The dance, which depicted the story of a main dancer, or swan, falling and rising, opened with a quote by modern dance icon Martha Graham about an artist's relationship with their craft: "A dancer dies twice — once when they stop dancing, and this first death is the more painful." Fittingly, the song spends its length as an artistic confessional of sorts, focusing on BTS's relationship with music. Opening with slinking, plinking, traditionally inspired strings and then shifting into a haunting melody propelled by trap beats and rising to emotional heights with terse, orchestral reflections about how there are moments when the act's members face concerns over their long-term relationship with the very music that they love, "Black Swan" is exquisite in its poignant meditation on artists' relationship to their art.

With a festive, Latin sound propelling his solo, Jimin's "Filter" offers a swaying melody and lilting, romantic thrills that evoke a cinematic tango performance as he uses the photo-enhancing feature as a metaphor for what it means to exist in relation to others: "What sort of 'Filter'" – or persona – "do others want of him today?" he contemplates. Witty in its usage of the metaphor, and filled with depth regarding how the way individuals interact with one another is affected by the perceptions and actions of others, it's a song that shines a spotlight both on Jimin's expressive vocals and the way he views the world.

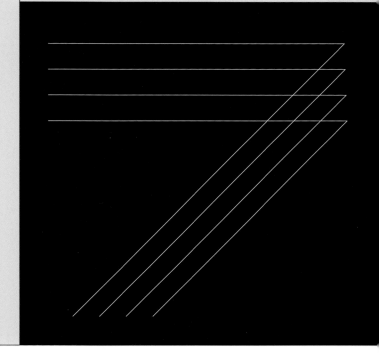

④ My Time

⑤ Louder than bombs

The euphoric, uplifting EDM-R&B hybrid melody of Jungkook's "My Time" seems anachronistic with the lyrics, in which Jungkook questions whether he'll be able to recover the lost time of his youth, which has been focused on his career versus the typical experiences of others his age. Only 24-years-old in Korean age (or 22 internationally) when the song was released, Jungkook acknowledges the movie-like elements of his life – after all, he's a global superstar before his 25 birthday – but still wonders what it means to experience "My Time" when walking a path different to your peers. Contemplative and wistful, though not necessarily despondent, it sheds light on the relationship BTS's youngest has with his career and how it has shaped his adolescence.

One of several songs on the album with an affecting, almost gloomy yet breathlessly rousing feel to it, "Louder than bombs" is an emotional high of *Map of the Soul: 7,* through which the septet expressively relay how speaking and singing can make one "louder than bombs." Utilizing layered, echoing vocal effects throughout, and modulating the delivery of the rappers to reflect the emotional turmoil of their verses, the song, which was co-written by Troye Sivan, is almost ironic in the way it uses silence – especially in how it leads off into a black sonic space after the final croon – to share how as artists able to inspire and bring about change they have become "Louder than bombs."

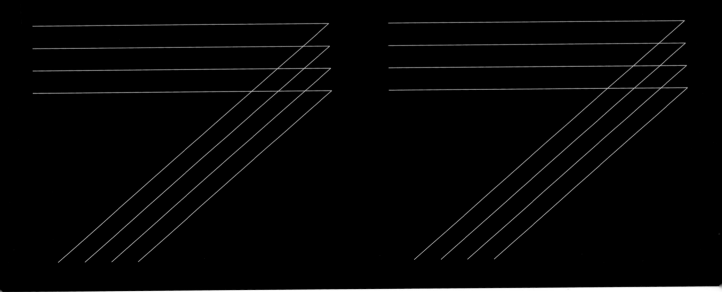

Anthemic and boisterous, the drumline-featuring "ON" is an inspirational tune about how BTS can never be held down, and how pain can become motivational. A fitting lead track for an album series that spends its time philosophizing on the relationship between an individual's light and shadow, "ON" follows in the path of other BTS releases like "Dope," "Fire," and "Not Today" as singles that lay forth the act's *raison d'être*, serving as an expression of what they have done and how they hope to inspire their audience. A parallel to "N.O" the way "Boy with Luv" was a foil to "Boy in Luv," "ON" reveals how the past has shaped and changed BTS, bringing them both pain and success, and how those experiences have enabled them to rise.

"ON" was released through two music videos, one that focused on the dynamic dance and drumline performance and one that told a series of intertwined stories as BTS performed for the first time on television during the act's appearance on *The Tonight Show starring Jimmy Fallon* at Grand Central Station in New York City, reflecting how BTS's reach had grown so far beyond Seoul that they're able to premiere a new performance in the very heart of New York City, and thus western, culture.

A gunshot-fueled rap response to online haters, "UGH!" returns BTS's rappers to the place in which they thrive: bombastic, swaggering takedowns. With mellow, creeping trap elements driving the cypher-like tune, "UGH!" features the trio expressing disgust towards those who spend their days driving pointless anger and hatred on the Internet, with a specific emphasis on how people troll celebrities, disregarding their humanity with the idea that public persons are fair game to criticize publicly. Full of outrage, it ends with a series of gunshots, which could be interpreted either as the trio's feelings towards the people they're singing about, or else serving as a metaphor for the pain and suffering those behind keyboards can cause to the targets of their derision.

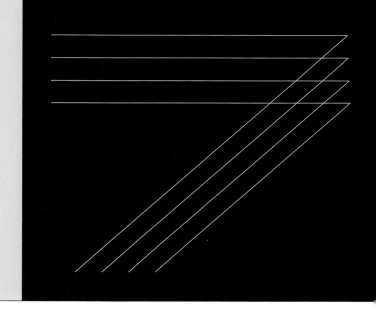

⑧ 00:00 (Zero O'Clock)

⑨ Inner Child

After the drama of "UGH!" comes the vocalists' "Zero O'Clock," a sweet tune about how, despite whatever else is going on, life always resets at midnight. Hopeful and optimistic, the tune is a promise of tomorrow's future potential, propelled by the harmonious voices of BTS's four singers. A comforting lullaby, it's introspective and thoughtful, and a song to listen to late at night after a tough day.

Like other solos on the album, V's "Inner Child" is a beautiful retrospective on himself, which parallels Jungkook's "My Time" in the way it looks back on his past self and the person he has become. The focus on this track, however, is the changes a person goes through to grow into who they are at present. Utilizing sweeping synths and soaring strings to create an ambient, uplifting feel that is altogether full of promise for what is to come, the vocalist simultaneously gets in touch with his past self, lovingly referring to his childhood self, recalling how "My boy" has grown and changed in a charming way.

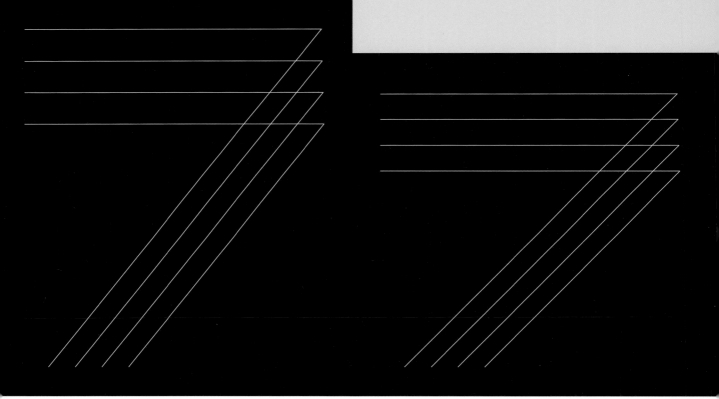

10 Friends

The first duet on the album, "Friends" is the vibrant soundtrack to Jimin and V's friendship, with the duo endearingly singing about how they have done this all together, bonding with one another and growing because of their relationship. A fitting reflection for *7*, the pair sing about how they came to know one another, despite being so divergent as if from completely different celestial homes, thousands of miles apart. But when it comes down to it, they have stayed together side by side throughout it all, lifting one another up, and becoming soulmates, which has helped them to thrive and become better for it.

11 Moon

Jin's "Moon" fittingly arrives towards the end of the album as an homage to ARMY and his relationship with BTS's beloved fandom. The song sweeps along with a clap-happy beat and vibrant harmonies to give it an overall bright and euphoric feel. "Moon" expresses Jin's happiness at being able to give back to audiences as a bright light, akin to the moon, shining his worth and music onto those who benefit from it. The metaphor is as poignant as it is beautiful, and it is an intensely touching tune from BTS's eldest member.

12 Respect

What does it mean to "Respect" someone, wonder Suga and RM in this sonorous old-school hip-hop-feeling track. Almost like a trip back to the early days of BTS, and before, when the pair had to prove their street cred as both artists and rappers, "Respect" – which is often used in Korean despite being an English word – weighs the way people earn respect, and how people view others, with Korean and English wordplay breaking the term down into the "re" of "return" and "spect," such as in "inspect" to relay an idea of looking back and reconsidering or re-observing how one perceives those worthy of respect. With a bright trap beat propelling much of the tune and the pair's discordant rap styles playing off of one another, with vocal modulation adding weight and depth to their deliveries, "Respect" is almost like a four-minute resume of why the pair are deserving of "Respect" both as artists, and as humans who spend their time ruminating on important philosophical ideas. The track ends with a conversation between RM and Suga, with the latter using *satoori,* as they discuss the meaning of "respect," before comically concluding that English is difficult, a valid point for a group that has been able to break into the English-dominated global music scene regardless of their usage of English in their music.

13 We are Bulletproof: The Eternal

"We are Bulletproof: the Eternal" essentially summarizes the time from the release of *2 Cool 4 Skool* on June 13, 2013, to the release of *Map of the Soul: 7* on Feb. 21, 2020. Perhaps more than any other on *Map of the Soul: 7,* "We are Bulletproof: the Eternal" feels the most like a closing chapter to the first seven years of BTS's career. Though seven was historically a cursed number for K-pop groups, as seven-year contracts are common, often leading to disbandment at that time, BTS have taken ownership of the number and turned it into a celebratory milestone and reflection of their career. "We are Bulletproof: the Eternal" is the bookend to "We are Bulletproof, Pt. 2" from their very first album, and fittingly revels in how far the act has come in their quest to grow from being "only seven" to becoming eternalized in the hearts and ears of their beloved ARMY and listeners in general. With lyrical parallels to "Pt. 2" the song reflects on how they have reached heaven due to being eternally immortalized in music canon and how they have grown from being only seven to being more than just seven.

With samples from the intro of *2 Cool 4 Skool* and other outside sources, the upbeat and funky "Outro : Ego" puts a close to *Map of the Soul: 7*. J-Hope gets the final wholly original number on the album, reflecting on the "Ego" part of the *Map of the Soul* while he explores how "J-Hope" and "Jeong Hoseok" are different people, but have essentially become one, and how hardships have eventually turned into sources of comfort and confidence. A declaration of trust in both himself and where fate will take him, J-Hope sings about getting to know himself and how the *Map of the Soul* has become the "map of all" and his "ego." It's introspective and celebratory, and the perfect finale for the album.

Though "Outro : Ego" is the true conclusion, *Map of the Soul: 7* was released digitally with another additional track, "ON," featuring none other than Australian singer-songwriter Sia, who adds added weight and depth to the chorus and on a brief verse adds her own take on the song's message to bring on the pain.

FURTHER DISCOGRAPHY

(JAPANESE RELEASES, SOLOS, COLLABS, AND COVERS)

Chapter Twelve

Though this book primarily focuses on BTS's formal Korean discography, the group has also released a significant amount of content outside of their primary releases, through solo and joint songs and albums in both Korean and Japanese, as well as numerous collaborations and covers. Each of these releases is important and worth highlighting for its place in the act's discography and identity, at least briefly.

BTS'S JAPANESE MUSIC

Over the years, many of BTS's singles have been remade into Japanese, and "Boy In Luv" earned a remake in Mandarin, but the septet have also released numerous original songs in Japan, many on brief singles albums, but also on full-length releases. The original songs featured on their Japanese albums revealed a more romantic, rock-ish side to the group than they typically emphasize on their Korean discography.

Wake Up, their first Japanese album, was released on December 24, 2014, and showed how immensely popular the group was in the country already: the album debuted at No. 3 on the Oricon weekly album chart, and No. 2 on the daily one. The album introduced Japanese audiences to BTS's *Skool*-era music through remakes of "Jump," "Danger," "Boy In Luv," "Just One Day," "Like," "No More Dream," "Attack on Bangtan," and "N.O," as well as five original tracks: an intro and outro, "The Stars," the titular "Wake Up," and "I Like It, Pt. 2—At That Place—," a sequel to the group's "I Like It" from debut album *2 Cool 4 Skool.*

Each of these five new songs did something to introduce BTS to Japanese listeners, offering a new take on what BTS was all about. First up was the groovy scratch of the first track, adding an old-school hip-hop meets funk vibe to the group's "Intro" into a new market. "The Stars," the following song on the album, similarly works to explain exactly who and what BTS are and where they fit into hip-hop history, this time with a first verse from Japanese rapper KM-MARKIT, who would collaborate with the group by songwriting on future Japanese releases as well, before featuring the septet singing and rapping about their dreams and desires, using celestial metaphors to emphasize the brightness of their forward momentum to the future, regardless of the hard times.

Following several remakes of the band's Korean songs, the Japanese version of "Like" led into its sequel on the album. With a groovy, clapping beat, "I Like It, Pt. 2—At That Place—" continued to explore the emotions of looking at the social media account of an ex-girlfriend, as one hopes to return to a relationship that's over. After more remakes, the album begins to approach its close on "Wake Up", the lilting alt-R&B tune which gives the album its title. It fittingly serves up a typical BTS message, urging listeners to wake up, live their lives with pride and pursue their dreams. The album finishes with a piano-melody-fronted "Outro," repeating the refrain of "Wake Up," leaving listeners with the motivation to *Wake Up* and live their lives in the way they want to.

It would take another two years for BTS to follow *Wake Up* with their next Japanese LP *Youth* in September 2016, this time following the release of their *HYYH* era. Fronted by the June 2015 release of the single "For You," the 13-track album featured Japanese variants of the group's "Run," "Fire," "Dope," "Save Me," "Boyz with Fun," "Silver Spoon," "Butterfly," "I Need U," and "Epilogue: Young Forever" along with three other tracks.

Opened by "Introduction: Youth," the album began with a short snippet of samples from the era's singles and a voiceover from RM explaining the theme in a wider, ageless context: "Youth has no age, it just stays there beautifully. And it's everyone who's chasing their dreams, like Rap Mon, Jin, Suga, J-Hope, Jimin, V, and Jungkook. We're one of them who is chasing our stars. So you can call us young, and we'll never get old."

The first full-length new song on the album, "Good Day," is a sprightly pop-rock-influenced song that features the seven men bouncily laying out an optimistic worldview, both for listeners and for themselves. It features a reference to the Oath of the Peach Garden sequence from the famous 14th century Chinese novel *Romance of the Three Kingdoms*, during which men become sworn brothers to do good, a nod to the bond among BTS to succeed in their career and "be okay."

The next new song, "Wishing On A Star," arrives a few tracks later, reiterating the overall positive message of the original tracks on *Youth*, this time serving up a mellow, jazzy pop-rock tune about following dreams and wishes. It references the Greek myth of Pandora, who let negativity loose in the world—which is also the inspiration behind J-Hope's stage name: the dancer-rapper combined the first initial of his last name, Jung, and the idea of hope, the final thing left in Pandora's box, to create his new identity, aiming to bring hope to the chaotic world as a member of BTS.

The final new song on the *Youth* album, "For You," sweetly rounded things out. Guided by a lilting piano melody and scattered synths and trap beats, "For You" might be one of the most endearing moments of BTS's group discography, in part thanks to a music video that featured Jungkook dressing up as a teddy bear mascot, working hard to give out flyers. The song itself is a heartwarming expression of wanting to be together with a loved one even though distance keeps them apart. A straightforward love song featuring the members' warm vocals and expressive raps, it also can be interpreted as a message to ARMY, expressing the desire to be together despite being geographically dispersed, brought together by the Internet and music.

Like its tie-in, *The Most Beautiful Moment in Life* trilogy, *Youth* was a major success, and went on to become the group's first album to be certified gold by the Recording Industry Association of Japan.

After a *Best of BTS* album in 2017, the group would return with their *Love Yourself*-era Japanese tie-in *Face Yourself* in April 2018, just four months after they put out a single album for *MIC Drop/DNA/Crystal Snow*, which was certified double platinum by the RIAJ. The original song from the trio, "Crystal Snow," would be featured on the 2018 *Face Yourself* LP along with a handful of other brand-new Japanese songs as well as remakes of several songs from *You Never Walk Alone* and *Love Yourself: Her.* The album began with the chilling, echoing "Intro: Ringwanderung," a reference to a German term with multiple meanings including a reference to walking in circles and a wedding game during which guests make wishes on the wedding bands. The song served as a quasi-remix of "Best of Me" to create a haunting start to the album, and then led into that track before putting forth other Japanese variants of previously released BTS hits. The album then arrived at the first original full-length Japanese track on the album, "Don't Leave Me."

A sweeping, ambient electronic track, the members expressively exude desperation and desire through their verses and raps over snapping beats and off-kilter synths. The album's main single, it was the theme for the Japanese drama *Signal*, a remake of a 2016 Korean show. The song's popularity helped propel the album to go double platinum.

"Crystal Snow" followed two tracks after "Don't Leave Me." A soft, wintery ballad, "Crystal Snow" emphasizes the vocalist's sweet tones over a rock-meets-EDM melody that flits freely between full moments and lighter, emptier ones, adding spatial depth to the tune.

BTS served up one final full-length new track on the album in the form of "Let Go," a free-flowing alt-R&B track that brought the relationship to a conclusion, expressing determination and acceptance when something comes to an end. The album ended with "Outro: Crack" that, like the "Intro," was an echoing song that reframed another album track, this time giving a jazzy, woozy vibe to the repeated refrain of "Let Go."

SOLO
EFFORTS

RM

Sweat

The most prolific songwriter and soloist in BTS, since the act's debut RM has put out two solo album-length releases, his 2015 mixtape *RM* (still as Rap Monster) and 2018's *mono.* playlist. He has also featured on a variety of one-off collaborations with other artists.

As a soloist, RM's identity has vacillated over the years from the hard-hitting hip-hop featured prominently on *RM*—where the rapper spent much of the time declaratively exploring his identity and what it means to be an idol rapper coming out of the hip-hop underground scene—and his more introspective, philosophical side, as seen on *mono.*, which he largely spent reflecting on his life and maturing worldview while leaning more heavily into electronic, alt-R&B, and rock elements.

Each of his songs, both as a soloist and as a collaborator, reflect RM's perspective on the world, with the artist instilling his songs with his worldview: in 2012, prior to BTS's debut, "Party (XXO)" from Big Hit's girl group GLAM was co-written by RM and featured a fluid approach towards love, unrestricted by gender limitations. A rare example of a K-pop song positively depicting same-sex relationships, it's often heralded as a sign of RM being an LGBTQ+ ally, along with things like him posting a Troye Sivan song from the soundtrack of *Love, Simon*; Sivan is publicly out as a gay man, and the film is a gay rom-com meets coming-of-age story.

RM's political leanings have also filtered into his music, perhaps most notably on "Change," a 2017 collaboration with Wale where the pair discussed social issues that they felt needed to result in change. On the track, Wale rapped about police brutality in the U.S. while RM explored the harsh realities of student life and social media in the modern age.

Both *RM* and *mono.* reflect the artist's path in life: the former explores who he is, largely spending time addressing his role in BTS and as an idol, while the latter ruminates on how he is, and his mental state. Each fitted into the timeline of his career in BTS not only lyrically but also stylistically. *RM* drew heavily on the group's hip-hop roots, and freely sampled and covered songs from an array of rappers as RM showed off what he had to offer through tracks that varied from emotive to explosive. By comparison, *mono.* is more in line with the group's sound in 2018 when it was released, leaning more heavily into synth-pop and reflective alt-R&B balladry.

Over the years, the star has also collaborated with a wide range of artists, both Korean, such as MFBTY, Drunken Tiger, Nell, and Primary, and otherwise, like Fall Out Boy and Warren G, honing his craft and widening his reach all the while showcasing his flare for bombastic, sleekly phrased hip-hop.

SOLO
EFFORTS

SUGA

Sweat

Suga's solo work and songwriting career began when he was part of the underground scene in Daegu before joining Big Hit Entertainment, and continues in the present. He has worked on many songs for BTS since the group's early days, but truly put himself front and center with the 2016 release of *Agust D*, a mixtape in which he bared his soul.

With a combination of aggressive bluster and despondent expressiveness, Suga took the opportunity of his first solo release while in BTS to share his thoughts and personal experiences. *Agust D* vacillated between explorations of who Min Yoon-gi is as Suga of BTS, and who he is as a human being. Like early BTS albums, it leaned heavily into his hip-hop roots and included both an intro and a skit, and featured a variety of collaborators, including DJ Friz, Yankie, and Suran, as the rapper flitted between sonic styles on the mixtape. Things started off brashly, with sampling "Intro: Dt sugA" introducing his alternate persona, Agust D, in a way reminiscent of BTS's first-ever intro track from *2 Cool 4 Skool*; it also featured DJ Friz, just like that early BTS song. The album worked its way through a series of emotions, ending on the final notes of "So Far Away," a dreamy electro-rock tune featuring Suran's rich vocals that would later be re-released featuring Jin and Jungkook.

A testament to Suga's artistry, *Agust D* was revolutionary for its intensity and earnestness about life's issues, including the star's struggles with mental illness, as relayed through "The Last." Openly addressing his depression and anxiety, as well as how he sought out medical treatment, the song alluded to having responded "yes" when a doctor asked him if he'd considered self-harm. In the track, the artist reassured

listeners regarding his current state, but also emphasized how his struggles have shaped him. Throughout the album he opens up about the contradictory nature of being an idol rapper, his difficulties at home growing up, an accident during his pre-debut period where he injured his shoulder while working a part-time job, and more. Each of these hardships have led him to where he is now, a major star breaking down barriers in the world.

Along with his *Agust D* album, Suga's released a handful of other tracks over the years. Aside from his early underground days and SoundCloud releases, in 2017 he gained renown as a producer after crafting Suran's award-winning alt-R&B hit "Wine." Then in 2019 he featured on LeeSoRa's "Song Request," and co-wrote Epik High's "Eternal Sunshine," not only confirming his role as a worthy collaborator beyond BTS's work, but also working with two legendary Korean artists, including one of his key musical inspirations. Suga was also featured on Halsey's 2020 Manic album, with the 2019-release "Suga's Interlude" bringing the pair poignantly together to ruminate on dreams. From a hopeful in Daegu to a world star songwriting for those who shaped his love of hip-hop, the glow-up has been real for Min Yoongi, and he's now regarded as one of South Korea's most prominent young songwriters.

SOLO
EFFORTS

J-HOPE

Sweat

BTS's third rapper, J-Hope also came up through the underground hip-hop scene but as a dancer, and grew over the years into his role as a rapper. Ironically enough, he was the first member of BTS to get his own distinct pre-debut solo on a track with a labelmate ahead of the group's formal start in 2013. He appeared on the single "Animal" by Jo Kwon of 2AM, released in 2012 on Jo's *I'm Da One* album. A confident electropop track, J-Hope was credited by his given name Jeong Ho-seok, and performed alongside Jo during his promotional period, delivering a swaggering rap about dominating the stage.

After making his debut as a featured artist, it would take J-Hope another six years to release his mixtape, *Hope World*, though it was preceded by the release of "Verse 1," a remake of "El Chapo" by The Game & Skrillex. Put out in 2015 through the group's SoundCloud, the song was a boisterous trap anthem for J-Hope detailing his success as an artist and member of BTS, all of which he credits to his fans.

He later created a vibrant, funky hip-pop soundscape for his 2018 solo mixtape *Hope World*, which opened with the literary-inspired single "Hope World," featuring references to the Jules Verne character, explorer Captain Nemo who J-Hope told *Time* was his inspiration for starting the album off with a title track through which listeners could begin to explore his *World*, while the album's groovy single "Daydream" similarly referenced Hogwarts from the *Harry Potter* series and *Alice in Wonderland*, as the artist sang about all the dreams he wanted to achieve, ending with the whisper of "wake up" and the sound of an alarm, as if emphasizing that one cannot live without dreams, but nor can one succeed without acting on them.

Throughout the album, the BTS member hopped through genres, expressing his desire to bring hope and happiness to others through songs like the steel drum-utilizing "P.O.P (Piece of Peace)" pt. 1 and getting his groove on in the trap track "Base Line," which revels in J-Hope's time as a dancer, while he and Supreme Boi teamed up on "HANGSANG" to celebrate their successes. The album ended on a typical BTS outro track, "Blue Side," but not before J-Hope dropped "Airplane," a dreamy, breezy tune about the extreme heights his career has taken him to, emphasizing that he's able to travel across the globe thanks to his success. It was later recalled on the *Love Yourself: Tear* track "Airplane, Pt. 2," reflecting on how the group has traveled the globe as musicians spreading their sound and message.

As a testament to J-Hope's artistry, *Hope World* shared a bit more of the star with his fans, putting the spotlight on his distinctly upbeat, forthright worldview.

VOCALISTS

The vocalists of BTS have had less of an opportunity to share their personal styles up to this point, as none have yet released their own albums or widely worked with other artists, however they have released a handful of original songs outside of BTS's discography.

JIN

Along with a variety of covers and remakes, Jin was featured with V on the song "It's Definitely You" for the *Hwarang* television show soundtrack in 2016. It marked the first time the pair, or any member of BTS, had been featured in a Korean television show soundtrack (aka K-drama OST), and emphasized the contrast between the pair's tones: V, who appeared in the show, fronted the jazzy pop-rock track with his breathy, deep tone while Jin's sweet mellow flow parried with it, with the pair joining together to expressively declare their love. "It's Definitely You" put a new emphasis on Jin's crisp vocals, showing fans another side to his musicality beyond the BTS repertoire.

In June 2019, Jin released his first non-album solo track, the tender ballad "Tonight" as part of that year's *Festa* celebrations. Shared through SoundCloud, he evocatively sang about his affection for his pet sugar gliders and dog, including those who had passed away. Tender and heartfelt, it was a sweet, emotive tune that shared a bit more of the BTS member's life with his audience.

Sweat

V

V has released three original songs on BTS's SoundCloud account, "4 O'Clock" with RM, "Scenery," and the English-language "Winter Bear." Each of the songs are expressive ballads through which the vocalist's sweet baritone tone breathily relays his romantic emotions. "Scenery," which arrived at the end of January 2019, drew on his long-term passion for photography, with shutter clicks incorporated into the soft, orchestral instrumental melody, which is driven predominantly by piano and strings. Forlorn and evocative, it has a similar feel to "4 O'Clock" with that collaboration featuring a bit more of a pop-rock melody as V's tone and RM's blend together to reflectively express their contemplative feelings right around dawn, as the sky begins to turn blue. "Winter Bear," meanwhile, arrived in August 2019 and was an ambient track about wanting to spend good days with a loved one, with him wishing the listener a cozy night's sleep. Each song wrapped listeners in V's warm tone, as he painted sonic pictures full of warmth and love.

JIMIN

A self-composed song, Jimin's "Promise" arrived on the last day of 2018 (in South Korea) as a source of comfort. In a V Live in January a few weeks after its release, he revealed that the mellow tune was originally dark and featured negativity aimed at himself, but as the months passed and he worked on it, his mood shifted and he was inspired to write something more positive. Inspired by the feelings he had while performing at Citi Field, the gentle acoustic guitar melody and his sweet tone join together in the inspirational track. "I had the thought while performing at Citi Field that I wanted to make a promise to myself," he said. "Even if life makes things difficult, I won't make things difficult for myself. I won't insult myself."[34]

JUNGKOOK

Jungkook is yet to release an original solo effort but has released many covers over the years. He's performed and shared renditions of songs by some of his favorite artists, like Justin Bieber and IU on YouTube, and gained a lot of attention for his cover of BIGBANG's "If You" on *The King of Masked Singer* television show in 2016. His covers have even led to collaborations, with a joint performance between BTS and Charlie Puth during the 2018 MBC Plus X Genie Music Awards of "We Don't Talk Anymore."

OTHER SONGS OF INTEREST BY BTS

Pre-debut collaborations as BTS:

"Ashes"
by Lim Jeong-hee
FEATURING BTS

"Love U, Hate U"
by 2AM
FEATURING BTS

"Bad Girl"
by Lee Hyun
FEATURING BTS AND GLAM

"Because I'm a Foolish Woman"
by Kan Mi-youn
FEATURING BTS

"Song To Make You Smile"
by Lee Seung-gi
FEATURING BTS AND HAREEM

"Perfect Christmas"
by RM, Jungkook, Jo Kwon, Lim Jeong-hee, and Joo Hee of 8Eight

NON-ALBUM SINGLES

"Come Back Home"
2017

A remake of Seo Taiji and Boys' 1995 hit, "Come Back Home" emphasized BTS's role as the latest in the musical lineage that started with Seo Taiji and Boys, who are considered the precursors to modern K-pop. The song was released as part of a special album full of remakes by popular artists in commemoration of Seo's 25th year in the music industry.

"Withseoul"
2017

A promotional track released through the official Visit Seoul tourism website. A music video showing off BTS interacting with the city was later released.

"Waste It On Me"
BY STEVE AOKI, 2018

A collaborative track featuring RM and Jungkook as representatives of the group, it is notably the first song released under the name BTS that was sung entirely in English. A music video featuring many Asian-American stars was later released in what was considered a major win for diversity.

"Ddaeng"

2018

Released as part of BTS's 2018 *Festa* celebrations, "Ddaeng" is one of the most important non-album tracks from BTS, and a fan favorite for all that it encompasses about BTS's legacy. Featuring traditional instrumentals, it's a song that draws on the legacy of BTS's rap line's cyphers, the frequent use of wordplay, and their identity as a hip-hip idol group that takes inspiration from the lives and identities of the very Korean members, who have regularly incorporated their pride in being Korean into their discography.

Using the term "Ddaeng" to mean several different things, including but not limited to school bells, wrongness or ending, a type of play in the Korean card game go-stop (also known as *hwatu*), and more, the rap line take their haters to task, asserting that they—BTS—are "three-eight," or the best, unbeatable move in *hwatu* regardless of what others are saying about them. The numerous meanings are interspersed throughout the raps, with each witty turn of phrase driving home the main point of the song: BTS are thankful for the animosity expressed towards them, since it's helped foster their passion and simultaneously bolstered them because only those who are worthy of attention get naysayers. RM even mentions that rappers without haters should be quiet, as only those who are worthwhile have naysayers. Throughout "Ddaeng," the trio seem to refer to real-life criticism they've heard as they each get their own chance to rap, riffing on different rap styles as they languidly taunt those who were wrong about BTS.

LOVING YOURSELF THE BTS WAY

3

BTS & THEIR ARMY

**Chapter
Thirteen**

When Drake took to the stage at the 61st Grammy Awards on February 10, 2019, to accept his trophy for "God's Plan" being named the best rap song of 2018, he had a message for every music-lover out there, subtly criticizing the long-standing representation and diversity issues stemming from the awards and the music industry in general: "You've already won if you have people singing your songs word for word, if you're a hero in your hometown," he said, before the Grammys cut him off for speaking publicly during the live broadcast against trophies and awards in favor of valuing listeners. "Look, if there's people who have regular jobs who are coming out in the rain, in the snow, spending their hard-earned money to buy tickets to come to your shows, you don't need this [trophy] right here. I promise you, you already won."

Though his speech was cut short, it had an impact, and was particularly relevant to BTS—who were in attendance to present the best R&B album to H.E.R.—and their fan ARMY. Drake's message felt especially apropos when applied to a group whose following had propelled them to the top of the international music scene. When BTS and Big Hit named their fandom "A.R.M.Y" back in 2013, it was prophetic regarding the scale and impact their fans would have on their career.

An acronym for "Adorable Representative M.C. [master of ceremonies or, alternatively, mic controller, both used to refer to rappers, and also spelled emcee] for Youth," BTS's ARMY are quite unlike any force ever seen before. While one can point to Beatlemania's effects on fans, Lady Gaga's Little Monsters, Taylor Swift's Swifties, EXO's EXO-L, One Direction's Directioners, Girls' Generation's S♡NE, Beyoncé's Beyhive, and so on as examples of fandoms that have affected the careers of their favorites through developing a proactive fan culture, ARMY's role in BTS's career is something different again. This is because BTS and ARMY grew up in a time of social media, connecting artists and fans of all kinds across the globe, and both ARMY and BTS took advantage of this. Brought together by their love for a seven-member group from Seoul, ARMY has not only created its own fan culture and bolstered BTS's career, they have taken on a co-creator role. If BTS and Big Hit Entertainment are two points of a triangle surrounding the group's success, then ARMY are the third part of the holy trinity of Bangtan.

The beauty of fandom in the digital age is that you can connect with people from across the globe who share your love and with whom you have something in common. In this case, ARMY's shared creed is the love of BTS. Regardless of where you live, the language you speak, and what else you believe, if you find yourself enthralled by BTS, their music, and all they have achieved, then you, too, can become part of what is currently one of the most active communities in the world. Its members are spread far and wide across the globe, but everyone in ARMY is connected.

Though not all ARMY activity takes place in online interactions, BTS's following is most active in digital spaces. The *lingua franca* is typically Korean or English, but many geographic factions pop up as local fans bond together over further aspects of shared identity. Though BTS are immensely popular across social media platforms and they have official accounts, the group and Big Hit primarily interact with audiences on Twitter and that's where ARMY traditionally keeps its base, as it is the most direct way to share BTS-associated content immediately, although pools of ARMY are found just about everywhere across the Internet. Twitter is widely acknowledged as ARMY's playground, where they trend hashtags daily worldwide in relation to BTS, the members, their activities, their music, ARMY, Big Hit Entertainment, and many other related entities.

Though there is no way to truly count how many hundreds of thousands if not millions of fans BTS have, on social media platforms at least one thing is clear: on Twitter and Tumblr, since 2017, BTS have been the single most talked-about artist each year. They are discussed more than news topics and even the likes of Donald J. Trump, across the globe in terms of social media interactions, and it's all due to the passion of their fans. And this may be one of the most important, unique elements of ARMY: the fandom acts as a form of social media marketing for BTS.

When people log on to Twitter, Facebook, Tumblr, Instagram, Weibo, or Naver, see something trending, and don't know what it is, they often look at it. Even if they don't, when the same, associated terms trend regularly, it's time to take note. And that's exactly what many people have done, and reacted accordingly. In a day and age where social media is the prevalent form of advertising and gaining traction is key, being the most talked-about topic of the day, and year, is a major selling point. And by bolstering BTS's career with constant trends on American-oriented social media sites as they cheered on various career points, ARMY single-handedly made the septet one of the most marketable entities on social media; since BTS entered *Billboard*'s Social 50 ranking at No. 1 on October 29, 2016, at the time of writing they haven't ever dropped below No. 2, and have spent well over 150 weeks at No. 1, revealing immense momentum in digital spheres.

The power of fan mobilization to support and promote their faves—ARMY regularly prep social media hashtags in advance of an event so that all fans know to use the same hashtag—and garner attention in different markets has played a major role in BTS's career, with ARMY fighting tooth and nail for the group, their music, and their efforts to be acknowledged.

One such example was when Stateside Twitter fanbases contacted radio stations and requested that they play BTS songs and promote their albums, with *Yonhap*[35] reporting that *Love Yourself: Her*, the group's first album to rank in the Top 10 of the Billboard 200 chart, saw a particular push in this way from ARMY. By making industry insiders recognize that BTS's fans were not just digital pixels but actual people with spending power, ARMY were able to make America's media scene take note of what many had perceived to be a small, Internet-based niche. Although the group only saw minimal radio play in the U.S. during the *Love Yourself* era, it was a start at breaking into the heavily guarded American music market, through which most listeners become familiar with new acts.

Like a populist movement taking to the streets, ARMY taking to communication channels en masse, of their own free will and without pay, shook the American media scene, demonstrating how little comprehension there was in the West of the size of the group's fandom. This activity resulted in a general reshuffle of the American music industry, as media entities realized that BTS was just one of many acts coming out of Asia with a significant following in the U.S., leading to a flurry of pushes, both from Korean companies and American ones, to try and re-create BTS's traction. Fittingly, by the end of 2018, many more Korean and Chinese acts started pivoting into the U.S. market, opening up a 2019 Asian concert touring season in the country unlike anything it had ever seen. At the same time, streaming services and media platforms increasingly aimed to grow in Asian markets. Forging a path into the Western market for an increasing number of Asian acts, BTS have changed the way that the largest music industry in the world is approaching international music, although no other Asian artists aiming for the English-language music world have yet been able to gain even a small fraction of the popularity BTS have built up naturally.

Fandoms, particularly fandoms built around boy bands, have been underestimated for decades in the U.S., most notably when the Beatles were initially marketed as a group primarily targeting young women. "Sorry girls, he's married," read the screen on *The Ed Sullivan Show* when John Lennon appeared during the Beatles' first Stateside television performance on February 9, 1964.

This condescending attitude to the audience, which was indeed primarily female, was not only a disservice to the Beatles and their music but also to their tastemaking listeners who had, like fans of BTS and countless other boy bands, made the music world take note of quality artists via their intense dedication. It wasn't just about their sex appeal. Since the earliest days of mass media, good looks and sensual appeal have been part of entertainers' armories, but the quality of the music still matters. By not giving credence to female-dominated fandoms of male artists as tastemakers but instead assuming that it is lust, not listening, that makes them fans, the music world does a great disservice to a good portion of the world's population.

It's the music itself and the impressive coordination of the fans that have been responsible for BTS's success. "ARMY" isn't just a nickname. In a fandom of this scale, there are dedicated commanders tracking BTS's career and records, with numerous accounts on social media devoted to promoting the group to their hundreds of thousands, if not millions, of followers. Many proscribe goals and guides to ARMY, setting new and bigger aims for each BTS comeback for followers to help the group achieve a new record with each step of their career. Whether they're on Instagram, Tumblr or Weverse, sharing photos or fan art, or running Twitter accounts that track streams of BTS's music videos, or creating YouTube videos that provide translations, ARMY are some of the most active netizens of this day and age.

While their audience is largely concentrated in the U.S.,[36] BTS fans are difficult to stereotype: anyone can fall for the group and support the septet in their own way, whether it's casually listening to "Fire" on their daily commute or coordinating fundraisers to celebrate a member's birthday. There are ARMY communities and accounts dedicated to bringing together older fans, LGBTQ+ fans, black fans, Latinx fans, Muslim fans, male fans, and more. Like any community, different groupings of fans don't necessarily all agree on how to achieve their goal—loving and supporting BTS—but ultimately, it is the combined ARMY that BTS acknowledge for their success. In a day and age when everyone and everything is subject to questioning, BTS have provided a forum in which fans from around the globe can rally and share their thoughts. There are plenty of opinions

Fandoms, particularly fandoms built around boy bands, have been underestimated for decades in the U.S.

on how to be part of ARMY and, as in many digital communities, there is often infighting over how to be the best ARMY you can be. Perhaps the biggest argument within ARMY is whether or not you can wholeheartedly support BTS while supporting any other K-pop group, as many ARMY don't believe BTS to be part of the K-pop paradigm any longer but "Beyond The Scene." This conversation surrounding K-pop versus "BTSpop" has in turn opened up numerous discussions about BTS's place in the South Korean music scene and the future of Korean music in the English-language market.

Fandom squabbles and debates aside, ARMY is generally quite set in its ways of behaving towards the seven men that they love, and, when it matters, ARMY have never failed to support BTS to the best of their ability. And BTS have showered ARMY with love in return, thanking their fandom regularly, and creating a wide range of material and content to entertain fans, ranging from terms of endearment like "I purple you" replacing "I love you," and the annual *Festa* and Muster events.

Along with creating a community of supporters and working as an unofficial marketing arm for BTS, ARMY serves another essential purpose: translating BTS's words and work into other languages. Whereas it is increasingly more typical for K-pop groups, including BTS, to upload translations of their lyrics to YouTube music videos in other languages—often English but increasingly others as well—and occasionally V Live livestreams will get official subtitles, for years K-pop-related content has largely been translated by fans, with many "fansub," or fan translator accounts popping up over the years. In multiple interviews, including one in 2018, Bang Si-hyuk reportedly credited BTS's success to the dedication of fan translators, saying, "The fandom was able to grow because videos related to BTS were translated into many different languages and posted to sites

like YouTube or Twitter in real time."[37] It is this last bit that seems particularly important: the ability of ARMY to support BTS "in real time" via translations, and it is made possible by the media landscape in which BTS exists.

Before social media became such a prevalent aspect of people's daily lives, accessible at any moment of the day or night, K-pop fandoms were dominated by a series of fanbases, with fansubbers joining together to translate particular content, like episodes of television shows on which acts appeared, or blog posts. But it wasn't until the mid-2010s that K-pop fans began to translate every word and phrase uttered in public by their favorite acts, translations that were more accessible than ever before thanks to social media and digital streaming platforms making content instantly available to international fans. The early days of YouTube saw famous Korean television shows spliced into eighths and famously hidden behind symbols so that fans in the know could find them but algorithms and copyrights wouldn't remove them (such as popular shows like *Strong Heart* (2009–2013) being famously posted on YouTube in parts with names like, "$+r0n5 h34r+ 1/8"). By the time BTS was formed in 2013, Korean content had already started systematically filtering through into English-language audiences, through sites like DramaFever, Viki, Hulu, and Netflix legally licensing Korean television shows even as Korean television stations and entertainment companies were beginning to upload content, only occasionally adding subtitles on YouTube. Fanbases adapted to this evolving media scene: as official content was made available more quickly to international audiences, so, too, did fansubbers have to keep up with the increase in information. By the late 2010s, just as BTS were beginning to peak with the *HYYH* series, it was the norm among K-pop fandoms to have multiple fanbases translating content for fans in varieties of languages, whether on Twitter or Tumblr. BTS's fans were particularly active in this, and in translating in real time.

Online presences reflect the numbers of offline fans—and few fandoms can compare in scale to BTS's ARMY in digital spaces. BTS are the leader of a generation of K-pop groups whose fandoms are dominated by social media. When discussing K-pop, the idea of "generations" often comes up, and there's a lot to be discussed when considering which generation of K-pop we are currently experiencing: first-generation acts of the '90s and early '00s set the groundwork, while those of the second generation in the '00s and early '10s helped it spread throughout the globe. The third generation of the '10s led,

280

and continues to lead, K-pop to become a global phenomenon, and the burgeoning fourth generation is likely to see it continue to reign and become further enmeshed with global music.

Ultimately, however, each "K-pop generation" is not only defined by its trends and successes, but was formed and actualized more by the media in which these artists operated more than anything else. Whereas the first generation of K-pop idoldom was primarily analog—with the groups of the '90s and early '00s relegated to television, VHS, and radio in South Korea and, later, throughout Asia—by the time the mid-00s kicked off the digital era had arrived, and by 2009 K-pop had firmly made itself known as a musical entity that thrived in spaces like YouTube and social media platforms, steadily growing its presence throughout Asia.

BTS, who arrived in 2013, came just as social media platforms truly began to hit their stride internationally. Whereas social media platforms in the mid-00s and early '10s were primarily based around individuals' personal lives and peer groups, by the mid-10s, social media habits had changed and had become such a functional part of people's daily lives that they naturally led to a shift in fandom behavior and, fittingly, over the past half-decade or so, there has been a notable shift in fandom interactions rising to the mainstream where fan behaviors, formally considered geeky or nerdy, have now become part of the mainstream culture throughout the world, and fan communities are now stronger and more impactful than ever.

Though not necessarily unique to fans of K-pop, ARMY's passion and drive coincided with improvements in technology and the streaming age. These combined to create the perfect storm of a growing fandom that worked together to bring access to fans from across the globe, and made it almost seamless for fans, both those familiar with the K-pop industry and new fans who had never encountered it before, to get BTS-related content almost instantaneously. Rather than have to wait months, weeks, days, or even hours, ARMY's hard work and dedication meant that fans could actively participate, via commentary, in events taking place across the world at a moment's notice. This communal, conversational element of ARMY is perhaps one of the most significant elements in the fandom's ascent beyond that of other K-pop followings: inadvertently, small conversations would grow like wildfire among ARMY, where even a single day without any BTS updates feels lacking. While previous generations tuned in to radio shows to hear the latest songs or turned on the TV at a certain time each week to get a new episode of a program, in the digital age when everything is at your fingertips, BTS,

BTS & their ARMY

281

via ARMY mobilization, have become one of those Must-Not-Miss entities that seemingly everybody is talking about.

Even beyond BTS themselves, the culture surrounding the group has spread: fan creations like artwork, games, and fan fiction are immensely popular among ARMY, and in January 2018, a single Twitter-based work of fan fiction titled *Outcast* trended worldwide on Twitter as fans of BTS tuned in daily for real-time updates from the author, known only by the Twitter handle @flirtaus, to see how the story would progress. Other social media accounts have similarly dominated ARMY attention, gaining followers for their creative, charitable, educational, and other efforts related to BTS and ARMY.

ARMY, especially Stateside ARMY, have been particularly active in spreading the gospel of BTS, using social media as a tool to bring the group's message to more people. In the early days when BTS weren't yet selling out arenas, their fans were creating a community based around the idea of bolstering BTS by the simplest of digital currencies: engagement. Just as BTS took to Twitter to talk to fans, so too did fans take to social platforms to tell people about BTS and what they love about their music. Fortuitously, almost by accident, as the group's musicality developed and their fandom grew, these conversations developed on a massive scale, and eventually led to the social media landscape that saw BTS gain presence in just about every corner of the worldwide web. Most notably, a person might be casually looking through YouTube, and the comment section, often ones of behind the scene, or "bts," footage, would contain something along the lines of, "Any ARMY here?" By reaching out to find one another, ARMY rapidly created a tight bond and became the foot soldiers of BTS's message to the world. They would participate en masse in voting campaigns for events that digital media platforms were hosting; trend hashtags to celebrate birthdays and music releases; create streaming guides; reach out to individuals, asking them to support BTS; and more. ARMY would do what BTS and Big Hit couldn't: quite naturally they became the street team on social media for BTS in a way that no other fandom had ever done to such a degree.

When considering why it was BTS and not any other band—K-pop or otherwise—out there that saw such immense online fervor, there are likely many elements involved beyond the group's musicality and innate charm. But a few specific things helped: firstly, the group's underdog narrative, as a group that exists within an industry but beyond its mainstream, is appealing to many, particularly in the U.S., where authenticity is valued intensely even in a day and age when few artists get to the top of the industry without corporate help. Having

282

Tears

gone through struggles like ordinary people and weaving that into their musical identity, BTS were more accessible to new fans at a time of growing political discontent when love songs alone don't cut it. With a hip-hop focus, the most popular genre of the streaming age, they could similarly resonate with more audiences than general, poppish boy bands, so even when they would later veer towards trendier pop sounds it felt like it was coming from a place of authentic, artistic growth, which in turn led to their fandom increasing.

And as the group's following grew, so, too, did fans' fervor. It was important for ARMY to listen to songs on release day. It was important to buy multiple copies of albums. It was important for ARMY to engage in social media conversations. By doing so, they were showing up and showing others that ARMY exist, and that ARMY exist because BTS are worthy of fans. And, eventually ARMY became so ample in size that it was impossible to miss their expressions of love in their various activities supporting and promoting BTS and their music.

BTS will now forever be known as the barometer of success for all Asian musicians in the U.S. While Psy once held that distinction, BTS blew the viral hitmaker out of the water, instead proving that time, patience, and communication between fans and artists could eventually pay off. Which means that the pressure is very, very real for BTS and ARMY to continue proving their worth. It is not enough that BTS have the best-selling South Korean album of all time in the form of *Map of the Soul: Persona*; there is always room to grow. Yes, they topped the Billboard 200 three times, but maybe they can do it a fourth. Or a fifth. They got a No. 1 in the UK with *Map of the Soul: Persona*;[38] maybe they can get another. Maybe they can top every world music chart at once. Maybe they can be the first Korean group to win a Grammy. Whatever the case, ARMY's support of the group has enabled BTS to become the unmitigated benchmark of success when it comes to breaking into the Western market. ARMY are BTS's *Wings*, and they're dedicated to seeing how far they can help the group continue to soar.

When considering this passion, it's important to recognize that, like BTS's name itself, the name "ARMY" has multiple meanings. First, there's the literal meaning of the acronym: "Adorable Representative M.C. for Youth." Broken down, it essentially translates to an "adorable" fandom related to hip-hop and youth culture, a counterpart to BTS's suave hip-hop and youth-oriented concept. But taking a step back, the acronym itself, "A.R.M.Y," the term that both BTS and fans use rather than the long version, reflects a specific idea. BTS's fandom is called after a sizable military unit made up of a variety of different elements and peoples, each smaller legion built upon different needs, and it can be either a powerful force of protection or expansion, which similarly ties in to BTS's very own ethos of protecting and serving as the Bulletproof Boy Scouts. And BTS's fandom, with their ARMY bomb lightsticks in hand, has lived up to each of these elements at different points of the band's career, as ARMY have helped to expand BTS's reach via guerilla marketing, as is now popular in the social media age, and helped to protect the band from dangers, whether its competition, naysayers, or bad news. With multitudes of fans willing and able, ARMY are the writers, fact-checkers, and editors of BTS's narrative as it spreads throughout the world, with fans ready to set the BTS story straight as per the ARMY narrative at every opportunity so that new audiences learn what it means to truly love and know BTS, their music, and their career.

And, of course, aside from all the digital elements of ARMY and their telling of the BTS story, there are also the offline elements, which ultimately lead back to the online ones. BTS's ARMY are immensely capable at coming out and supporting the group not only from behind screens but also offline, whether it's selling out concert tours throughout the world, buying millions of copies of albums, creating charity funds donated in members' names, or buying ads in Times Square to celebrate BTS's members' birthdays. To be a member of BTS's ARMY is to be part of a whole world, and as they walk the path of Bangtan, fans are able to carve out their own direction.

ARMY have BTS's back, and BTS have recognized this time and time again. They are two halves of a whole, or two-thirds if Big Hit's team and the rest of the creatives BTS work with are considered, and there is a bond there that ties together the septet and their millions of fans around the world. Though BTS might never know each individual fan's name, they know their collective name: you can call BTS idols, you can call them artists, but their fans have one name, and that is ARMY.

BTS BREAKS
THE INTERNET

Chapter
Fourteen

When BTS appeared at the Billboard Music Awards on May 21, 2017, to receive their first Top Social Artist award, it was a huge moment. In their first true introduction to Western television audiences, the group of seven men stood up on the stage and RM gave an acceptance speech—and most viewers had no idea who they were. The group had little, if any, radio play prior to their appearance at the 2017 BBMAs, and if you weren't tuned in to streaming platforms or social media sites, there was little to make you aware of who BTS were and what their impact was. But standing on stage, beating out Justin Bieber for the social media-based award, one thing was clear: even if people offline didn't know who the group was, they were being talked about in digital realms, which are more expansive and far-reaching and enable the kinds of dialogue that would never be possible offline.

In the modern age, social media presence is a form of currency, and few can compete with the wealth amassed by BTS, at least across American-based social media platforms such as Twitter, Instagram, and Tumblr. On those sites and others, the septet dominated conversations throughout 2016–2020 and were the most talked-about music group/general entity. BTS's rise in digital spaces grew out of the group's own inclination to use social media as a way to connect with audiences across the world. Abetted by technological advancements, BTS experimented throughout the years and became dedicated to different media platforms, most prominently Twitter and YouTube, and in later years Naver's livestreaming app, V Live, as a way to share their career and daily lives with fans. Eventually Big Hit released its own Weverse, or community, app for its artists and fans to communicate on directly. These brief windows into BTS's world are a key factor in the act's appeal, with the septet sharing elements of themselves and fans reveling in this access point into the lives of their faves.

BTS have used social media to connect and open up their world to ARMY in a variety of ways. Even before their debut, the group was active on Twitter, sharing aspects of their trainee life with audiences. The official account shared by the seven men (@BTS_twt) was opened in July 2011, and BTS's first recorded tweet is dated December 17, 2012. Translated from the original Korean, it reads: "Wassup! We're BTS. Finally, the BTS Twitter account is official open ~ Clap clap clap! We will be uploading fun things beyond your imagination here until our debut." That same day, RM's "닥투" (shorthand for the phrase "닥치고 투표" or "shut up and vote"), an inflammatory track urging people to vote or stop complaining about societal ills, was uploaded to the group's BANGTANTV YouTube channel as their first video.

"Beyond your imagination," indeed. The phrase might as well have been the group's slogan rather than "Teamwork makes the dreamwork," which they tweeted on March 19, 2013, and has become a rallying cry of both the group and ARMY. But BTS truly were setting off on a career that would lead them, and the global music scene, to a place that would have been hard for anyone reading that tweet to imagine back at the end of 2012.

Over the years, the band grew to utilize Twitter as their primary mode of interaction with international ARMY, sharing snippets of their daily lives via pictures, short posts, and screenshots, and occasionally directly engaging with fans.

At the start of their career, BTS were, and remain, one of numerous Korean groups to utilize social media on non-Korean platforms while simultaneously connecting with local fans through official blogs, fancafes, and other localized sites. But, given the limited potential of the Korean music market as a revenue source, getting a message across to both Korean and international fans through globalized social media platforms is important for anyone hoping to connect with international audiences. This is one of the primary reasons that K-pop stars have public social media accounts across a variety of platforms. Facebook and Instagram were dominant areas for K-pop companies to focus their attention on, as on the former they could share vast quantities of information at once, whether it was text, videos, or images; for briefer updates, Instagram was better. Tumblr was largely seen as a site for fans, not public persons or companies. Twitter, however, was still relatively unpopular among celebrities at the start of BTS's career, used more as a news aggregation app than anything else, but it proved to be the ideal outlet for BTS and ARMY.

While the group have never explicitly discussed why Twitter works best for them, the platform allows for a different kind of conversation than other internationally focused platforms do. Facebook is largely seen as a personal platform, for people to interact with those to whom they are closely connected, and both Instagram and Tumblr are limited in their conversational aspects. However, Twitter is a fast-paced platform where micro-conversations can be had with anyone from across the globe. Facebook was either too intimate or too corporate a platform and Instagram was too limited in scale, with the comment section on posts hardly facilitating lengthy dialogue or sharing. Twitter gave BTS the opportunity to essentially throw conversation starters out into the world, and decide to participate in these discussions if they so desired. It was brief, but conversational. Active with updates that engage fans, BTS use Twitter as a multi-faceted, real-time, dialogue-oriented window through which ARMY can see into their lives and careers.

One important element of BTS's Twitter usage is that it distinctly separates the seven men and their career: the group itself operates the @BTS_twt account, whereas @bts_bighit is the official BTS-associated account run by their company, which also operates @BigHitEnt. Each of the three accounts operates differently, providing different sorts of updates. But for that fleeting sense of intimacy that social media platforms enable influencers to share with their followers in the digital age, it is the account operated by the septet themselves that fans turn to, as the others are primarily business-oriented.

An important element of BTS's Twitter account is that it truly belongs to BTS as a whole. Rather than each member having an individual account, BTS's identity as a cohesive unit was introduced and perpetuated through their Twitter account, sharing not only their career but also their individual voices with the world. Each member made use of the platform, sharing moments from their lives. Over the years, the conversation became more one-sided as their popularity grew and it was impossible to truly engage with fans, but the sense of connection via social media is a major one for BTS and ARMY.

The group's YouTube videos and, in latter years, Naver's V Live, are similarly forums through which the seven men of BTS connect with their fans, though in a more planned, coordinated way. Partially entertainment, partially an informative look at BTS's behind-the-scenes workings, the group shared hundreds of videos throughout their early career, offering ARMY a look at their dynamic and what makes them tick—usually with random, hilarious shenanigans involved. Through their BANGTANTV channel, BTS were able to utilize the power of YouTube to reach their fans directly, in comparison to the limited opportunities available through traditional broadcast media. Not only did traditional media limit their direct access primarily to South Korean audiences, but coverage was hard to come by in the early days of their career.

In the relaxed, self-curated environment of BANGTANTV, BTS could show different sides of themselves. But, tellingly, the very first video upload to BTS's group YouTube channel wasn't an introduction to the act, or one of the humorous behind-the-scenes clips they often share. Instead, the first video available was the aforementioned political song by RM, "Shut Up and Vote." The song, a cover of Kanye West's

"Power," is the BTS rapper's message to listeners to use the small amount of power that's granted to them in society to make a difference, and to go out and vote. As the launching point for BTS's presence on YouTube, this was significant as it was immediately clear that this was a group with an impactful socio-political message for listeners.

"Shut Up and Vote" was one of several videos released ahead of BTS's debut by the members, with all but V—the "hidden" member of the group, only revealed just before the act's first album came out—sharing behind-the-scenes videos of themselves working on their performances and skills, and introducing themselves to their audience. After the group debuted, they started a variety of series, most prominently *Bangtan Bomb* and *Episode*; the former are brief videos of the group ostensibly doing whatever, often having fun and playing around with one another, and the latter takes fans behind the scenes of performances or projects the group was working on or had just released. Other things, like *Eat Jin*, Jin's *mukang* series, and *Hope on the Street*, where J-Hope shares his dances, have also been featured, and over the years the group's members have shared a whole range of content.

Like their Twitter account, BANGTANTV was set up as a different sort of platform from Big Hit Entertainment's formal YouTube channel, where the group's official content was released. This was, essentially, a channel for the group, by the group. While many videos were coordinated, and often filmed, by staff, it helped create yet another connection between BTS and their fans, and in later years Jungkook began sharing his G.C.F videos. Like YouTubers who gain followings by letting audiences watch their daily lives and hear their thoughts, BANGTANTV provided further insights into the men of BTS. It was a place for BTS to be humans, rather than idols. It served as a more down-to-earth counterpart to their official music video content and appearances on television, showing the men of BTS to be just average teenagers and twentysomethings having fun with one another rather than professionally marketing themselves to audiences through glossy music videos.

Though they are not the only K-pop artists to make use of streaming platforms as a way to showcase their identity and career, BTS were innovative in their approach of creating a distinct brand on BANGTANTV, providing easy access to the sort of content fans want, namely a behind-the-scenes look at BTS's career and lives. Though their counterparts in the industry typically had to wait until the next promotional cycle to appear on television, BTS took content directly to fans, and have set a standard in the industry as more and more

K-pop acts turn to YouTube and livestreaming, with newer acts dropping multiple videos and airing several livestreams a week, if not in a single day.

As livestreaming became more popular, BTS gradually shifted much of their video content to Naver's V Live app, where the group regularly held sessions in which they spoke to fans about their work. Things like live post-album release videos, where the members address the inspiration behind their latest new music, became a normal occurrence rather than the pre-recorded ones previously uploaded to YouTube, and the group even started *Run BTS*, a weekly variety series where the members typically participate in challenges and competitions to receive prizes or punishments. V Live also served up another reality series, the travelogue *Bon Voyage*, where the septet are seen traveling to different countries.

Through these videos and, to a lesser degree, televised appearances, BTS steadily grew their fanbase, which turned to the group's social media platforms as a way to be both entertained and to learn more about the men with whom they felt such a bond. As BTS became more popular, each of their social media platforms began to attract huge numbers of fans: the band's @BTS_twt account, the official BTS account, and Big Hit Entertainment have the three most-followed Twitter accounts in South Korea as of June 2019, and their V Live channel became the first channel on the site to surpass 10 million subscribers in August 2018.

This sharing of every step of their careers with fans via videos and social media posts, whether it's the inspiration behind an album or something as simple as the song they're listening to at the moment or a picture they've taken that they think fans might like, is integral to the group's success. BTS share a part of themselves through social media and successfully market their identity as a relatable, hardworking boy band to millions of fans worldwide who are ready to cheer them on and support them. There is nothing arrogant about their social media posts: everything about BTS appears to be driven by their hard work and relatability, their love of music and their love for fans. While they are certainly entertainers and there is always an element of curation to their posts—after all, social media culture in the modern age is largely about showing off the best version of oneself to the world, often with the intent to monetize a following—everything about the way BTS tells their own story through social media posts and videos comes across as earnest and wholesome. They are idols, here to entertain, with income to earn—and Big Hit Entertainment's website homepage explicitly calls fans "customers" in recognition of this—but they're also young men setting out to have a good time. They are artists sharing their music; they're also tastemakers sharing their inspirations. Throughout all of their content, there's a sense of approachability and authenticity. Much of BTS's social media content isn't as tightly curated as is typical of K-pop stars; it feels like something that they want to share with fans in that moment, not because they have to but because they want to. Whether it is a brilliant approach to transmedia marketing or truly reflects the desires of the members doesn't matter: BTS's social media presence has resonated with audiences around the globe, making everyone take note.

It's unfair to BTS, their artistry, and the team of creatives they work with to claim that their success is solely driven by their social media presence, but there is much to be said about how impactful ARMY have been as a way to raise awareness of the group through social media, and the impact that's had on their career. In a day and age when everyone is trying to monetize social media traction, BTS have done just that, almost by accident. By creating content—both their music and their visual content, whether it's the BU narrative, their various videos and music videos, or their social media posts—that simultaneously entertains and resonates with fans, BTS were primed as a Topic of Discussion, and ARMY's digital-based culture of conversing with intent made it thrive beyond digital spaces. Both formal campaigns by ARMY, particularly those based in the U.S., to raise awareness of the group, and general, everyday interactions by ARMY with BTS and related content paid off. Like a game of Telephone, the message got through, as people began to pay attention. All of this momentum led to the moment when the 2017 Billboard Music Awards opted to give out the Top Social Artist award on-air rather than off-air as in the past. Prior to BTS, only Justin Bieber had received the award, and BTS overtaking his record was impressive enough for the BBMAs to bring the septet on air to recognize them for their impressive reach and following. And from then on, people who hadn't been paying attention to BTS took note, and haven't turned away since. That, as much as BTS's musicality, played a role in the group's crossover to become a headline act, resulting in their performing at events like the 2017 American Music Awards, where they were one of the night's final acts, and *Dick Clark's New Year's Rockin' Eve* to ring in 2018. The next year, they would hold stadium shows on multiple continents.

It is worth noting at this point that almost every single appearance by BTS on American television through to the end of 2018 was brought about by Dick Clark Productions, which is owned by the same parent company as *Billboard*, Valence Media, with their charting presence and social media presence simultaneously serving as evidence of the group's popularity to decision makers in Hollywood. Whereas radio play, and, increasingly, streaming counts, have traditionally been gauges of musicians' traction in the U.S., the group's seemingly sudden rise on music charts was bolstered by their widespread fanbase, and their fans' presence in digital spaces. BTS represented a new paradigm of what it means to be "mainstream": they were arguably more popular than just about any other musician across social media platforms, and their music was achieving astronomical sales, yet the average American had never heard of them. They were, quite literally, Beyond The Scene.

Counter-cultural in a way, BTS's digital presence provided them entry into an industry that has often resisted outsiders and continues to struggle with a lack of diversity due to historically racist institutions. With the support of ARMY, BTS demanded attention, and the American music industry could not reasonably ignore them, even though the radio industry by and large overlooked their success, limiting their airtime on traditional radio platforms. It would not be an overnight shift; for years the group was only recognized for social media awards and, at the very end of 2018 with the Grammy Nominations, for their album packaging rather than their music, though in 2019 the members would each individually be invited to join the Recording Academy, which votes for the Grammys. The industry would grapple with wanting BTS's presence to bolster views and social media numbers, but not being quite sure how to deal with a Korean boy band that so thoroughly proved to the American music industry that it was no longer the primary tastemaker of the music universe: in the digital age, fans control narratives in a way that has previously been impossible. Across the board, fans have increasingly proven that their voices can be heard through social media in a way typically limited to mail-in and phone-in campaigns.

Social media proved to be the great equalizer for BTS, showing the industry that geographic boundaries no longer have the impact they once did. The strings of the worldwide web have pulled together cultures and industries in a way that was formerly impossible, and in 2018 this band from South Korea were able to top the Billboard 200 albums charts on two occasions, propelled by dedicated fans, only to repeat the feat again the following year with their next album. Reframing what it means to be popular, there was nothing traditional about BTS's rise, a fitting feat for a group that has spent its career inspiring fans to look critically at the world around them and try to overturn it to become a better place.

MESSAGING THROUGH MUSIC

Chapter Fifteen

Since the start of their career, BTS have had something to say. Matching the ethos of the company under which the band was formed, there is intent flowing throughout BTS's discography as the septet sing and rap their way through a multitude of emotions, serving up artistic music meant to "heal" its listeners.

A lofty goal, the idea of music that serves as sustenance for the soul is typical in South Korea, and is even considered a distinct genre of music. "Healing music" is essentially any inspirational song—often a soft pop ballad—that resonates within your heart of hearts. Within BTS's repertoire, Jin's "Epiphany" from *Love Yourself: Answer* might be considered a typical healing song, as it clearly expresses a sense of understanding and hope, or something like *HYY2*'s "Whalien 52," which relays a sense of hope in the face of loneliness. The group's most famous "healing" song, however, is *You Never Walk Alone*'s "Spring Day." Reflecting on the sorrow of missing someone, "Spring Day" ends on an emotional high, promising that spring will arrive and wipe away the chilly feelings that accompany this visceral lack.

BTS excel at creating songs packed full of meaning; both straightforward messages for the general public, and alternative, hidden meanings that fans can draw from the lyrics. The *Wings* album is a particularly good example, with each of the seven solo tracks serving as both a reference to the BU narrative and an autobiographical look at individual members' states of mind and artistry, while all of their album series spent time exploring dedicated socio-cultural or philosophical themes. BTS are not revolutionary in this; music has always been about touching its listeners' hearts. But coming out of the South Korean pop world, a generally conservative sphere, it has been immensely impactful.

The history of K-pop boy bands using their music as a platform for social criticism is a long one, with the likes of Seo Taiji & Boys, H.O.T, Sechs Kies, g.o.d, Shinhwa, TVXQ!, Super Junior, and other formative acts leaving their listeners not only with dynamic hit songs but also something to think about. But few in the modern era of K-pop made it their group's driving motive and concept. BTS did just this and the septet's music is largely meant to provoke thought. As the years progressed, this intention became more and more pronounced, and by the time the *Love Yourself* series had come around it was a mainstay in BTS's public narrative. Part rebellious advocates against societal ills, part philosophers of love—as well as opposing the industry ills that they've encountered—BTS's identity as they rose to global awareness has been built on the idea that this is a boy band with a purpose. The *Love Yourself* series was the culmination of this, shifting attention directly to the overall intent of BTS's career, with *Map of the Soul* following along to continue this pursuit of using music to understand the world and oneself.

What does it mean to love yourself in this day and age? According to BTS's music, it's getting in touch with one's own deepest, darkest emotions and innermost secrets and taking ownership of them. It's taking pride in your hard times, and revelling in your successes. It's speaking up when you see something wrong in the world. It's becoming an advocate for both yourself and others. At times aggressive, at times sentimental, BTS's music is meant to relay all of this.

And it's not just the music; BTS have continually lived up to their messaging, most prominently with their UNICEF (United Nations Children's Fund) initiatives, though the members and ARMY alike have also been involved with a wide range of charitable giving and donation campaigns. UNICEF has long worked with South Korean entertainers on various initiatives, but BTS were the first to launch their own campaign that tied directly into their artistry. Launched on November 1, 2017, shortly after the release of *Love Yourself: Her*, the Love Myself charity campaign organized by BTS and Big Hit Entertainment was created to support UNICEF's ongoing global #ENDViolence campaign.

#ENDViolence is the U.N. initiative to reduce violence towards young people across all walks of life, whether at home, in school, or in their communities. According to UNICEF,[39] every 7 minutes an adolescent is killed by an act of violence, and over half of the world's teens experience peer violence in or around schools. Millions of children each year face corporal punishment, and, according to a 2014 report from the organization, around 120 million girls under the age of 20, or about 1 in 10, have been forced into sexual intercourse or other forced sexual acts at some point in their lives. Love Myself was created by BTS as a campaign "pursuing love and a better place to live for all" in line with #ENDviolence's aims, and planned to raise funds in a variety of ways over the next two years, including through direct donations from Big Hit and BTS, as well as 3 percent of the income from the physical album sales of the *Love Yourself* series. Upon the anniversary of Love Myself the following November, UNICEF Korea announced that the charity initiative had raised over 1.6 billion KRW, or upwards of 1.4 million USD, and had accrued over 6.7 million uses of the hashtag, #BTSLoveMyself.

298

Along with raising awareness and funds to #ENDviolence, the primary factor behind #LoveMyself was the theme of self-love, which ties directly into the *Love Yourself* series. Throughout its run, the campaign would promote certain hashtags, like #BTSLoveMyself and #ARMYLoveMyself, suggesting that ARMY use them on social media to share what they love about themselves. Regular updates helped reaffirm Love Myself's efforts, and on August 10, 2018, a new post on the Love Myself website offered up words of wisdom from RM, J-Hope, and Suga as they shared ideas on how to internalize the feelings of Love Myself.[40] Suga suggested, "Not comparing myself to others," while RM said, "Telling myself that I'm doing well, and that I love myself," and J-Hope said, "Finding something of my own while doing what I want to do."

Promoting self-love to fans while simultaneously raising funds for a good cause, the Love Myself campaign was only one way that BTS spread their positive messaging through a UNICEF collaboration: the group was given the opportunity to speak at the U.N. on September 24, 2018, during the launch of UNICEF's Generation Unlimited campaign at the U.N.'s 73rd General Assembly. An expansion of previous UNICEF initiatives, Generation Unlimited is aimed at battling "the global education and training crisis currently holding back millions of young people and threatening progress and stability." While UNICEF typically uses its platform to address problems faced by children and adolescents, Generation Unlimited expanded UNICEF's mission to support young adults, and "aims to ensure that every young person is in education, learning, training or employment by 2030."

With RM representing the group, the rapper took to the podium at the U.N. and gave a speech in front of global dignitaries who craft the future. During his speech, dubbed the "Speak Yourself" speech, he reflected on his own life and career, and called for youth around the world to listen to their heart of hearts and become advocates for themselves while carving out their own distinct path in the world.

The self-affirming theme of his speech would carry over into the following year when the group brought the second leg of their *Love Yourself* world tour to stadiums across Asia, Europe, and North America under the name *Speak Yourself.* They then followed it up with the *Map of the Soul* era, expanding the search to self-understanding.

And though both Love Myself and the "Speak Yourself" speech tied directly into the *Love Yourself* era, BTS's depth of messaging outside of their lyrics drew fans in across the eras, and even before their debut. Perhaps most notable was the group's subtle support of

At the heart of everything BTS does is a message about bringing change, whether it's in society or about oneself and one's relationships.

LGBTQ+ relationships, despite it being a taboo topic among most young Korean entertainers. Even prior to the group's career, RM was tweeting positively about same-sex relationships, and in March 2013 he praised Macklemore and Ryan Lewis's "Same Love" for its positive messaging. "This is RM," he wrote on March 6 of that year, just three months before BTS released *2 Cool 4 Skool*. "This song is about same-sex love. It's good even if you don't listen to the lyrics, but if you look at the lyrics and listen it'll make you like the song twice as much." A conversation then took place between RM and Bang Si-hyuk, during which the pair spoke about the song and its message in a positive light. When asked about the tweet and the group's point of view on gay rights in general in 2017 for a *Billboard* cover story, Suga declared, "Everyone is equal."

The idea of equality plays a major role in BTS tracks that address societal ills, particularly with their frequent references to being born with a silver spoon versus a dirty one. But as their career has progressed and they've reached immense heights, the group haven't turned away from this. Instead, along with the Love Myself campaign, they've continued to support causes that are important to them. In 2017, it was reported that the band, with Big Hit Entertainment, had donated 100 million KRW to a charity supporting the families affected by the tragic sinking of the Sewol Ferry in 2014. At the time, Korean media reported[41] that Big Hit had stated the donation was meant to be made privately.

One of the most interesting aspects of BTS's career is the dichotomy between their positive messaging, and that of the intense anger apparent within much of their music. Throughout the act's discography and cinematography, a sense of disgruntlement and outrage with both the world and their own personal experiences, aimed particularly at those who have criticized them and their career paths, is pervasive. From day one, the seven men were protesting ills within society, and each and every album release of theirs since then has featured at least a song or two where they are criticizing either something or someone. Even relaying the romantic, philosophical elements of their *The Most Beautiful Moment in Life*, *Love Yourself*, and *Map of the Soul* eras, many of their songs are full of anger. As they express both love and anger, BTS come across as a Janus of sorts, the two-faced Roman god of beginnings and time, tempestuous in nature.

At the heart of everything BTS does is a message about bringing change, whether it's in society or about oneself and one's own relationships. And changes don't come about by happenstance or complacence but out of intense emotions. Anger is one of those impassioned feelings that help drive change and is innately tied into BTS's career, as they use it as motivation to keep pushing forward to make the world a better place. In February 2019, Bang Si-hyuk reflected on how anger has affected his career and thus his efforts working with BTS during a commencement speech he gave addressing the graduates of Seoul National University, his alma mater and South Korea's most prestigious university.

"I feel that anger has become my calling," he said. "Getting angry for people in the music industry to receive fair evaluation and reasonable treatment, getting angry for unfair criticisms and belittling against artists and fans. Fighting for what I regard as common sense to be realized, is the tribute to music which I loved and was with me for my entire life, as well as in respect and gratitude for fans and artists. And lastly, it's the only way for me to be happy." He went on to explain how anger leads to happiness, as the source of inspiration for him and his artists: "I am happy when my company spreads good influence in the society, and especially gives positive influence to our customers who are young people, helping them create their own world view. Going further, I feel happy when I can be part of changing paradigms of the music industry for development and take part in improving qualities of life of the professionals in this industry. My happiness is when Big Hit and I achieve this kind of change."

Anger as an impetus for change is an important element of being BTS and, by association, ARMY. It is anger with the state of the Korean music industry, where there is widespread corruption and disparity, and with the state of the workforce and student life in the country, where hard work is expected to result in little payoff, and the world at large, that drives much of BTS's messaging. It is anger, essentially, that facilitates all the other emotions they express; by harnessing rage to gain artistic momentum, BTS, and Bang Si-hyuk, are able to turn that energy into something positive. ARMY similarly behaves this way; while large-scale fandoms have a huge potential for toxicity, the intensity comes out of defending and protecting BTS and their message. By streaming en masse, by rallying around and refuting negativity towards the group, by spending time and energy defending BTS in both digital and real-world spaces while simultaneously hyping up every instance of positivity, ARMY are following in BTS's path and taking that anger as a way of approaching the world to benefit BTS. Two sides of one coin, positivity and fury propel BTS's career in a brilliant meshing of energy that has led to one of the most powerful forces this world has ever seen.

Throughout their career BTS have come to represent this wholesome inspiration that fans could look to, not only for emotional support through their music but also for literal guidance regarding how they approach life. Like all great musicians, their artistry has grown beyond a simple form of entertainment to encapsulate the act's worldview and relay it to their listeners, who in turn internalize it. A movement as much as a musical act, BTS's impact will be felt for years to come as fans reassess the way they approach life, using BTS and their music as a lens through which they can shift their worldview.

OUTRO

The question that will forever surround BTS will be: "Why?" Why did they and their music resonate with so many fans across the globe? Why them and not another group?

It's their lyrics. It's their melodies. It's their raps. It's their dancing. It's their bravado. It's their humor. It's their good looks. It's their attitude. It's their message. To the millions of ARMY across the globe, it's all of the above, and so much more. They're the group from South Korea that has continued to push forward with a distinct idea of the type of music they want to share with listeners, and what that music should be about. The group that has closely interacted with fans in a changing, disjointed entertainment environment. The group that has dedicated itself to intense, interactive storytelling that parallels the emotions their songs express, and who have built a whole fictional narrative out of it. The group that has made the impossible possible regardless of international and linguistic barriers, and that now has the attention of the entire world. All of that made BTS an act that drew fans to them, building up a dedicated fan ARMY that has thrived in the digital era when the click of a button could bring them into the daily lives of their favorite stars, and their news could run around the world in a split second.

All of these elements combined at a time when the world was primed and ready for it. Before the rampant spread of social media and the rise of streaming, BTS might not have flourished as they did. But circumstance is a powerful force, and the universe came together to create the perfect balancing act, where BTS's career unfolded at exactly the right moment, with the act learning something from every hardship. A hint of serendipity has permeated BTS's career, where the group's members and those around them came together at the perfect tipping point. Seven men representing different parts of South Korea, each bringing their own personality and distinct artistry into the mix, set off down a path with a talented creative team at their back and an ARMY defending their front.

In an era where information is at your fingertips and people can fly across the globe in a matter of hours, limitations and boundaries that once existed have started to fade away. BTS have succeeded in a way previously unheard of, breaking down walls in the global music scene, and setting all eyes on the South Korean music industry as the world tries to figure out "Why?" In years to come, when we look back on what BTS did, the real answer will be, as it is now, none other than, "Why not?" They put their blood, sweat, and tears into pursuing their goal of making it to the top of the music game and succeeded, because they alone are BTS.

ACKNOWLEDGEMENTS

Thank you to everyone, both named and unnamed, who has supported me throughout the ups and downs of this journey.

As always, thank you G-d for all you give and put before me, and thank you to my family, especially my parents Ira and Dina Herman, who have cheered me on throughout it all. Thank you Sarah Fairhall for being an amazing editor and making this all happen, thank you Josh Getzler and Jon Cobb for representing me at Hannigan Getzler Literary agency, and thank you Katherine Barner for your fact-checking expertise. Thank you to everyone at Billboard and Macaulay Honors College who gave me opportunities to get to this point in my career.

Thank you so much to all of my wonderful friends. I'm so blessed that I have so many, and I know I'm inevitably going to forget a few and be haunted by this forever, so I apologize in advance... Lots of love to Alexis and the entire KultScene family, Anna, Rosanna, Sydney, Jean, Kat, Jenna, Rebecca, Cat, Sandra, my motivator of a roommate Lexi, Mara, Marni, Monique, all of the supremely talented members of the New York K-Pop writers crew, NJF, and so, so many more. You have gifted me such amazing support over the years, whether it was with motivational talks, letting me ramble through a thought, sending me care packages, or coming to my apartment with bagels and a cactus... It's been an honor to discover your friendship and be part of your lives—thank you for letting me in, and thank you for all your love and support.

And last but certainly not least, thank you BTS for everything you have given this world, and for showing us how to spread our wings and fly.

1   Keith Caulfield, "BTS, Selena, The Singing Nun & More: Non-English No.1 Albums on the Billboard 200 Chart," *Billboard: Chartbeat*, June 2, 2018. URL: https://www.billboard.com/articles/columns/chart-beat/8458997/bts-selena-non-english-no-1-albums-on-billboard-200-chart

2   Xander Zellner, "BTS' 'Fake Love' Becomes 17th Primarily Non-English-Language Top 10 on Hot 100," *Billboard: Chartbeat*, May 29, 2018. URL: https://www.billboard.com/articles/columns/chart-beat/8458242/bts-fake-love-17th-primarily-non-english-language-top-10-hot-100

3   Re-uploaded by HCZA89x (@zeng_ann), original source: kbs.co.kr, "130629 KISS THE RADIO with Bangtan Boys," *YouTube*, video, 0:55, June 30, 2013. URL: https://www.youtube.com/watch?v=z9fXjHqyMyY

4   Rapper B-Free's public apology on Twitter, photograph taken by @seoulbeats *Twitter* account, January 26, 2016. URL: https://seoulbeats.com/wp-content/uploads/2016/02/2016_seoulbeats_B-Free.png

5   Tamar Herman, *Billboard*, pub date: December 2019.

6   Gaya, "BTS Highlight Tour 2015: A Rundown of Events," *Seoulbeats*, October 4, 2015. URL: https://seoulbeats.com/2015/10/bts-highlight-tour-2015-a-rundown-of-events/

7   Eric Frankenberg, "BTS Moves 600,000 Tickets in 6 Markets on the Love Yourself: Speak Yourself Tour," *Billboard: Chart Beat*, June 14, 2019. URL: https://www.billboard.com/articles/columns/chart-beat/8516047/bts-600000-tickets-six-markets-love-yourself-speak-yourself-tour

8   Tess Cagle, "BTS just became the first K-pop group to reach No. 1 on U.S. iTunes chart," *The Daily Dot*, November 24, 2017. URL: https://www.dailydot.com/upstream/bts-top-itunes-chart/

9   Hong Dam-young, "President Moon Jae-in congratulates BTS for achieving No. 1 on Billboard 200," *The Korea Herald*, May 29, 2018. URL: http://www.koreaherald.com/view.php?ud=20180529000293

10 Grammy-nominated singer-songwriter Halsey, "BTS," *Time 100* (tribute in honor of BTS's inclusion into *Time* magazine's "100 Most Influential People of 2019" list), April 17, 2019. URL: https://time.com/collection/100-most-influential-people-2019/5567876/bts/

11 In the Korea Music Copyright Association (KOMCA) database, ADORA (ID no. 10006011) is credited by her given name, Soo-hyun Park, as the composer for the song "*Playground*" from Topp Dogg's debut album released in October 2013, and for at least one BTS song, "*Euphoria*". URL: https://www.komca.or.kr/foreign2/eng/S01.jsp (insert "SOOHYUN PARK" in the Writers & Publishers search

box to find entry.) URL: Twitter thread by @ADORA_base. February 14, 2019. URL: https://twitter.com/ADORA_base/status/1096019654374551552?s=20

12 (Press Release) Big Hit Entertainment, March 6, 2019, "Big Hit Entertainment Appoints Lenzo Yoon as Co-Chief Executive Officer." The press release was picked up by Forbes on March 7, 2019. URL: https://www.forbes.com/sites/tamarherman/2019/03/07/big-hit-entertainment-appoints-new-co-ceo-following-rise-of-bts-launch-of-txt/#7cdfdd442f79

13 BangtanSubs, "180223 Good Insight Season 2: Producer Bang Sihyuk Episode," *Daily Motion*, video, 52:59, November 2018. URL: https://www.dailymotion.com/video/x6y2b23

14 1theK, "I'M: BTS_N.O Pop Quiz Event," *YouTube*, video, 9:27, September 15, 2013. URL: https://www.youtube.com/watch?v=g6b87itlfl4

15 1theK, "BTS_War of Hormones," *YouTube*, video, 4:58, October 21, 2014. URL: https://www.youtube.com/watch?reload=9&v=XQmpVHUi-0A

16 (Statement by Son Ji-hyoung, Big Hit Entertainment) "Big Hit Entertainment apologizes for BTS' misogynistic lyrics (full translation)," The Korea Herald, July 6, 2016. URL: http://kpopherald.koreaherald.com/view.php?ud=201607061726135533447_2

17 K Do, "MOT's eAeon Reveals How BTS's Rap Monster Is Dealing With The Misogyny Controversy," *Soompi*, July 6, 2016. URL: https://www.soompi.com/article/874109wpp/mots-eaeon-reveals-btss-rap-monster-dealing-misogyny-controversy

18 Jiwon Yu, "BTS Explains the True Meaning Behind Their New Title Track," *Soompi*, November 27, 2015. URL: https://www.soompi.com/article/792787wpp/bts-explains-the-true-meaning-behind-their-new-title-track

19 BTS, "BTS Live: WINGS Behind story by RM," *VLIVE*, video, 41:25, 2016. URL: https://www.vlive.tv/video/15694

20 Big Hit Entertainment, *BTS Wings Concept Book* (Play Company Corp, June 30, 2017). Jimin also alludes to feelings of "not being good enough" during his interview in this concept book where he discusses the process of writing the song. URL: http://playcompany.kr/portfolio-items/bts/

21 Choe Sang-Hun, "Korean Official, Calling for Class System, Hears Woofs, Oinks and Outrage," *The New York Times*, July 12, 2016. URL: https://www.nytimes.com/2016/07/13/world/asia/south-korea-education-ministry.html

NOTES

22 Ock Hyun-ju, "[Newsmaker] Official apologizes for 'dogs and pigs' remarks," *The Korea Herald*, July 11, 2016. URL: http://www.koreaherald.com/view.php?ud=20160711001026

23 Refer to page 168, for the initial discussion about "Omelas" signage.

24 Chang Dong-woo, "(News Focus) How BTS's stardom kindled misogyny debate in K-pop scene," *YONHAP NEWS AGENCY*, March 17, 2017. URL: https://en.yna.co.kr/view/AEN20170316010900315

25 Manthan Chheda, "BTS's 'Interlude: Wings' banned from KBS due to obscene language," *YIBADA*, February 8, 2017. URL: http://en.yibada.com/articles/192706/20170208/bts-interlude-wings-banned-from-kbs-due-to-obscene-language.htm

26 Translated by K Do, "Suga Talks About How BTS Songs Address Social Issues," *Soompi*, September 18, 2017. URL: https://www.soompi.com/article/1045527wpp/suga-talks-bts-songs-address-social-issues (Original article posted in Korean on *Naver*: https://entertain.naver.com/read?oid=277&aid=0004078493)

27 HuskyFox, "BTS 'LOVE YOURSELF' SERIES Album Identity," *Behance*, March 28, 2019. URL: https://www.behance.net/gallery/77735237/BTS-LOVE-YOURSELF-SERIES-Album-Identity

28 HuskyFox, "BTS 'LOVE YOURSELF' SERIES Album Identity," *Behance*, March 28, 2019. URL: https://www.behance.net/gallery/77735237/BTS-LOVE-YOURSELF-SERIES-Album-Identity

29 Jin, English translation of the song "*Epiphany*" from the BTS album: *Love Yourself*, Genius lyrics database. URL: https://genius.com/Genius-english-translations-bts-epiphany-english-translation-lyrics

30 Big Hit Entertainment, early version of BTS's *Love Yourself* poster, Genius lyrics database. URL: https://images.genius.com/d110e520527239f57c116fe58f7e61bb.640x400x1.jpg

31 Murray Stein, *Jung's Map of the Soul: An Introduction* (Open Court, December 30, 1998).

32 BTS, "RM - MAP OF THE SOUL: PERSONA Behind," *VLIVE*, video, 1:10:08, May 2019. URL: https://www.vlive.tv/video/15694

33 Laura London, "Episode 42: Jung's Map of the Soul," podcast audio, *Speaking of Jung*, MP3, 01:02:29, March 23, 2019. URL: https://speakingofjung.com/podcast/2019/3/25/episode-42-jungs-map-of-the-soul

34 E Cha, "BTS's Jimin Opens Up About The Personal Struggles That Inspired His Self-Composed Track "Promise," *Soompi*, January 19, 2019. URL: https://www.soompi.com/article/1295447wpp/btsss-jimin-opens-personal-struggles-inspired-self-composed-track-promise

35 Chang Dong-woo, "(News Focus) Catching fire: Grassroots campaign that sold BTS to mainstream America," *YONHAP NEWS AGENCY*, December 22, 2017. URL: https://en.yna.co.kr/view/AEN20171222003200315

36 "BTS: YouTube Music Charts & Insights – Global," *YouTube*. URL: https://charts.youtube.com/artist/%2Fm%2F0w68qx3

37 E Cha, "Bang Shi Hyuk Shares The Secret To BTS's Success And His Ultimate Goal For The Group," *Soompi*, January 6, 2019. URL: https://www.soompi.com/article/1104305wpp/bang-shi-hyuk-shares-secret-btss-success-ultimate-goal-group

38 Jack White, "BTS set for their first Number 1 on the UK's Official Albums Chart with Map of the Soul: Persona," *Official Charts*, April 15, 2019. URL: https://www.officialcharts.com/chart-news/bts-set-for-their-first-number-1-on-the-uk-s-official-albums-chart-with-map-of-the-soul-persona__26072/

39 "Campaign: #ENDviolence; Children should feel safe at home, in school and in their communities," *UNICEF*. URL: https://www.unicef.org/end-violence

40 BTS, "5 Ways to Love Myself," *Love Myself*, August 10, 2018. URL: https://www.love-myself.org/post-eng/bts_5ways_eng/

41 J Lim, "BTS And Big Hit Entertainment Make Generous Donation To Families Of Sewol Ferry Victims," *Soompi*, January 21, 2017. URL: https://www.soompi.com/article/940069wpp/bts-big-hit-entertainment-make-generous-donation-families-sewol-ferry-victims

BTS

Blood, Sweat & Tears

Written by **Tamar Herman**
Design by **Evi-O Studios**
Production by **VIZ Media**

Images on pages 2-3, 75, 76, 80, 91, 95, 96, 309, and 310-11
© Peter Ash Lee / Art Partner Licensing.

Images on pages 4, 48-49, 72, 79, 84, 92, 193, 284-85, and 304
© David Cortes Photography.

Images on pages 8, 11, 14, 20-21, 24, 33, 45, 53, 58, 67, 70-71, 74, 78,
82, 83, 86, 87, 88, 90, 94, 98, 99, 106, 111, 112, 119, 127, 128, 137, 138,
149, 150, 159, 166, 175, 176, 188, 194-95, 197, 204, 216-17, 225, 226,
232-33, 242, 252, 256-57, 268-69, 272, 278-79, 286, 294-95, and 296
courtesy of Getty Images.

Images on pages 34, 120, and 186 © ArtygirlNYC.

Image on pages 40-41 © 2020. MRC Media LLC. 2140552: 0220DD.

Images on pages 50, 157, 212-13, and 302-03 courtesy of AP Images.

Published by VIZ Media, LLC
P.O. Box 77010
San Francisco, CA 94107

Printed in South Korea

ISBN: 978-1-97471-713-2

Library of Congress Cataloging-in-Publication Data

    Names: Herman, Tamar (Journalist) author.
    Title: Blood Sweat & Tears : BTS & Their Music / by Tamar Herman.
    Description: [First edition.] | San Francisco : VIZ Media, 2020. | Includes
      bibliographical references and index.
    Identifiers: LCCN 2020013490 | ISBN 9781974717132 (paperback)
    Subjects: LCSH: BTS (Musical group) | Singers—Korea (South—Biography |
      Boy bands—Korea (South)
    Classification: LCC ML421.B79 H47 2020 | DDC 7
    LC record available at https://lccn.loc.gov/202001

This book is not an official publication of BTS or Big H

10 9 8 7 6 5 4 3 2 1
First Printing, August 2020

viz.com

$27.99